CHARLESTONIANS
IN WAR

Flag of the Charleston Light Infantry, the only surviving company flag of the Charleston Battalion. Its pristine condition and lack of additional battle honors indicate that it may have been retired early in the war or produced as a relic after the war. Courtesy The Museum of the Confederacy, Richmond, Virginia. Photograph by Katherine Wetzel.

Charlestonians IN WAR

THE CHARLESTON BATTALION

W. CHRIS PHELPS

FOREWORD BY JOSEPH P. RILEY, JR.

PELICAN PUBLISHING COMPANY

Gretna 2004

Library of Congress Cataloging-in-Publication Data

Phelps, W. Chris.
  Charlestonians in war : the Charleston Battalion / W. Chris
Phelps ; foreword by Joseph P. Riley, Jr.
      p. cm.
Includes bibliographical references and index.
  ISBN 1-58980-166-0 (alk. paper)
  1. Confederate States of America. Army. South Carolina Infantry
Battalion, 1st. 2. Charleston (S.C.)—History—Civil War, 1861-
1865—Regimental histories. 3. United States—History—Civil War,
1861-1865—Regimental histories. I. Title.

  E577.51st .P48 2004
  973.7'457—dc22

                                                          2003026780

Printed in the United States of America

Published by Pelican Publishing Company, Inc.
1000 Burmaster Street, Gretna, Louisiana, 70053

In memory of the citizen soldiers of Charleston

"All honor to the glorious name and deathless fame of 'Gaillard's Charleston Battalion'"

Contents

Foreword

For more than 320 years, generations of Charlestonians have rallied to the defense and preservation of their city in many different ways and for many different reasons: hurricanes, earthquakes, tornadoes, disease, and war. Indeed, the remarkable restoration movement that reclaimed Charleston and its splendor during the last century was the result of citizens coming to its defense in the cause of historic preservation.

Perhaps, however, the most interesting and extraordinary story of Charlestonians defending their city is the story of the Charleston Battalion during this city's most difficult period, the 1860s and the American Civil War. The men who filled the ranks of this hometown unit came from everyday life in Charleston and bonded and trained together to form a most effective and successful military unit. For almost two years the Charleston Battalion defended this city against an invading enemy in campaigns and engagements at Secessionville, Battery Wagner, Morris Island, and Fort Sumter before being sent off to other fields of battle in Virginia and North Carolina. Charleston was understandably a most important target for the Union forces, having been the place where the Ordinance of Secession was signed and furthermore being one of the most prominent Southern ports and arguably the most prominent city in the Confederacy. To many in the North, Charleston was the bull's-eye.

The story of the Charleston Battalion brings to life the fact that these men were most obviously ordinary citizens who had professions, careers, and responsibilities that were quite diverse. In addition, the battalion represented every race, religion, ethnic group, and social class found in Charleston's society.

It is an interesting irony that, literally translated, the motto on the city seal of Charleston is "Regard our buildings, customs and laws," meaning to protect them, which was the task presented to the men of the Charleston Battalion during the war. It is also interesting and not at all surprising that the Charleston Battalion's commander, Peter Charles Gaillard, later became the first postwar mayor of Charleston, charged with the same task in a civic role. His grandson, J. Palmer Gaillard, Jr., two generations later also served the city as mayor for almost sixteen years.

Charleston is a most remarkable city with a rich and exciting history. A study of the men in the Charleston Battalion and their efforts during the Civil War reveals yet another interesting and meaningful chapter of Charleston's history. In a broader, more modern sense, the valor and sacrifices of these men are a reminder of the American heritage of citizen soldiers. As this is written, that is very much in evidence as our military forces, men and women from Charleston, are engaged in battle for our country, state, and city in another part of the world.

JOSEPH P. RILEY, JR.
Mayor of Charleston

Introduction

The memoirs of Brig. Gen. Johnson Hagood, prewar planter and lawyer as well as postwar governor of South Carolina, were published in 1910, twelve years after his death, under the title *Memoirs of the War in Secession*. Presented in this record is an intimate and detailed history of the battalions and regiments that served in General Hagood's brigade during the last year and a half of the Civil War and the campaigns in which they fought. Reminiscing on his defense of Charleston, July 1863 through the spring of 1864, Gen. P. G. T. Beauregard remembered Hagood's brigade as "the best troops I had." The present writer became intrigued by Hagood's short sketch of the Twenty-seventh South Carolina Infantry in large part owing to the unique if not peculiar characteristics assigned to it by the general, but most interesting of all was that he asserted that this unit "was especially claimed by Charlestonians as *their* regiment." In the well-documented annals of Charleston's Civil War history, no other South Carolina regiment has been given the distinction of being native to Charleston: the third-largest city in the South; per capita the wealthiest city in the nation; the city where secession first became a reality and in whose harbor the war was thus inaugurated.

Upon examination of General Hagood's two-page sketch of the Twenty-seventh, it becomes quite clear that such an exclusive nom de guerre as the *Charlestonians Regiment* was applicable to this regiment solely due to its core element known as the "Charleston Battalion," which provided seven of the regiment's

11

ten companies. Indeed, here was the quintessential, native Charlestonian organization. As its name would suggest, this battalion "was originally raised in Charleston," according to Hagood. "Its officers were almost without exception Charlestonians, and the city element largely predominated in the ranks." Virtually every Southern city fielded a company, battalion, or regiment that was distinctively native. From New Orleans, by far the largest Southern city, came numerous such units, like the Crescent Regiment of Infantry, the Orleans Guard Infantry Battalion, and the Washington Artillery. From Richmond came the Richmond Blues and the Richmond Howitzers, from Mobile the Mobile Cadets, and from Charleston the Charleston Battalion.

Generations before the war, the individual companies of the Charleston Battalion had existed as volunteer city militia companies, some even predating the American Revolution. Ultimately these companies mustered in defense of their city and state in December of 1860, when South Carolina seceded from the Union. In the spring of 1862 these companies came together to form the "First South Carolina Infantry Battalion," a unit specifically created to defend Charleston and forever after known as the Charleston Battalion. The Charleston Battalion had been in Confederate service for a year and a half by the autumn of 1863, when Hagood's brigade was created, and in that time had amassed a battle record unmatched by any other unit in the defense of Charleston. The battalion was only part of General Hagood's brigade for little more than a week when three additional companies—collectively known as the First Battalion of Sharpshooters—were consolidated with the Charleston Battalion, giving it enough companies to form a new regiment designated as the Twenty-seventh South Carolina Infantry. According to Capt. Julius Blake of the Charleston Battalion, many of his men rejected being consolidated with the Sharpshooter Battalion because they desired to remain "a distinctive City Battalion." The die was cast, however, and the battalion was supplemented to create the new regiment. A later chapter of this work will illustrate that there was even disaffection on the part of the Sharpshooters—only one of whose six senior officers was from Charleston and the preponderance of whose men were from other parts of the state—at joining with the Charleston Battalion. It therefore becomes obvious that when Hagood describes in his memoirs specific characteristics of the Twenty-seventh Regiment relative to its Charlestonian or urban composition, he is actually regarding that regiment and the Charleston Battalion as one and the same.

The Charleston Battalion did not storm the Peach Orchard at Shiloh nor did it participate in Pickett's charge at Gettysburg, but it is remarkable nonetheless that this unit has escaped study. The men who formed its rank and file were Charlestonians who in one way or another had been participants in—or at least front-row spectators to—the events that led the United States down the tragic road to war. In addition, more so than any other South Carolina unit, the Charleston Battalion embodied the spirit, determination, and diversity of Charleston. Sadly, there is not even a plaque or monument in Charleston that honors these men.

With that in mind, the purpose of this work is threefold. First and foremost it chronicles the part played by these Charlestonians during the War Between the States. Secondly this work strives in some degree to flesh out General Hagood's observations of the relationships that existed between Charleston society and the Charleston Battalion. In doing so, the battalion's rank and file is surveyed by examining age, race, occupation, and nationality. The city of Charleston was well known for its diverse population of native whites, slaves, free blacks, and immigrants. The Charleston Battalion was a true cross section of Charleston society and not surprisingly it will be shown to have contained elements of each race and class found in the city as well. Lastly, it is hoped that this quasi-prosopographic examination may also be regarded as a useful genealogical resource for the present generation of Charlestonians, South Carolinians, and Americans who are able to trace their lineage back to this forgotten group of patriots and that tumultuous era.

CHARLESTONIANS
IN WAR

CHAPTER 1

Citizen Soldiers: The Militia Legacy

The roots of the Charleston Battalion lay in the state militia, a national defense system adopted in the earliest years of the Republic. Following the American Revolution, the United States Congress chose to set up a defense system based on individual state militias rather than a national army. A professional army would have bankrupted the fledgling nation and was simply too reminiscent of the British habit of quartering troops amidst the general public.

In May 1792, Congress established guidelines for the independent state forces by passing an official act.[1] Within the guidelines of this act, the militia structure adopted by South Carolina in 1792 called for two divisions of infantry troops consisting of nine brigades amounting to approximately twenty thousand men. Each brigade consisted of three to five regiments depending on the white male population of a certain locality. Each regiment had two battalions, and each battalion contained five companies. A company numbered between a set minimum of thirty and a maximum of sixty-four officers and enlisted men. Four of a battalion's five companies were "beat" or "line" companies made up of the general male population obligated by law to serve, while the fifth was a "light infantry," "grenadier," or "rifleman" company considered to be a more elite unit. These more prestigious companies fell under the heading of "volunteer" companies and typically consisted of "men of economic, cultural, and social status." The volunteer companies chose their own unit name, paid for their own uniforms, made their own organizational rules, and generally took their drill and muster much more seriously.[2] During drill and parade exercises, or when facing the enemy on the field of battle, the volunteer company was placed on the right of a battalion's line. Typically this right company carried rifles, weapons of superior range to that of the smoothbore muskets carried by the line companies, thus the right company was the flanking company because it protected the flank of the battalion.

For the first forty years, the state militia served as a "territorial and administrative institution" charged primarily with the registration of the male population of a certain geographic area as well as a local police force for that area. They also frequently patrolled at night to catch fugitive slaves. The "beat" or "line" companies of infantry maintained a force of the minimum thirty to the maximum sixty-four officers and men. They also furnished their own weapons and, with the exception of their officers, usually wore no particular uniform other than what the state furnished in times of active service. The volunteer companies, on the other hand, had specific training and classification as cavalry, artillery, or rifle companies. Due to the specialized nature of the volunteer companies, and the necessity of privately footing the bill for uniforms, rifled muskets, artillery, and horses, usually only men of means filled the ranks of such units. In 1848, the average cost to outfit a volunteer militiaman in Charleston was between ten and fifty dollars, a hefty sum. Because of expense and frequent population shifts that reduced company strength below the allowed minimum, volunteer companies often disbanded. On the other hand, new volunteer companies often materialized in times of worry or crisis.[3]

When the United States initiated war with Mexico in 1846, the state militias could not supplement the small U.S. army because legally those commands could not be forced to serve outside of their respective states for any practical period of active campaigning. Accordingly, a national call was made for 20,000 volunteers from the states of Alabama, Arkansas,

Georgia, Illinois, Indiana, Kentucky, Mississippi, Missouri, Ohio, Tennessee, and Texas to serve for either one year or the duration of the conflict. Not surprisingly, most volunteered for the minimum one-year service. Though South Carolina was not officially asked to forward volunteers, a "Palmetto Regiment" was organized from members of the state's volunteer militia companies and the regiment served with distinction. Among this regiment's eleven companies, Company F consisted of volunteers from Charleston[4] and sixteen years later a few of these veterans could be found on the rolls of the Charleston Battalion. In this way, volunteer companies rose to supplement the U.S. Army and by the 1850s many states, North and South, had altered their militia structures to rely more heavily on the volunteer companies than the beat companies. As a result, many state militias became largely "voluntary and selective rather than compulsory and universal."[5]

By the time of the Mexican War, many states had passed new laws to improve the effectiveness of their militias. On the eve of secession, South Carolina's most recent militia law— passed in 1841—had divided the state into five military districts defended by a citizen soldiery filling the ranks of ten brigades and forty-six regiments. According to this law all of the state's white male citizens between the ages of sixteen and sixty were eligible for some degree of militia service, but those aged eighteen to forty-five could be activated at a moment's notice for a period of three months inside the state and two months outside of its borders. Individual companies were required to assemble four times a year to drill. Regiments were required to have a formal review in front of their brigade commander and his staff at least once a year, and once every two years the officers of each brigade were required to encamp for five days of instruction. Many were exempted from militia service, however, including the lieutenant governor, secretary of state, treasurers, clerks of court, and sheriffs. Also exempted, except in times of alarm, were members of the clergy, doctors, schoolteachers, and students.[6]

By 1860, much of South Carolina's militia had lapsed into a

condition of ineffectiveness; some companies were hardly anything more than social clubs. Their poor condition was for the most part the fault of their officers, who were more interested in political station than battlefield effectiveness. Naturally, though, as South Carolina moved toward secession, its male population became galvanized by the patriotic rhetoric of their leaders, and as a result, many of the volunteer units began to organize and drill seriously, even attracting new recruits to their organizations.[7]

The general lax attitude that had prevailed over much of the state's militia prior to 1860 was not evident in Charleston, however. Here the more affluent volunteer companies were always eager to drill and parade on just about every occasion, taking it very seriously as well. When South Carolina seceded on December 20, 1860, by no surprise, of all the state's militia, its best-organized and most well equipped element was the Fourth Brigade of Charleston. Besides the four rifle companies supplied by the city's volunteer fire departments, the infantry of this brigade consisted of the First Regiment of Rifles, numbering seven companies, and the Seventeenth Regiment of Infantry, with ten companies.

FIRST REGIMENT OF RIFLES

This regiment was organized on December 20, 1853, and was commanded by Col. J. J. Pettigrew. In December of 1860 it contained the following officers and volunteer companies.

Col. J. J. Pettigrew
      Lt. Col. John L. Branch
      Maj. Ellison Capers
      Adj. Theodore G. Barker
      Q.M. Allen Hanckel
      Commissary L. G. Young
      Surgeon George Trescot
      Assistant Surgeon Thomas L. Ozier, Jr.

Companies:

> Washington Light Infantry, organized 1807
> Capt. C. H. Simonton
>
> Moultrie Guards, organized before 1845
> Capt. Barnwell W. Palmer
>
> German Riflemen, organized 1842
> Capt. Jacob Small
>
> Palmetto Riflemen (German), organized 1858
> Capt. Alex. Melchers
>
> Meagher Guards (Irish), organized 1860, in
> May 1861 renamed "Emerald Light Infantry"
> Capt. Edward McCrady, Jr.
>
> Carolina Light Infantry, organized 1858
> Capt. Gillard Pinckney
>
> Zouave Cadets, organized 1860
> Capt. C. E. Chichester

SEVENTEENTH REGIMENT

In the early militia structure this regiment was originally designated the Twenty-ninth Regiment. By far the older of the two infantry regiments in the Fourth Brigade, the Seventeenth had the peculiar distinction of having a beat regimental organization yet containing only volunteer companies. In 1860 it was commanded by Col. John Cunningham and contained the following officers and companies:

Col. John Cunningham
Lt. Col. William P. Shingler
Maj. J. J. Lucas
Adj. F. A. Mitchell

Companies:
Charleston Riflemen, organized 1806
Capt. Joseph Johnson, Jr.

Irish Volunteers, organized before 1798
Capt. Edward MaGrath

Cadet Riflemen, organized 1820
Capt. W. S. Elliott

Montgomery Guards (Irish), organized 1860
Capt. James Conner

Union Light Infantry (Scottish), organized 1807
apt. David Ramsay

German Fusiliers, organized 1775
Capt. Samuel Lord, Jr.

Palmetto Guards, organized 1851
Capt. Thomas W. Middleton

Sumter Guards, organized before 1822, reorga
nized 1860
Capt. John Russell

Emmet Volunteers, organized 1860
Capt. P. Grace

Calhoun Guards, date of organization unknown
Capt. John Fraser

VOLUNTEER CORPS IN THE FIRE DEPARTMENT

Vigilant Rifles
Capt. S. Y. Tupper

Phoenix Rifles
Capt. Peter C. Gaillard

Aetna Rifles
Capt. E. F. Sweegan

Marion Rifles
Capt. C. B. Sigwald

Six companies from the militia's Seventeenth Regiment would eventually form the Charleston Battalion. These were:

Charleston Riflemen
Irish Volunteers
Union Light Infantry
German Fusiliers
Sumter Guards
Calhoun Guards

An additional volunteer company known as the "Charleston Light Infantry" helped form part of the battalion as well. The name Charleston Light Infantry was revived from that of an old military organization dating back to the Revolution, though in name it was not active during the nineteenth century until 1862, when it mustered into the Charleston Battalion. Peter C. Gaillard, captain of the fire department's Phoenix Rifles, would eventually lead the battalion.

CHAPTER 2

The First Year of War: Pre-Charleston Battalion

From Abraham Lincoln's election in November of 1860 through the firing on Fort Sumter in April 1861, the city of Charleston was center stage to all the events that led the United States down the tragic path to fratricidal war. The citizen soldiers who filled the ranks of the volunteer militia companies of Charleston now became performers in the all-important first act of the drama. The war began earlier for Charleston than for any other Southern city, with the conflict's first military operation occurring on November 12, 1860, just after Lincoln's election, when a small detachment of South Carolina militia peacefully surrounded the U.S. Arsenal in Charleston.[1] In a halfhearted effort to mask the truth, the U.S. officer in charge of the arsenal, Capt. C. F. Humphreys, was told that the state troops were guarding against a possible slave insurrection.[2]

Infuriated by Lincoln's election, South Carolina held a secession convention in Charleston on December 20, 1860. All 169 elected delegates to the convention unanimously voted to withdraw from the Union. Perhaps as a subtle harbinger of things to come, the day before the ordinance was signed, an earthquake rumbled through Charleston, breaking windows and startling the city's inhabitants.

Anticipating the actions of their state, the recently reorganized Sumter Guards were ordered to hold their company drill at Institute Hall at seven o'clock the night of December 20. This was just hours after the Ordinance of Secession was signed, and in the same building where the signing had taken place. Also holding drill that evening were the Charleston Riflemen, at their "Drill Room" at 292 King Street. The Riflemen were ordered to wear their full uniform and carry their rifles and pistols.[3] The next day, the Union Light Infantry, composed of Scotsmen, held their drill at 120 King Street in full dress parade uniform, including their Highland trews—tight-fitting tartan trousers.[4]

Unfortunately, there are few records describing the uniform styles worn by many of the Charleston Battalion's individual volunteer companies in December of 1860. It is well known, however, that all volunteer companies typically outfitted themselves with any style of uniform and headgear they chose, the only consistency being the ever-present palmetto insignia. Often, uniform selection was intended to reflect the nationality or unique characteristics of a certain company.[5]

Based on the surviving collection of 1840s hand-colored lithographs by Charleston artist William Keenan entitled *Southern Military Sketch Book*, we have a reasonable idea of what the dress uniforms of both the Union Light Infantry and Charleston Riflemen might have looked like in December of 1860. In my illustration here, the Union Light Infantryman, variously known as a "Highlander" or "Lowlander," is depicted wearing a green tailcoat with two rows of twelve buttons down the front. Gold embroidery and lace ornament the collar and epaulets. The Scotsman's pants are the trews and his headgear is a bonnet of red-and-white-checkered pattern with a red and white feather on the front.[6] Though it is a common misconception that this company wore kilts, the unit did have accompanying bagpipers, who may have donned kilts on special occasions.[7] The Scotsmen's fatigue uniform featured a distinctive blue hunting shirt.

The other illustration represents the complete opposite in uniform fashion, that of the Charleston Riflemen. The rifleman's frock coat and pants are dark brown, and the raveled fringe around the coat's collar, cuffs, and skirt, as well as the

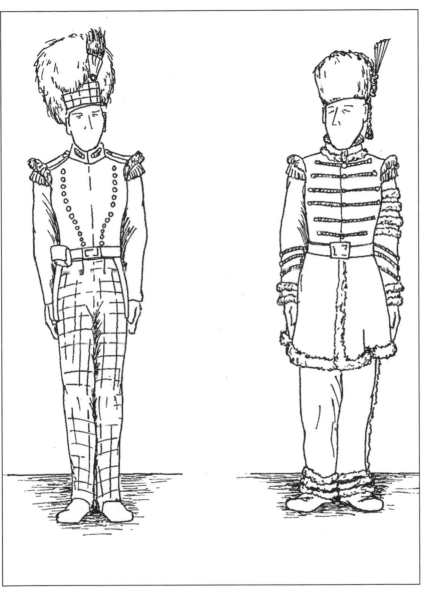

Left: Union Light Infantry.
Right: Charleston Rifleman. Illustration by author.

pants' outer seams and cuffs, is dark green. Above the cuffs of his coat are three chevrons of green cord with brass buttons at each apex, and down the front of his coat are six to seven rows of brass buttons similarly connected with green cord. The rifleman's headgear is known as a "shako," also dark brown, with a green brush and a green tassel hanging alongside.[8]

There is no definite record of the dress uniform worn during the winter of 1860-61 by the other companies of the future Charleston Battalion, though it is believed the Irish Volunteers uniform resembled the uniform of the Montgomery Guards, a recently organized Irish company. The Montgomery Guards uniform consisted of a green coat with three rows of buttons, blue pants, and a leather or cloth cap.[9] The postwar uniform of the Irish Volunteers was that of a gray coat and gray pants trimmed with green, and a gray hat with a green and white plume. It is likely that this was reminiscent of their wartime uniform. The same may hold true for the Sumter Guards, whose postwar uniform consisted of gray pants and a gray coat trimmed in black, with a gray hat sporting a white pompon.[10]

No records exist for the German Fusiliers either, but it is believed that their dress uniform was probably the standard 1840s dress uniform of the United States Infantry,[11] because the Fusiliers' postwar uniform was very similar, with a gold-trimmed, dark-blue coat, dark-blue pants with a red stripe, and a regulation hat.[12]

When in the fall of 1860 Charlestonians began to realize there was a distinct possibility of the election of a Republican president, which might bring secession from the Union, many volunteer companies began to consider the need for the more practical "fatigue" or "undress" uniforms for service in the field to defend their state's borders. After Lincoln's election, the *Charleston Mercury* noted that "the majority of our volunteer military companies . . . have been, for five or six weeks past, preparing themselves for the contingency of war, by . . . changing their stylish uniforms for more serviceable articles of clothing."[13] By the spring of 1861 most volunteer companies had outfitted themselves, at their own expense, with undress uniforms of green, gray, tan, and even blue cloth. William Russell, British war correspondent for the *Times*, wrote from Charleston that spring, "There is an endless variety—often of ugliness—in dress and equipment and nomenclature among these companies. The head-dress is generally, however, a smart cap like the French kepi; the tunic is of different cuts, colors, facings, and materials."[14]

To establish some sort of uniformity under orders from Gov. Francis Pickens, a pamphlet was published entitled *Uniform and Dress of the Officers of the Volunteer Forces Raised Under the "Act to Provide an Armed Military Force."* This pamphlet was the first step toward standardizing the uniforms of state officers. According to the document, company officers were to wear a single-breasted frock coat, dark blue, with one row of nine buttons down the front and a standing collar. Shoulder straps were dark blue and bordered with silver embroidery. Pants were also blue with a one-inch-wide white stripe down the outer seam and hats were to be a dark-blue military cap with a silver palmetto tree on the front. Undress uniforms were virtually identical to the dress uniform minus the frills of epaulets, swords and belt, sash, gauntlets, and so on.[15] Probably, however, such prescribed uniforms were worn only by the officers of six-month and one-year volunteer companies and regiments, not those companies still in service as state militia.

The United States Army, however, *did* have a regulation uniform, and at Fort Moultrie on Sullivan's Island guarding the entrance to Charleston Harbor, there were eighty-six officers and men in U.S. blue who opposed the idea of secession. Six nights after South Carolina seceded, their commander, Maj. Robert Anderson of the First United States Artillery, skillfully transferred the garrison from Moultrie to the much more defensible Fort Sumter. Though Sumter was empty and still under construction, it at least enjoyed the protective isolation of being situated in the middle of the channel entrance to the harbor. Suspecting such a move, a state coast-guard patrol was sent out on a steamer each night to watch the channel. On the night that Major Anderson transferred his garrison to Sumter, one of these patrols was manned by the Charleston Riflemen, commanded by Capt. Joseph Johnson, Jr., and Lt. Thomas S. Mills. Unfortunately for the state authorities, this patrol boat apparently did not leave the city docks until the garrison transfer had been successfully completed.[16] The next morning, December 27, 1860, a member of the Irish Volunteers who resided on Sullivan's Island was the first to notify the city officials of the "aggressive" move made by Anderson and his U.S. forces.[17] The governor immediately activated several rifle companies to take possession of the abandoned Fort Moultrie, as well as Castle Pinckney in the Cooper River only a mile from Charleston's waterfront.

The *Charleston Daily Courier* wrote that, enraged by Anderson's move, "instinctively men flew to arms."[18] One Charlestonian woman remembered:

> Every man volunteered. Some were officers, more were privates—the private everywhere the favourite. The militia companies grew sixty to a hundred strong in a day. New companies were formed: the old ones split into first and second corps, their recruits were so many.[19]

Eager to have a part in the drama, the Irish Volunteers, led by Capt. Edward MaGrath and numbering more than sixty men, paraded through town during the evening of December 27, headed to the Mills House Hotel, where they "paid their respects to the Governor" and tendered their services. The *Courier* wrote, "We feel assured that these 'sons of Erin' will shrink from no position of peril or danger when their adopted State demands their services."[20] In the next few days, Governor Pickens placed Lt. William H. Ryan of the Irish Volunteers along with a detachment of twenty men on board the guard ship *General Clinch* as lookouts against any effort by U.S. forces to resupply Fort Sumter.[21]

Volunteer rifle companies from Charleston's Fourth Brigade occupied the abandoned Fort Moultrie late on December 27, but the first fortification to be forcibly occupied by South Carolina troops was Castle Pinckney, an outdated masonry fort practically within musket range of Charleston's bustling waterfront. Detachments from the city's rifle regiment, including the Washington Light Infantry, Meagher Guards, and Carolina Light Infantry, were assigned to take possession of Pinckney, and though none of these companies was to serve in the Charleston Battalion, at least one person among them would.[22] Escorting the militia in case of any casualties was Francis Tourquand Miles, a notable Charleston physician who afterward joined the Phoenix Rifles from the Fire Department's Volunteer Corps, at that time commanded by Capt. Peter Gaillard. Dr. Miles was later offered the post of surgeon in the Washington Light Infantry in 1862 but declined, choosing instead to accept the captaincy of the Calhoun Guards.[23]

Occupying every military installation in and around Charleston was of paramount importance now that South Carolina was a sovereign entity, and on December 29, 1860, Governor Pickens ordered that the U.S. Arsenal (under "siege" since November) finally be taken into possession due to the "excited state of public mind."[24] The order was quickly and discretely executed by a twenty-man detachment of the Scottish Union Light Infantry under the command of Capt. David Ramsay.[25] Having no sizeable force with which to contest such action, U.S. captain C. F. Humphreys quietly surrendered the arsenal to Captain Ramsay on December 30. The Scotsmen hauled down the Stars and Stripes and replaced it with the Palmetto banner, exclaiming that they were "soldiers of a new State."[26] Perhaps along with the Palmetto flag the Scotsmen flew their own banner bearing the thistle of Scotland.

On James Island sat the unoccupied ruins of Fort Johnson, the oldest fortification in the harbor and the only military installation remaining that needed to be occupied by state troops. In this era Johnson was overrun by cattle and weeds, but still its position commanded the inner harbor and Fort Sumter, and shortly after the arsenal was taken, Governor Pickens dispatched the Charleston Riflemen under the command of Capt. Joseph Johnson to occupy the fort and begin its repair.[27]

With only a few months left in office, Pres. James Buchanan reluctantly decided to covertly resupply the garrison of Fort Sumter via the *Star of the West,* a private steamer chartered for the purpose in New York City. The *Star of the West* arrived off Charleston during the night of January 8-9, 1861, and made for Sumter at first light. Posted on Morris Island as a lookout, a member of the Irish Volunteers was the first to sight the *Star* moving up the channel and sound the alarm,[28] and before long artillery pieces manned by cadets from the Citadel military academy were in action. The cadets scored several hits on the vessel as it pushed up the channel, and forever after they proudly claimed to have fired the first shots of the war. Fort Moultrie soon opened up with a few wild shots and the steamer headed back out to sea and returned to New York.[29] President Buchanan's first and only effort to aid Major Anderson and his garrison proved a dismal failure. No further effort would be made to help Anderson until Lincoln took office.

About the time that the *Star of the West* was fired on, the Sumter Guards, under their commander, Capt. John Russell, paraded through the city to their campgrounds at the old U.S. Arsenal. This was the first time the guards had held a formal parade since their recent reorganization.[30]

During this anxious and exciting time, new recruit Charles Kaufman wrote home proudly stating:

> I have joined the Charleston Riflemen and as soon as I can get my uniform I will be into service. I'm ready if we have to fight. The company is on duty at Fort Johnson.[31]

At their own expense, the Riflemen may have purchased gray undress uniforms by that time. On February 5, Kaufman wrote that he and a portion of the Riflemen were "on a steamer one night last week . . . acting as a Coast guard."[32] All told, there were eight of these guard boats, most painted black to provide camouflage at night.[33] Kaufman continued, "The Company has been drilling and meeting, so my time has been devoted to the State. . . . Tomorrow afternoon we parade as an escort to the Aetna Guards."[34] Like the Phoenix Rifles, the Aetna Rifles was a volunteer company from Charleston's fire department.

By the end of the month, some of the twelve-month volunteers called for by an act of the state legislature were reaching Charleston to help man the harbor forts. Private Kaufman wrote:

> All the city Companies except the Artillery have been withdrawn from the various posts in the Harbor. The "enlisted" Volunteers and Regulars are in possession now. There is a strict watch kept every night on board the steamer. The Riflemen take a turn tomorrow night. We are armed now with the Minie Rifle and Sabre bayonet.[35]

The first week of February, a detachment of the Sumter Guards was seen marching through the city and it was noted, "They were well equipped, and presented a substantial appearance." Capt. Peter Gaillard and his Phoenix Rifles were also seen drilling that week and it was reported, "Their ranks were full, and their appearance soldierly."[36] In mid-February, Gen. D. F. Jamison presented the Sumter Guards with a new company flag from the balcony of the Charleston Hotel on Meeting Street. Jamison presented the flag on behalf of a number of "lady friends" of the Guards who had sewn and stitched it themselves. The Guards were escorted to the hotel by the Cadet Riflemen. After a lengthy speech, General Jamison presented the flag to Capt. John Russell of the Guards, saying, "I have great confidence that it will never be surrendered while one of the Sumter Guards lives to defend it." The flag's field was dark blue, with a green palmetto tree in the center backed by the state's arms and a silver crescent moon in the upper hoist corner. On the reverse side was a gamecock with the words *In Statione Nostra Parati* ("We are ready at our post").[37]

On the last day of February, Charleston's Seventeenth Regiment of militia held a formal review at the Citadel parade grounds. Among the multitude of admiring ladies was twenty-two-year-old Miss Emma Holmes of Charleston, who recorded in her diary the sight of "ten or eleven companies in their plain dress uniforms, their bayonets glancing in the bright sunshine, the bands of music . . . with throngs of spectators in all directions."[38] On this occasion the Charleston Riflemen under Capt. Joseph Johnson numbered fifty-eight men, the Sumter Guards under Capt. John Russell numbered forty-eight, Capt. Edward MaGrath's Irish Volunteers numbered sixty-five, the German Fusiliers under Capt. Samuel Lord, Jr., numbered sixty, the Calhoun Guards under Capt. John Fraser numbered the minimum of thirty-six, and the Union Light Infantry under Capt. David Ramsay numbered forty-eight.[39]

Additional twelve-month regiments from the upper counties of South Carolina arrived almost daily to supplement the city force. Later a brigadier, but at that time a colonel, Johnson Hagood arrived from the interior during this period with his First South Carolina Volunteers. Hagood remembered, "The regulars and six months' volunteers provided for by the Convention were rapidly enlisted or accepted, respectively, and placed in service in Charleston harbor or on the adjacent islands. These, together with the volunteer militia from the city of Charleston, were employed in pressing forward the works projected for the reduction of Ft. Sumter."[40]

During the evening of March 4, the ladies of Charleston "devoted to arming and equipping the Sumter Guard" enacted a fundraiser performance of *Lady of Lyons*. Among the ladies who played both the male and female roles was Susan Petigru-King, wife of the Sumter Guards' Lt. Henry C. King and daughter of the distinguished attorney James L. Petigru, who despite his staunch Unionist views was one of the most respected and influential Charletonians of the age.[41] Though all in attendance had a wonderful time, Miss Emma Holmes noted in her diary that the performance was "murdered" rather than acted.[42]

South Carolina was quickly joined in secession by six other Southern states, and with delegates from the "Palmetto State" they formed a Confederate government situated in Montgomery, Alabama. The new government prudently took control of the events unfolding in Charleston Harbor, and by the end of March, newly appointed Confederate brigadier general Pierre Gustav Toutant Beauregard arrived in Charleston to assume command of the state forces and the military situation surrounding Fort Sumter. With the city's militia supplemented by newly raised twelve-month volunteers, there was an aggregate of 3,027 South Carolinians and Charlestonians at the general's disposal.[43] Upon inspection of the harbor batteries, General Beauregard concluded that much work still needed to be done if Sumter was to be reduced and its garrison forced to surrender. However, the general was impressed with the progress made thus far by the state officers and their troops. According to Alfred Roman in his contemporary biography of the Creole general, Beauregard praised the patriotism of Charleston's citizen soldiers. The city's militiamen were described as "gallant and sensitive gentlemen who had left their comfortable homes, at the call of their State, to vindicate its honor and assert its rights . . . they had endured, for weeks, the privations and exposures of a soldier's life, on the bleak islands" about Charleston Harbor.[44] Roman reinforced the social and economic level of these men, many of whom were to fill the ranks of the Charleston Battalion, stating, "Among the privates there assembled for duty were planters and sons of planters, some of them the wealthiest men of South Carolina."[45]

Early in April, after three months with no real succor from Washington and running dangerously low on supplies, Major Anderson was notified that the new president was dispatching a flotilla of warships, tugboats, and supply vessels to relieve Sumter's garrison. General Beauregard was also informed by Lincoln that a Union fleet was headed south to Charleston. A little before midnight on April 8, seven vessels believed to be of Lincoln's fleet appeared off the entrance to Charleston Harbor. Though it proved to be a false alarm, instantly the state and city troops were summoned into action by the bells of St. Michael's church and the firing of seven cannon from Citadel Square. City resident Emma Holmes remembered, "All night the tramp of armed men were heard marching to the boats and the streets were thronged and bustling with the preparation for war."[46]

When Lincoln's real fleet arrived, it ultimately failed in its military mission to relieve Sumter's garrison, though it was successful in its political mission of forcing the South to inaugurate civil war, with the resulting thirty-four-hour Confederate bombardment of Fort Sumter. The firing of the first shots against Sumter was the culmination of decades of sectional bitterness between North and South, and the Charlestonians and other South Carolinians who participated in the event had full knowledge of the ramifications of their actions.

Among the Southern commanders who praised the conduct of their men in this first engagement of the war was Col. Wilmot G. DeSaussure, a prominent Charleston attorney and commander of the artillery on Morris Island. In his report, DeSaussure mentioned Capt. John Russell and his Sumter Guards for their support of the Marion Artillery at Fort Johnson. During the night of April 12-13, the Guards had helped construct embrasures for the Cumming's Point Battery on Morris Island nearest Sumter while under fire from Anderson's guns. The Guards were also kept busy placing sandbags on a portion of the Iron Battery. In addition, Colonel DeSaussure thanked Dr. Francis Tourquand Miles, future captain of the Calhoun Guards, for his preparedness in the event of casualties, though none occurred.[47]

Capt. J. Gadsden King, commanding the Marion Artillery at

Fort Johnson on James Island, reported, "My thanks are due to the detachment of fifteen men from the Sumter Guards, Capt. John Russell for services rendered the last three hours of the bombardment."[48] Though for some reason King did not elaborate on the matter, the Sumter Guards actually relieved the artillerymen from their work near the close of the bombardment. One eyewitness remembered, "During [the Sumter Guards'] good service here, taking into consideration their entire ignorance of gunnery, they made some very good shots, several of their shells falling into the magazine of the fort, and others dropping on the parapet."[49] While this detachment manned the mortars, the remainder of the Guards was probably on Morris Island, where much of the Seventeenth Regiment was placed to check a feared landing by forces of the Union Army and Navy. Within a few months, Captain Russell resigned because of poor health and Lt. Henry C. King advanced to fill the position as captain of the Sumter Guards.[50]

Pvt. George W. Alexander, a French teacher who lived at 48 Bull Street, recalled that his company, the Calhoun Guards, was stationed on Sullivan's Island near Fort Moultrie and was initially quartered in the comfortable Moultrie House Inn. Shortly before the bombardment, they were marched to the eastern end of the island in case the expected Union flotilla landed troops in that vicinity. If the enemy landed, according to Alexander his company was to "fire and fall back and so lure them under the guns of Ft. Moultrie." Alas, however, no enemy landed and Alexander later lamented that his position "offered little opportunity for witnessing the bombardment." Though neither he nor any of his fellows were involved in the fight, years afterward Alexander reflected, "There were many a hero in embryo, no doubt bumbling about the sands at the Myrtles and chasing Sand Crabs to their holes. Our Chances for immortality were still in the dim future."[51]

Other future Charleston Battalion companies, like the Irish Volunteers and the German Fusiliers, record having been active around the harbor during the bombardment but their exact locations are unaccounted for. Lt. Col. Ellison Capers, a Charlestonian and veteran of the action at Fort Sumter, recorded that during the bombardment the Seventeenth Regiment of state troops was stationed on Morris Island under the command of Col. John Cunningham.[52] Though Capers wrote from memory many years after the war, and was not himself in command of the Seventeenth Regiment, it does appear that all the future battalion companies except the Calhoun Guards were on Morris Island, including the Sumter Guards, who were shifted to James Island for part of the bombardment. It is no surprise that more infantry companies were not mentioned in the final reports simply because the action was an artillery operation from start to finish.

Having lost Fort Sumter, President Lincoln now resolved to suppress the rebellion. In reaction, Virginia and the upper South seceded, and thousands of South Carolina's volunteer soldiers—the first Southern troops prepared for extended service—were immediately loaded on trains bound for the "Old Dominion." There were ultimately two great armies that defended the South during the Civil War: the resilient "Army of Tennessee" and General Lee's "Army of Northern Virginia." Thousands of Charlestonians and South Carolinians formed the core element of Lee's army. In an address given to the Virginia Division of the Army of Northern Virginia in 1886, Charlestonian Edward McCrady, Jr., claimed that the gallant army in Virginia owed its origins to the militia companies of Charleston. When Union forces abandoned Fort Moultrie and occupied Fort Sumter during the night of December 26-27, 1860, "the State of South Carolina had but the volunteer companies of Charleston available for seizing and occupying the other strategic points around Charleston harbor," McGrady stated. "They thus took the field without an hour's notice . . . and indeed were on duty with but little intermission until the fall of Fort Sumter on the 13th April, 1861."[53] McCrady commanded the Meagher Guards, one of the three Irish companies in the Charleston militia. The Meagher Guards took the field in December of 1860 with all the other city companies, and like many of those companies, they eventually made their way to Virginia in the weeks following the firing on Sumter. When the Guards reached Richmond, they joined Col. Maxy Gregg's First South Carolina Regiment and were quickly dispatched to Suffolk, Virginia and the department of Charlestonian general Benjamin Huger.[54]

Because South Carolina's troops, and those from Charleston in particular, were prepared for service long before any from other Southern states, they were the first to reach the Old Dominion when Northern troops crossed the Potomac River from Washington and invaded that state. As a result, by the end of May 1861, the only well-drilled and -equipped body of troops in Richmond was half of Gen. Milledge L. Bonham's South Carolina brigade, some 1,500 men. Detached from Bonham were his two remaining regiments at Suffolk, Virginia, including Gregg's Regiment with Colonel McCrady and the Meagher Guards, numbering another 1,500 muskets. At points across Virginia, raw troops were being organized and drilled by cadets from the state military academy, but few of these had been forwarded to the capital at Richmond.[55] On June 20, 1861, the assembling Virginia army was designated as the Confederate "Army of the Potomac", and Governor Bonham's Brigade, consisting of Gregg's, Bacon's, Kershaw's, and Cash's South Carolina regiments, was bestowed the honor of forming the first brigade of its first division.[56] When General Lee took command in June of 1862, he officially renamed the army the "Army of Northern Virginia," and these earliest South Carolina regiments retained the honor of forming the first brigade of the first division of the first corps.

Probably expecting to travel to Virginia as well, at six o'clock P.M. on July 4, 1861, at Institute Hall, the Charleston Riflemen, under 1st Lt. Julius Blake, received their company flag. On this occasion the Washington Light Infantry escorted the Riflemen to the ceremony. The banner was manufactured by the firm Hayden & Whilden and was described as "probably the most handsomest which has been presented to any of our city companies"—a gift from the ladies of Charleston. Another one of the state's "Blue Banners," the flag had on one side the classic palmetto tree and crescent gorget, but under the tree was a rendering of the Riflemen's January 1861 camp with a sentinel at his post and cotton bales lying at his feet. On the reverse side were the encircled words *Presented by the ladies to the Charleston Riflemen, July 1861.*[57]

To be sure, caught up in the enthusiasm of the war's early days, so many of the city's volunteer companies joined regiments headed for Virginia that it looked as though there would be no troops to defend Charleston and its coastline. South Carolina's governor Francis Pickens had not initially insisted on retaining local troops for this purpose, and soon he realized that he had few troops on hand.[58] Pickens finally forbade any more city companies from leaving the Charleston region, "lest the acclimated force in the city should, in too large numbers, be withdrawn to distant service during the ensuing summer."[59]

Those city companies remaining were relieved of their mandatory four months of service shortly after the fall of Fort Sumter. Throughout the summer of 1861, the volunteer companies held frequent drill and dress parades. Following the battle of Manassas, in which South Carolinians and Charlestonians played a conspicuous part, the Palmetto State's dead were shipped back home, and on July 27, 1861—a week following the battle—the bodies were escorted to City Hall, where the caskets lay draped in black. The Charleston Riflemen and Charleston Mounted Guard escorted the body of Georgian colonel Francis S. Bartow, also killed at Manassas, to the Savannah Railroad station for shipment to that city. Later that afternoon, the body of Gen. Barnard Bee—the man credited with naming General Jackson as "Stonewall" Jackson—was carried to St. Paul's Episcopal Church in the upper part of town for burial. The honor guards for General Bee were the Charleston Riflemen and Washington Light Infantry, with the entire Seventeenth Regiment of militia following.[60]

During the fall of 1861, men were detached from the Charleston Riflemen, Union Light Infantry, Calhoun Guards, Irish Volunteers, Sumter Guards, and German Fusiliers because they possessed skills needed to help manufacture everything from soap to ammunition in the Confederate shops at Charleston. One disgruntled and apparently untalented Charleston Rifleman wrote home, "I think it rather hard—those that happen not to be directly engaged in C.S. work must do the 'sojering.'"[61]

Capt. Edward MaGrath of the Irish Volunteers and Capt. Julius Blake of the Charleston Riflemen were detailed for court-martial duty in late September.[62] Blake's Riflemen were then encamped at Fort Pickens on Battery Island, a sandy strip of ground detached from James Island by marsh and tidal creek and resting on the Stono River eight miles south of Charleston. Though the island was isolated and infested with fleas and mosquitoes, Riflemen private Charles Kaufman wrote on October 6, "We live high sometimes. In fact it's higher than most of the mess do."[63] They ate roast beef, ham, "very fine" chickens, blackbirds, shrimp and every variety of fish with egg sauce, okra soup, and cake. But used to finer living, Kaufman was also engaged in fixing the platform of a big gun at Fort Pickens. He complained about the heat being intolerable, and that for once in his life his clothes "did not smell like 'otter of roses.'"[64]

Before long, Union naval vessels were spotted along the coast. In response to this threat, General DeSaussure, commander of the Charleston militia, issued Order No. 46 on October 11, 1861, which put the militia back on a "war footing" in preparation for an attack. The next day, DeSaussure issued Order No. 49, establishing an alarm system by which the militia would form in case of attack: fifteen strokes on St. Michael's bell, repeated five times with one-minute intervals, meant that all companies were to assemble under arms at their respective grounds. In section two of the same order, the city troops were ordered to assemble under arms the next day for inspection. On October 19, provision was made to equip the 863 men of the Seventeenth Regiment with knapsacks, blankets, drawers, haversacks, canteens and straps, plates, cups, knives, etc., meaning that active campaigning against the enemy lay ahead.[65]

In early November, a Federal fleet numbering seventeen vessels, mounting 200 guns, and transporting 12,000 infantry concentrated off of Port Royal Sound sixty miles south of Charleston. On November 7, in one of the war's earliest naval operations, the fleet managed to bully past the two Confederate forts flanking the entrance to Port Royal. Confederate resistance was admirable but not coordinated, and with little effort the U.S. government won an impressive holding along South Carolina's lower coast.[66] Charleston's Fourth Brigade was again activated for four months' service in response to the Union attack on Port Royal. The companies of Charleston's Seventeenth Regiment were shuffled from the city to Wadmalaw and John's islands just south of Charleston to block the expected approach of the enemy, but as autumn turned to winter with no action, the city's defenders realized that the Union forces at Port Royal had little intention of an offensive operation before spring.

That fall, the men around Charleston received a new commander, Gen. Robert Edward Lee, former United States colonel and late military advisor to Pres. Jefferson Davis. The Virginian was appointed to command the new geographical department of South Carolina, Georgia, and Eastern Florida, created on November 5, 1861, by Special Order No. 206.[67] Lee arrived in Charleston on November 6, and when he learned that U.S. naval vessels were off of Port Royal he wasted no time in boarding a train that would take him to the action.[68] It was too little too late, however, and Lee was powerless to stop the overwhelming Union contingent. His mission now was to consolidate his forces, recruit and arm new regiments, and prepare to meet the expected Union advance, wherever it might occur.

On November 19, Governor Pickens forwarded Lee a summation of the troops available for defending the coast. Of 13,000 troops on hand to meet the enemy, General DeSaussure's brigade of Charleston militia numbered 2,750 infantry, artillery, and cavalry.[69] This figure included men on detached duty, sick, or just plain absent and was later trimmed down to 1,531 officers, noncommissioned officers, and privates present for duty. This was a slim number for the two regiments of infantry in the brigade, also one each of artillery and cavalry plus the four rifle companies from the fire department. Approximately 1,219 militiamen were absent from duty for any number of reasons, and some who owned plantations along the Ashepoo, Pon Pon, and Combahee rivers near the enemy had been allowed furlough to go and secure their property and "negroes."[70] The larger of the two infantry regiments was the Seventeenth Regiment, purportedly numbering 803 men.

In anticipation of a Union advance, on November 24 the Calhoun Guards were ordered to be ready to move to James Island with five days' rations.[71] By a separate special order, Captain Dawson was to move the Guards from their camp at the racecourse (Hampton Park) and report to Brig. Gen. Roswell Ripley, who was in charge of the Charleston defenses. A few days later they were reported to be encamped on one of the islands south of Charleston, probably Wadmalaw Island, where they were "employed in guarding an important road" against the enemy just to their south. Also that November, Capt. Peter Gaillard of the Phoenix Rifles was commissioned lieutenant colonel of the Seventeenth Regiment, with his post on Wadmalaw Island.[72]

By Christmas Eve, all that the defenders of Charleston could do was watch and wait for a Federal advance, but for the moment the pressure seemed to be off. This relaxed attitude was exemplified in the Charleston camps, where a distressed General Lee found few troops. Lee wrote Governor Pickens complaining that on a visit to Charleston he could only locate

310 of DeSaussure's 1,531 city troops.[73] Of course, many men were distributed on sea islands guarding the southern approach to Charleston, while others were on detached duty, and some were simply evading their duty. But hundreds more were good soldiers on duty in their native city, and doubtless many of them had simply left their commands and gone to their homes to spend Christmas with their families. This was all the more probable owing to the fact that the Christmas of 1861 was anything but cheerful, for a catastrophic fire had ravaged Charleston during the night of December 11-12. The epic blaze, witnessed by General Lee and his staff from the Mills House Hotel, cut a swath of destruction across the city over a mile in length, running southwest from the Cooper River to the Ashley River and leaving over one-quarter of the city in ashes. Without question, many city troops were absent from their posts to assist friends and family in the wake of such a disaster. One Charleston woman recorded in her diary on December 16, 1861, "The past week will never be erased from the memory of Charlestonians. The terror! the misery, & desolation which has swept like a hurricane over our once fair city will never be forgotten as long as it stands."[74]

At the time the fire broke out, the Charleston Riflemen were encamped in the city and assisted the fire companies in combating the disastrous fire. Afterward the Aetna Fire Company presented a medal to the Riflemen for their conspicuous gallantry on that occasion. The Riflemen manned one of the Aetna's fire engines along the fire's southern boundary while that company was busy manning an engine along the northern boundary of the blaze.[75] Thus, without firing a musket at the enemy, the citizen soldiers of Charleston had fought their first battle, though it was against nature. And so ended their first full year of the war.

CHAPTER 3

The Charleston Battalion

The Union forces, occupying the relatively superfluous sea-island portion of the South Carolina coast, failed to develop an offensive against Charleston during the winter of 1861-62, and contented themselves instead with further establishing their position and raiding inland plantations. Their inactivity was fortunate for the Confederate defenders of Charleston because desperately needed reinforcements were not forthcoming, and the volunteer militia companies were due to muster out in February. With Federal troops just a few miles down the coast from Charleston, and an established blockade of the state's ports causing scarcities and rising prices, South Carolina authorities realized the likelihood of a prolonged war. They now endeavored to revamp their existing militia laws in order to force more men into military service for such a war.[1]

Aside from the volunteers on the coast and the twelve-month regiments in Virginia, South Carolina had filled only a third of its quota of "for the war" troops that the Confederate government in Richmond demanded. Granted, the state had sent 6,000 troops to Virginia in 1861 before any other state, but enlistment had waned, and early in 1862, state authorities took measures to enlist five new "war" regiments and reenlist enough twelve-month and volunteer units to make up the difference. For that reason, an appeal was made to South Carolina's twelve-month troops in Virginia to reenlist, and it was made known that on March 20 a new state law would take effect allowing all males between eighteen and forty-five to be conscripted.[2] Conscription was the absolute last resort in raising troops because it brought into the ranks those who previously had no intention of fighting. Units already in service could reenlist as volunteers—a much more favorable status—retaining their organization and either electing new officers or keeping their original officers.

The state's Executive Council resolved on February 4, 1862, that the volunteer corps of Charleston's Fourth Brigade be mustered into service for one year as "Local Defense Troops." A few days later the council issued a special order announcing that on the 19th of the month the city troops—volunteers and beat companies alike—must assemble at their camps, where "the Commanding Officers shall call for Volunteers to the number of TWO THIRDS of the original number of arms bearing men from each . . . and upon a failure upon the part of any Company to respond to such a call, he shall, ON THE SAME DAY, EXECUTE A DRAFT THEREFOR." When a sufficient number of men was obtained from each company, the company roll was to be deposited with the council and at that time "orders will be issued for rendezvousing of the Companies, and their organization into Battalions or Regiments." According to this resolution, battalions had to contain no less than four companies, and regiments exactly ten.[3]

In his farewell address to his troops, Order No. 231, dated February 7, 1862, Brig. Gen. Wilmot G. DeSaussure, commander of the Fourth Brigade of State Militia, thanked the volunteer companies of Charleston for their services and enjoined them to reenlist as volunteers: "Let it not be said that the citizen soldiery of Charleston were in vain called upon to volunteer for the completion of that Southern Independence which was there proclaimed and by them vindicated."[4] Reminding them that on February 19 they would be officially asked to reenlist or soon face conscription, DeSaussure appealed to their hearts: "Your Brigadier General indulges the hope that you will respond . . . & let your volunteering before that day be the reply of what part the citizen soldiery of the metropolis will bear in this their second war of independence."[5] DeSaussure's rhetoric simply echoed the will and civic pride of Charlestonians, who proclaimed:

> We trust, therefore, that Charleston will be prepared to respond nobly to the call for her quota, and that no draft will be necessary. . . . The country has furnished more than its quota. Let it not be said of Charleston that her people ever found wanting.[6]

So important it was to step forward of one's own accord that it was universally felt "the man capable of bearing arms, who stays at home in this emergency, is little better than a coward . . . and the man who waits to be drafted will be looked upon by volunteers with the contempt he deserves."[7] The February 19 deadline came to pass and, as instructed, the city companies assembled. Five days later, a list of twelve companies that were to be assigned to battalions and/or regiments was published. The list included the familiar volunteer companies as well as the beat companies.

Company No. 1: Calhoun Guards, Moultrie Guards, and Carolina Light Infantry (portion)

Company No. 2: Union Light Infantry

Company No. 3: James Rifles and Brooks Guard (becomes Charleston Light Infantry)

Company No. 4: Sumter Guards, Phoenix Rifles, Carolina Light Infantry (portion), and Beat No. 6

Company No. 5: Charleston Riflemen and Cadet Riflemen

Company No. 6: Jasper Greens (new) and Emerald Light Infantry (old Meagher Guards)

Company No. 7: Sarsfield Light Infantry (new) and Montgomery Guards

Company No. 8: Irish Volunteers

Company Nos. 9, 10, 11, and 12: Remaining beat companies

Now all that remained was for these companies to elect their officers. Already organized and with officers elected were two companies recruited under the banner of the Washington Light Infantry who were advertising as forming their own "Eutaw Battalion," as well as the new Beauregard Light Infantry, Arsenal Guards, and Washington Artillery.[8] The Beauregard Light Infantry chose to join forces with the Eutaw Battalion. Noticeably absent from this list were the German Fusiliers, who were also actively advertising for new recruits. Also curious was the fact that at this time the several companies containing Irishmen were promoting the idea of an independent "Irish Battalion," openly advertising the components of said battalion as being the original Irish Volunteers, the Emerald Light Infantry, and the Montgomery Guards. The latter two both recruited under the banner of existing companies serving in Virginia and lastly the new Sarsfield Light Infantry. For a brief period, even the Scottish Union Light Infantry was advertised as associated with these companies.[9]

The Eutaw Battalion was forming, and it appeared as though an Irish Battalion was in the works as well, but the first mention by name of a "Charleston Battalion" appeared in the February 24 edition of the *Mercury*, which exhorted:

> It has been proposed that a Charleston Battalion or Regiment be formed for the war. . . . It is due to the history and position of Charleston, to the part taken by Charleston in promoting secession, and to the alacrity with which our brethren and friends of the up country have rushed to our aid. Let Charleston be represented by a distinctive Battalion or Regiment or Legion.

The way had been paved for such a unit the week before on February 17, 1862, when the state authorized the formation of the "First Battalion of South Carolina Infantry," a unit specifically intended to represent the city of Charleston in the great struggle.[10]

On February 25, the results of the individual company

elections were published, revealing for the first time the officer corps of the intended Charleston Battalion as it was beginning to take shape. The results from the city companies numbered one through five were: Francis T. Miles, David Ramsay, Thomas Y. Simons, Henry C. King, and Julius A. Blake. Company Eight, the Irish Volunteers, was commanded by Edward MaGrath.[11] Capt. Samuel Lord, Jr., of the German Fusiliers, thus far absent from the roster of the city companies, was now listed as second in command of the Union Light Infantry behind David Ramsay, owing to a consolidation of these two companies.[12] At least in the case of the German Fusiliers, so many of their men were elderly and therefore restricted to guard duty that they counted less than forty men able to take the field in active campaigning. So Lord chose to join forces with the Union Light Infantry, resulting in a peculiar mixture of Germans and Scotsmen that on occasion presented a linguistic nightmare.[13]

Gradually, by the end of the first week in March, the Charleston Riflemen, Sumter Guards, Calhoun Guards, Union Light Infantry, Irish Volunteers, and Charleston Light Infantry had each individually been accepted by the state's Executive Council for twelve months' service. In addition to these, the four smaller Irish companies of the Emerald Light Infantry, Sarsfield Light Infantry, Jasper Greens, and Montgomery Guards had been consolidated into two new companies known as the "New Irish Volunteers."[14]

By the second week of March, the new Charleston Battalion, so far containing only four companies, was composed of the Charleston Riflemen, Sumter Guards, Calhoun Guards, and Charleston Light Infantry.[15] This battalion was encamped at Magnolia Camp Gist several miles southwest of the city along the Savannah & Charleston Railroad for the purpose of drill and recruiting only. "Those desirous of a pleasant time among friends for twelve months service"[16] and those who "wish to serve in this State, and in this way remain near their homes."[17] On March 14, 1862, Lt. Col. Peter Gaillard of the militia's Seventeenth Regiment was ordered to "take command . . . of the Camp of Instruction near Charleston, of the Charleston Companies," meaning those at Camp Gist, which he officially did on March 17.[18] The organization of the Charleston Battalion in this early period was: Charleston Riflemen, Company A; Charleston Light Infantry, Company B; Sumter Guards, Company C; Calhoun Guards, Company D.

Also encamped at Camp Gist were the companies intended to compose the Irish Battalion, including MaGrath's original Irish Volunteers and the Union Light Infantry.[19] As it turned out, however, the much-heralded Irish Battalion failed to materialize and the Union Light Infantry joined the Charleston Battalion on March 15, 1862.[20] MaGrath's Irish Volunteers held onto the dream of an Irish Battalion for a short time longer until it became clear that the legally required number of Irishmen could not be mustered to fill the ranks of such a unit. Finally MaGrath enlisted his company into Gaillard's battalion in April, almost a month after the other companies.[21]

On April 15, 1862, the Charleston Battalion—now six companies strong—"left the city . . . for the post of duty" on James Island with its organization complete and its officers elected for the period of one year's Confederate service in the defense of their city and state. In command of the battalion at this time were Lt. Col. Peter Gaillard and Maj. J. M. Harleston. As mentioned previously, the Seventeenth Regiment had a beat organization but contained only volunteer companies, and coincidentally consistent with antebellum militia structure, the new Charleston Battalion contained two companies of "Light Infantry" and one flanking company of "Riflemen."

The day after the Charleston Battalion took the field presumably for twelve months' service, the Confederate government passed a sweeping national conscription act, which declared every able-bodied Southern male between eighteen and thirty-five years old eligible for a compulsory military service of three years or the duration of the war, whichever came first. These Charlestonians were suddenly locked in for three years' service from the original date of their enlistments. As somewhat of a consolation in such cases, the Confederate government allowed all recently enlisted twelve-month troops to reorganize their companies and reelect their officers. By May all the battalion's companies were reorganized "for the war," with the most visible changes being that Capt. David Ramsay of the Union Light Infantry had been elevated to the position of major, unseating J. M. Harleston, who left the ranks of the battalion, and Pressley Smith had been appointed quartermaster of the battalion with the rank of captain. Additionally, the order of companies had been slightly altered. The unit's new organization was Company A, the Charleston Riflemen; Company B, the Charleston Light Infantry; Company C, the Irish Volunteers; Company D, the Sumter Guards; Company E, the Calhoun Guards; and Company F, the Union Light Infantry and German Fusiliers. The men were also extended the benefits of the previous December's national call for two- and three-year volunteers, which amounted to a fifty-dollar bounty and a sixty-day furlough with transportation furnished, which had more of an effect on morale than the reelecting of officers.[22]

Every volunteer company from the militia's Fourth Brigade that remained in South Carolina reorganized promptly for extended service. Some of these followed the lead of their earlier comrades and at this time attached themselves to existing South Carolina regiments already serving in Virginia, while others went to help form new regiments in the state like the Twenty-fifth South Carolina. Though many of this regiment's companies came from other corners of the state, its core was the Eutaw Battalion, and just as it had been in that battalion, Companies A and B of the new regiment were from the Washington Light Infantry. Much of the original prewar Washington Light Infantry militia company, which first organized in 1807, responded to the earliest call and went to Virginia in 1861 as Company A of the Hampton Legion. They served gallantly in nearly every major battle of that theatre all the way through General Lee's surrender at Appomattox. The two subsequent companies were recruited under the banner of the Washington Light Infantry during the early months of the conflict and by February of 1862 were filling the ranks of their Eutaw Battalion. This battalion remained in the Charleston theatre, where in July of 1862 the new Twenty-fifth South Carolina Infantry regiment was formed, thereafter often referred to as the "Eutaw Regiment." A fourth company was formed from the WLI, "composed mostly of aged and infirm members ineligible for active service" and charged with the task of protecting the records and property of the old organization.[23]

Another regiment formed during this season was the Twenty-fourth South Carolina Infantry, which has sometimes been mistaken for a city organization. The lieutenant colonel of the Twenty-fourth, Ellison Capers, was a Charlestonian and perhaps for that reason his regiment has often been thought of as having local roots. While the preponderance of the men in Company A of this regiment were indeed from Charleston, the men in the other nine companies hailed from Edgefield, Chester, Richland, Anderson, Abbeville, Colleton, Beaufort, and Marlboro, South Carolina.[24] One proud veteran of the Twenty-fourth hotly contested an article in the February 17, 1863, edition of the Charleston Daily Courier that claimed his unit was from Charleston, replying to the paper, "This we beg to correct. Of ten Companies composing said Regiment, there is only one from this city, and we think fully half of that is composed of country volunteers."

True to the design and desire of its officers and men, however, the Charleston Battalion managed to remain entirely native in its company organization. After the war, South Carolina brigadier general Johnson Hagood, a man who came to know the battalion well, recorded in his memoirs:

[It] was originally raised in Charleston . . . its officers were almost without exception Charlestonians, and the city element predominated in the ranks. . . . [It] was especially claimed by Charlestonians . . . and in consequence of its local popularity many of the best young men of the city were in its ranks. The average intelligence and social position of the rank and file were thus greater than most.[25]

APPROXIMATE UNIT STRENGTH

A battalion's strength was approximately half that of a regiment, and a typical regiment in the early days of the war numbered anywhere from 800 to 1,100 officers, noncommissioned officers, and privates. During the final months of 1860, when everyone was anxious to have a role in the exciting events that were unfolding, the city's volunteer companies numbered between 36 and 100 officers and enlisted men. The compiled service records of the battalion's companies reveal that the total number of officers, noncommissioned officers, and privates enlisted by the end of May 1862, including cooks and musicians, was:

Co. A = 93
Co. B = 97
Co. C = 98
Co. D = 83
Co. E = 74
Co. F = 113 (larger than the others due to the consolidation of ULI with GF)

Total = 558

CHAPTER 4

Charlestonians

In 1775, Charlestonians had organized themselves into the "Charles Towne Battalion" to defend the port city against the British, and counted among their number was Capt. Edward Rutledge, the youngest signer of the Declaration of Independence and brother of John Rutledge, president of the Republic of South Carolina and signer of the Constitution. Unlike the Charleston Battalion of the 1860s, the Charles Towne Battalion was an artillery battalion, which makes it an interesting coincidence that though the men of the 1860s battalion had been serving as infantry, due to the nature of Charleston's defenses several of the battalion's companies had advertised throughout February 1862 as recruiting for service as artillery. When British forces besieged the city in the spring of 1780, the Charles Towne Battalion engaged them north of the city along the siege lines near Charles Towne neck. The battalion along with 5,500 Continental troops were ultimately forced to surrender to the British on May 12, 1780, after nearly two months of fighting.

Following the Revolution, the city's name was changed from Charles Towne to Charleston and so too did the name of the artillery unit change to the Charleston Battalion. On May 2, 1791, the Charleston Battalion fired a fifteen-gun "Federal salute" to Pres. George Washington as he arrived at the city's Cooper River waterfront. In December of 1797, the unit was redesignated the "First Regiment of Artillery," and as such, sixty-four years later, the regiment's men were distributed between the city's "Washington Artillery" and "German Artillery" battalions. Regardless of any coincidental similarities, the Charleston Battalion of the 1860s was officially designated the First South Carolina Infantry Battalion and would serve as such until the close of the war.

General Hagood was not mistaken when he recorded in his memoirs that the officers of the 1860s Charleston Battalion were Charlestonians. Company A, the Charleston Riflemen, was under the command of Capt. Julius A. Blake and Lt. William Dove Walter. Blake, a commercial merchant whose office was at 13 Exchange Street along the city's Cooper River waterfront, resided at 10 Water Street near White Point Gardens.[1] At just thirty years old Blake had amassed a considerable fortune, having a real-estate worth of $10,000 and a personal wealth of $12,000.[2] Walter was a clerk for B. G. Heriot and lived at 65 Beaufain Street.[3] Under Blake and Walter were 2d Lt. Francis R. Lynch and Bvt. 2d Lt. J. C. Saltus. Twenty-nine-year-old Lynch worked at the Periodical Depot and lived on Meeting Street across from Burns Lane, and Saltus, a resident of 25 Mazyck Street, was a partner in Walker & Saltus sash and blind manufacturers.[4] In 1860 the Riflemen had been under the command of Capt. Joseph Johnson, Jr.,[5] a physician who lived at 107 King Street.[6]

As early as February 1, 1862, the Charleston Riflemen were advertising in the Charleston newspapers for volunteers to join their company; applications could be made at the company armory at 31 Broad Street between 10:00 A.M. and 2:00 P.M. Due to the nature of Charleston's defense, in a February 17 edition of the *Charleston Mercury* the unit was advertised as recruiting for artillery. The Riflemen went into camp of instruction on March 9, 1862, at Magnolia Camp Gist near Charleston. Eight days later, on the 17th, the company was mustered into Confederate service for a period of twelve months as local defense troops. On April 15, the company was ordered to the fortifications on James Island at Camp Royal, and then to the fortification at Secessionville on April 23.[7]

Company B, the Charleston Light Infantry, was captained

by Thomas Y. Simons, an attorney whose office at 63 Meeting Street was just around the corner from his home at 83 Broad Street.[8] Thirty-four-year-old Simons, like many Charlestonians, had attended Yale University and graduated in 1847 with a law degree. He returned to practice law in Charleston and later represented his native city in the state legislature from 1854 to 1860, also serving as a delegate to the Democratic National Convention in 1856 and the historic secession convention held in December 1860, to which document his signature is attached.[9] As one might expect of a Yale lawyer, Simons was fairly well off with a real property value of $18,000 and a personal property worth of $4,000.[10] Serving under Simons as lieutenant was Simons' own brother-in-law, thirty-year-old William Clarkson, a peacetime lieutenant in the city police department who lived on Limehouse Street below Tradd Street.[11] The Light Infantry's second lieutenant was twenty-seven-year-old William Sinkler, a wealthy planter who resided in Charleston with his wife and children and managed his plantation in St. John's Parish. No doubt much of Sinkler's wealth had been inherited, for at such a young age he had a personal worth of $50,000 and his land and other holdings amounted to $9,000.[12] Also serving as second lieutenant was twenty-six-year-old Alfred H. Masterman. Residing at 18 Vernon Street, Masterman had been born in England but had immigrated to Charleston with his family, several of members of which—including his own father—served under him in the company. True to the original tradition of one's surname being derived from one's occupation, Masterman was a jeweler and his father was a watchmaker.

The name "Charleston Light Infantry" dated to a militia company formed just after the Revolution but whose service was short-lived. In March of 1862 the name was revived and was applied to the remnant of city "Company No. 3," formed from the Jamison Rifles and the Brooks Guard. The captain of this company, Thomas Y. Simons, had been the captain of the Jamison Rifles. In February of 1862, Captain Simons was advertising for recruits, stating that he had "been requested to

take command of a Company for State defence" and that any-
one interested in joining him should call at his office across
from City Hall.[13] A month later the company was encamped at
Magnolia Camp Gist and applicants could inquire either at
the camp or with Mr. W. H. Boring on King Street.[14]

Company C, the Irish Volunteers, was commanded by Capt.
Edward Magrath. Like Captain Simons, Magrath was an attorney, with his office located at 45 Broad Street. Magrath lived
in the upper part of the city on Bee Street near Ashley
Avenue.[15] Though he had been in active service since secession, in April 1862 Magrath resigned his commission. A notation on his compiled service records indicates that he was
absent on sick leave in Charleston that month, his resignation
likely health related. Forty-year-old Magrath was replaced by
twenty-nine-year-old first lieutenant William H. Ryan, an engineer who lived at 89 Church Street.[16] Elevated to first lieutenant to fill Ryan's vacancy was thirty-five-year-old policeman
James M. Mulvaney, a resident of Horlbeck Alley.[17] Second
lieutenant of the Volunteers was A. E. Allemong, aged thirty
and another attorney, residing at 59 King.[18]

Magrath's "Old Irish Volunteers"—as they came to be
known in order to distinguish them as the original Irish military company—were organized sometime prior to 1798,
according to the *City Gazette* and *Daily Advertisers*, who advertised a meeting of the Irish Volunteers to be held on September 28, 1798, at the "Thatched Cabin." This structure sat at
the northeast corner of Meeting and Chalmers streets, opposite the site where Hibernian Hall would later be built. It is
believed that the Hibernian Society in Charleston originated
through these company meetings. The Volunteers tendered
their services during the War of 1812 but were not needed.
Again during the Seminole Wars in Florida the Volunteers
tendered their services, and under the command of "Captain
Henry" they served three months in Florida, where they
fought in a number of skirmishes with the Indians.[19]

When South Carolina seceded there were actually three

Irish companies in Charleston: the "old" Irish Volunteers, which joined the Charleston Battalion; the Montgomery Guards, newly organized in 1860 for the occasion of secession; and the Meagher Guards, also newly organized in 1860. The latter was renamed the Emerald Light Infantry in May of 1861 because its founder and namesake remained loyal to the Union. The Irish Volunteers were mustered into Confederate service as part of the Charleston Battalion for a period of twelve months on April 7, 1862.[20] After more instruction and drill, the company was sent to James Island and stationed at Legare's Point along the Stono River.[21]

Company D, the Sumter Guards, was commanded by Capt. Henry Campbell King and Lt. J. Ward Hopkins. Yet another attorney, forty-three-year-old King was a partner in Pettigru and King and lived at 68 Tradd Street.[22] King, whom most considered "national in his politics," had been for much of his adult life a Whig and had also frequently been elected to the state legislature.[23] Twenty-nine-year-old lieutenant Ward Hopkins was an accountant for C. T. Mitchell & Company and lived at 28 Church Street near White Point at the tip of the Charleston peninsula.[24] The company's second lieutenant was Peter J. Barbot, a forty-three-year-old accountant at North Commercial Wharf who lived at the corner of Montague and Smith streets near the College of Charleston.[25] Brevet second lieutenant was forty-one-year-old John J. Edwards, a partner in the commercial firm of Caldwell, Blakely & Company, located at 1 South Atlantic Wharf.[26] In the fall of 1861, Edwards resigned his position with that firm to enlist in the Sumter Guards, entering service as a third lieutenant.[27]

The Sumter Guards organized in 1812 under the name Jackson Guards, in honor of Gen. Andrew Jackson. General Jackson eventually became President Jackson, during which time he fell out of favor with South Carolinians due to his disrespect of John Calhoun and to his efforts to increase the powers of the federal government at the expense of states. As a result, in 1832, by "Act of Assembly," the company changed its name to Sumter Guards after Thomas Sumter, the famous South Carolina "Game Cock" during the Revolution.[28] During the Seminole Wars in Florida, the Guards offered their services but were not accepted.[29] The Sumter Guards indefinitely adjourned their drill and meetings in 1846 until the tumultuous election of November 1860, when on November 17 they officially reestablished themselves as a city militia company. In early 1862, the Sumter Guards advertised in the *Charleston Daily Courier* for recruits to join their command for twelve months' service in the state of South Carolina. All applicants were to inquire at 22 Broad Street.[30] Though they would serve as infantry, just three days later, on February 17, 1862, the Sumter Guards were advertising as recruiting for artillery.[31] In March of 1862, the Sumter Guards were officially mustered into Confederate service as part of the Charleston Battalion, and in April of 1862 they were stationed on James Island at the works at Secessionville.[32]

Company E, the Calhoun Guards, was under the command of Capt. Francis Turquand Miles and 1st Lt. Barnwell W. Palmer. At age thirty-five, Miles was a physician who lived at the corner of Calhoun and Lucas streets[33] and an alumnus of the College of Charleston and the Medical College of South Carolina, specializing in anatomy and physiology. He later studied in Cambridge, Massachusetts and Paris before returning to Charleston to teach anatomy. When the Civil War broke out, Miles "cast aside for the time the profession of his life and entered immediately into active service." During the spring of 1861 he enlisted as a private in the Phoenix Rifles, a volunteer militia company from the fire department.[34] Thirty-six-year-old Palmer, formerly the captain of the Moultrie Guards of the city's rifle regiment and a clerk for H. E. Vincent ship chandlers, lived at 3 King Street.[35] Second lieutenant of the guards was thirty-seven-year-old J. Waring Axson, a Hayne Street salesman who lived at 10 Hassell Street.[36] Third lieutenant of the company was forty-two-year-old John M. Easterby, who had served as fourth sergeant in Company F of the Palmetto Regiment during the Mexican War.[37] No longer on the roster was the Calhoun Guards' antebellum commander, Capt. John Fraser, a clerk with the Farmer's & Exchange Bank on East Bay Street.[38] The Calhoun Guards were mustered into Confederate service in March of 1862 and in April were stationed on James Island at the works at Secessionville.[39]

Company F was created by the consolidation of the Union Light Infantry and the German Fusiliers. The Union Light Infantry, known variously as the Scottish Company or the Charleston Highlanders, had a Charleston militia lineage dating back to 1806, when it was founded by the city's Scottish citizens. The captain of this company in 1862 was thirty-two-year-old David Ramsay, grandson of both Henry Laurens and South Carolina physician and historian Dr. David Ramsay. Laurens had been president of the Continental Congress and the only American ever imprisoned in the Tower of London. He was later exchanged for Lord Cornwallis after Cornwallis's surrender to General Washington at Yorktown. Dr. Ramsay was responsible for bringing the small-pox vaccination to the Southern colonies and writing a stinging history of the British campaign in South Carolina during the Revolution. Coincidentally, he served during the Revolution as surgeon of the original Charles Towne Battalion of artillery. Captured by the British when they occupied the city, Ramsay was imprisoned for eleven months at St. Augustine, Florida.

Grandson Capt. David Ramsay received his education from "the Universities of Europe and America," including the University of Heidelberg, and was an esteemed attorney, practicing with the firm Ramsay & Lockwood.[40] General Hagood rightly described him as being a "lawyer of high culture."[41] Ramsay had a real worth of $5,600 and personal value of $13,000[42] and lived on Broad Street between Meeting and King streets, probably in his grandfather's old apothecary shop.[43] Assisting Ramsay were twenty-one-year-old lieutenant George Brown, Jr., and twenty-five-year-old lieutenant Henry

Walker. Walker, a resident of 18 Magazine Street and business partner of Company A's 2d Lt. J. C. Saltus, became the battalion's adjutant.[44]

The German Fusiliers were commanded by Capt. Samuel Lord, Jr., a lawyer and commercial merchant with Whaley & Lord at 17 Exchange Street along the Cooper River.[45] The thirty-one-year-old lived with his elderly parents and several children of the Bloom family at 18 Society Street, north of the city market.[46] The German Fusiliers were organized in 1775 and participated in the defense of Charleston throughout 1776-77, the joint American-French assault against Savannah in 1779, and the siege of Charleston in 1780. During the British occupation of Charleston, the Fusiliers were forcefully disbanded for the remainder of the Revolution but reorganized as a militia company in 1782 and as such formed the honor guard for President Washington when he visited Charleston in 1791.[47] When in the 1830s the state of Florida asked for assistance from her neighbors in the Southeast to defend against the warring Seminole Indians, the Fusiliers immediately responded and saw active service defending St. Augustine. Their captain at that time was William Henry Timrod, father of future South Carolina poet laureate Henry Timrod. A decade later many Fusiliers volunteered for service in the Palmetto Regiment that went to fight in Mexico, and when John Calhoun died in 1850, the Fusiliers were appointed as part of the honor guard that escorted the great statesman's body through Charleston to Citadel Square.[48]

Like the Charleston Riflemen and Sumter Guards, the Union Light Infantry initially advertised as recruiting for artillery.[49] Under their new organization as Company F, David Ramsay became their senior officer. Under an Act of Confederate Congress dated August 21, 1861, the company mustered into Confederate service for a period of twelve months on March 15, 1862, and in April was stationed at Secessionville.[50]

For the next two and a half years, forty-nine-year-old lieutenant colonel Peter C. Gaillard would lead the Charleston

Battalion (henceforward often referred to as "Gaillard's Battalion") by example with his calm and disciplined manner. In December of 1860, Gaillard had been captain of the Phoenix Rifles, which he commanded until elevated to lieutenant colonel of the Seventeenth Regiment of militia in November 1861.[51] The Phoenix Rifles, along with the companies that joined the Charleston Battalion, had served under Gaillard in the Seventeenth Regiment until 1862, when the battalion was formed.

Peter Charles Gaillard was born in the village of St. Stephen's in St. John's Parish, Berkeley County, South Carolina, on December 29, 1812, at his father's plantation, Walnut Grove. He attended South Carolina College and in 1831 entered West Point Military Academy. Upon graduation in 1835, Gaillard was appointed brevet second lieutenant in the First U.S. Infantry and was officially commissioned as such in October 1836. Gaillard's pursuit of a military career followed in the footsteps of his grandfather, who had served alongside Francis Marion during the Revolution. The younger Gaillard's brief service in the U.S. Army took him across the country, first out to the northwest then back to the southeast to Florida, where he served under Zachary Taylor in the Seminole Wars. "Severe fevers" weakened his health, forcing him to resign his commission on April 30, 1838. He returned home and settled in Charleston, where he pursued commercial endeavors with the firm Gaillard & Snowden and, later that year, married Miss Anne L. Snowden.[52] Gaillard's firm was located at 5 Southern Wharf near the Exchange Building, and he and his wife lived at 5 Church Street.[53] In his memoirs, Johnson Hagood remembered Gaillard had "much of the old Roman type of character about him, had unbounded influence over his command, and was every inch a soldier."[54]

Officially ordered on March 7, 1862, Peter Gaillard received his commission in the Confederate Army as lieutenant colonel of the Charleston Battalion on April 18.[55] As a lieutenant colonel Gaillard initially received $194.16 per

month, plus expenses.[56] Second in command of the
Charleston Battalion, with his commission dated May 3, 1862,
was Maj. David Ramsay, who had been elevated to the position
from the captaincy of Company F.[57] Ramsay was to be com-
pensated $149 per month for his services, a good deal less
than his antebellum legal fees.[58]

BATTALION SURVEY

Slave Owners

In 1860, Charleston had a population of 40,522 people and
was the third largest city in the South, behind Baltimore,
which was a distant second to New Orleans. Of its citizens,
23,376 were white, 3,237 were free blacks, and the remaining
13,909—more than a third of the population—were slaves.[59]
Just prior to the Civil War, over 50 percent of Charleston's
white males over the age of twenty owned one or more
slaves.[60]

Though Company B's 2d Lt. William Sinkler was the only
bona-fide planter in the battalion's officer corps, he was *not*
the Charleston Battalion's only slave owner. Indeed, approximately one-third of the other officers, including Lieutenant
Colonel Gaillard, appear as slave owners on the 1860 Slave
Schedules. Sinkler was, however, by far the largest slave owner
in the lot, personally owning fifty-eight slaves ranging in age
from three months to fifty years.[61] This impressive holding
ranked Sinkler among the 200 largest slaveholders in the
Charleston area. The other officers were not planters, had far
fewer slaves, and therefore probably held theirs as domestic
servants and/or possibly, in the paternalistic sense, to ensure
them a better quality of life. Gaillard owned five slaves, and
based on their ages—three females aged sixty, forty-five, and
fourteen and two males aged forty and twenty-two—they
appear to have been a family.[62] Capt. David Ramsay owned
seven slaves, and again, judging by their ages, they seem to be

a family of two parents, three children, and one grandparent.[63] Capt. Thomas Y. Simons of Company B owned five slaves[64] and Capt. Henry C. King of the Sumter Guards—whose father-in-law was the staunch Unionist lawyer James L. Pettigru—owned ten slaves.[65] By owning fewer than twelve slaves, these officers, except Sinkler, were the typical urban Charleston slave owner and representative of at least half the slave owners in the South, who likewise owned fewer than twelve slaves.[66]

With the established statistic that over 50 percent of Charleston's white males over twenty years owned one or more slaves, it stands to reason that the ranks of the battalion were peppered with slaveholders like Pvt. Joseph Howell of the Charleston Riflemen, who owned seven slaves, and fellow rifleman Pvt. J. J. Laurens, who owned ten.[67] In the Charleston Light Infantry, Pvt. H. B. Cobia owned fourteen and in the German Fusiliers, Pvt. H. Schroder owned seven slaves.[68] Large-scale slaveholding was not restricted to Lieutenant Sinkler, however. Indeed, also ranked among the 200 largest slaveholders in the area were Pvt. A. Brown of the Charleston Light Infantry, who owned fifty-three slaves,[69] and W. Williams, a private in the Sumter Guards who owned a plantation in St. James, Goose Creek, where he held fifty-four slaves.[70] In addition, Calhoun Guardsman J. S. Tennent owned forty-one slaves at his St. James plantation.[71]

Just as one expects to find slave owners among the officers and enlisted personnel of any Confederate unit, 140 years of historical study ought to have equally revealed a few slaves and free blacks in the ranks as well. These men made contributions to the defense of Charleston just as valuable as those of their white comrades. The compiled service records of the men of the Charleston Battalion reveal at least thirty-three black Charlestonians on the rolls. Twenty-four of these were listed as cooks and eight as musicians or drummers. It should be noted that musicians often took on the role of stretcher bearers during an engagement and were thus exposed to their fair share of danger. Seven of these men were given the rank of private in addition to their status as cook or musician. It is interesting to note that the Confederate Congress allowed whites and free blacks to serve as head cooks for the equal wage of twenty dollars per month and as assistant cooks for fifteen dollars per month. Slaves could be enlisted as cooks also but only with written consent of their master. When in 1863 the Union Army began enlisting blacks as soldiers, they were only paid ten dollars per month; thus a freed black in theory made more money and was exposed to less danger in the service of the Confederacy than the Union.[72] There was only one black in the battalion whose muster card stated clearly only "private" and not also "cook" or "musician." He was Jacob of Company B—a slave.

Of these thirty-three black Charlestonians, only three were not regularly enlisted. Of these three, one was specifically listed as a slave and another as a free black. In all three cases, however, a notation on their muster cards clearly states, "not regularly enlisted," indicating that they may have been body servants of officers or other privileged soldiers.

Black Charlestonians in the Battalion

Company A:
    Johnson, cook, enlisted 3/17/62
    Ben, cook, not enlisted (slave)
    Fevers, cook, not enlisted (free black)
    George, cook, enlisted 3/17/62
    Cuthbert, G., musician, enlisted 3/17/62
    Middleton, drummer, enlisted 3/17/62
    March, musician, enlisted 3/17/62

Company B:
    Chase, W., private/musician, enlisted 3/25/62 (free black carpenter, home President Street)
    Edward, drummer, enlisted 4/16/63

Jacob, private, enlisted 6/62
Manly, cook, 3/62
Masterman, February, private/cook, enlisted 3/24/62
Masterman, Jacob, cook, enlisted 7/1/62
Phoenix, C., cook, enlisted 7/1/62
Ralph, D., cook, enlisted 7/1/62
William, cook, enlisted 3/63

Company C:
Bingo, Dick, cook, enlisted 4/62
Thomas, Dubose, cook, enlisted spring/62
Lewis, cook, enlisted 4/7/62
Henry, musician, enlisted 4/7/62
Pcter, cook, enlisted 4/7/62
Smith, J., cook, not enlisted

Company D:
Chase, Robert, musician, enlisted 3/24/62
Gadsden, Daniel, private/cook, enlisted 3/24/62
Jacob King, private/cook, enlisted 3/24/62*

Company E:
Cole, Thomas J., drummer, enlisted 2/18/63 (free
black drayman, home Line Street)
Cook, Moses, cook, enlisted 10/8/62

Company F:
Goings, A., private/cook, enlisted 3/15/62
Lee, Isaac, private/cook, enlisted 3/15/62
Marcus, K., cook, enlisted summer/62
Small, J., cook, enlisted 3/15/62

Company G (created in August 1863 from Company B):
Jeffery, cook, enlisted 8/14/63
Thomas, cook, enlisted 8/14/63

*Jacob King of Company D, Sumter Guards, may have been

a servant of the company's captain, Henry C. King.

Ethnic Diversity

The ethnic diversity of the men in the Charleston Battalion is also revealing. In times of peace, the volunteer militia companies served as social or fraternal organizations, but they also played a vital role as ethnic support groups for the influx of foreigners immigrating to Charleston. The English founded Charleston, but a considerable number of French Huguenots had helped establish the city in its earliest days. Lt. Col. Peter Gaillard, Capt. Thomas Y. Simons, Lt. William Clarkson, and 2d Lt. William Sinkler, along with many others in the ranks, were of French Huguenot descent. Gaillard, for example, had descended from Pierre Gaillard of the town of Cherneaux in Poitou, France. There were many collateral lines in South Carolina descended from Pierre Gaillard, and with Pierre being the French equivalent of Peter, there were, through the eighteenth and nineteenth centuries, many Peter Gaillards. Owing to their persecution in France generations before, the Huguenots of South Carolina intermarried with resolute consistency, making it sometimes difficult to sort through their lengthy hyphenated surnames to discern which line a person came from. In 1853, Lieutenant Clarkson, for example, married Miss Margaret Susan Simons, daughter of Thomas Y. Simons, a well-respected Charleston physician, and sister of Clarkson's superior, Capt. Thomas Y. Simons, making their command over the Charleston Light Infantry a family affair.

Along with the English and French Huguenots, many Scots contributed to the city's development. The Scots of Charleston organized a militia company, the Union Light Infantry, in 1807, and in 1862, when it mustered into the Charleston Battalion, it contained many recent Scottish immigrants as well as those who had lived in Charleston for generations.[73]

An unprecedented wave of immigration to the United

Sates occurred in the two decades before the war, particularly of Irish and Germans. This wave can be attributed to several factors, namely the Irish famine of the 1840s, European labor surpluses, land shortages, and the revolutions that swept over Europe in 1848. In 1845, approximately 150,000 immigrants came to America, but by 1855 the number had leaped to 425,000 each year, 87 percent of them, however, settling in free states. Fully two-thirds of these immigrants were Irish and the remainder German speaking.[74] The entire Southern United States in 1860 contained 84,763 Irish, 73,579 Germans, and 53,304 English and Scottish.[75] Charleston had felt the pressure of immigration during this period as well, and without question the two largest groups of newcomers were the Germans and Irish. The 1,944 Germans and 3,263 Irish made up more than 25 percent of Charleston's white population.[76] Most of these immigrants came to Charleston in search of a better life, and community organizations already established in the city such as militia companies served as welcoming committees and political machines. Two Charleston Battalion companies in particular were such organizations—Company C, the Irish Volunteers, and Company F, containing many Germans from the German Fusiliers.

One German newspaperman in Charleston wrote that many of the Germans arriving in the city were from northern Germany and that they engaged in "petty shopkeeping."[77] All told, during the 1850s, 68 percent of Charleston's German males were categorized as business owners or professionals, whereas only 22 percent of Irish males were in this class. Perhaps choice of occupation mirrored the desperation of the Irish, well supported by the fact that the Irish outnumbered the Germans nearly two to one in Charleston. Only 4 percent of Charleston's German males were unskilled, but nearly 52 percent of Irish males were unskilled.[78] The only category in which the two groups seemed equal was that of skilled labor/trade, with 22 percent of Irish males possessing skills or trades and 25 percent of German males, but the breakdown of their individual skills reveals their differing goals. For example, the skilled Irishmen were found largely in the occupations of brick masons, painters, and coopers, while skilled Germans tended to be bakers, shoemakers, and tailors.[79]

At least one soldier, Adolphus John Jager, broke the German-Irish barrier. Adolph Jager was born in 1844 in Hamburg, Germany and immigrated early in life with his family to Charleston, where they lived at 10 Rose Lane. Adolph served in the Sixteenth Regiment of South Carolina militia during November and December of 1862 but his service with the Charleston Battalion began on January 1, 1863, when he entered the ranks of the Irish Volunteers. Following the war, Jager, a Roman Catholic, married a Catholic Irish girl, Julia Mahoney. True to the occupational trends, he became a grocer, and as fate would have it, this German was ironically the last surviving member of the Irish Volunteers. Jager died on April 14, 1925, in Savannah, Georgia.

Occupations

The 1859 and 1860 city directories and census provide the occupations for many of the Charlestonians in the battalion. Unfortunately, as with modern phone books and directories, many residents chose not to be listed. Furthermore, others chose to list their home address but not their occupations, while often individuals who boarded at hotels or other private residences also do not appear in these records. In addition, many of the battalion's younger members do not appear in these directories as workers or homeowners. Yet the occupational data available remains telling. Interestingly, this data falls somewhat in line with the conclusion stated in the previous section that the largest concentration of men represented from the Irish Volunteers were indeed unskilled laborers and that the largest concentration of men from the German Fusiliers were indeed merchants and storekeepers. Aside from these employment tendencies, however, virtually every other

Pvt. Adolph Jager. Courtesy Tom Walsh.

occupation was represented in these two companies. Examples include: John Burke, forty-seven-year-old harbor pilot; Egan Thomas, thirty-five-year-old artist; Henry W. Hendricks, thirty-five-year-old deputy sheriff; John May, undertaker; twenty-three-year-old porter John Dwyer; and James Grey, "Master in Equity." In addition, a ship's mate, gas worker, newspaper owner, lawyers, scavengers, clerks, and cotton factors were scattered among the two companies.[80]

A survey of Company A, the Charleston Riflemen, for example, reveals that this company would have been more appropriately named the "Salesman Company" or the "King Street Legion" since more of its men were King Street salesmen than any other single occupation. Of course, a few salesmen appear on the rolls of Companies C and F as well, but very few, and far fewer unskilled laborers, appear on the rolls of Companies B, D, and E.[81]

While the Charleston Light Infantry, Company B, contained a few King Street salesmen, it is interesting that, unlike in the other companies, there is no one particular occupation that stands out as more represented than the others. Indeed, there seems to have been three of each of the following: policemen, clerks, and blue-collar workers. Virtually every other occupation was also represented, including two jewelers, Alfred H. and William Masterman, two fruiterers, several accountants, a tavern owner, a cigar-store owner, a boat captain, and a cotton shipper.[82]

Company D, the Sumter Guards, contained a few salesmen too, as well as planters, a doctor, a butcher, a night watchman, at least three policemen, the secretary of the Palmetto Savings Bank, and a couple of attorneys. The largest single occupation represented in this company, however, appeared to be that of clerk/accountant.[83]

Similarly, a survey of Company E, the Calhoun Guards, revealed a wide variety of occupations. There were at least one barroom owner, a photographer, a planter, and the familiar crowd of commission merchants, factors, and bankers, plus a shoemaker, two "makers of fine hats and caps," and the construction foreman for the incomplete U.S. Customs House. But as with Company D, the largest occupation represented was that of clerk/accountant.[84]

Maturity

General Hagood remembered of these men: "The average intelligence and social position of the rank and file were . . . greater than most."[85] In a December 1862 letter, Capt. Julius Blake of Company A urged Major Ramsay to consider the wishes of the men on a particular issue because "though they be in the ranks . . . many of them are intelligent gentlemen and holding in civil life social position equal to the officers."[86] One such example was thirty-seven-year-old Pinckney Brown—a private in Company E, Calhoun Guards—known as "a gentleman of means and literary culture."[87] Brown was a signer of the Ordinance of Secession who refused promotion and served for two years as a private in the ranks. Wounded in June of 1862 at Secessionville, Brown was killed in a skirmish on May 14, 1864, at Drewry's Bluff, Virginia.[88] Another example from the same company, and no spring chicken, was fifty-four-year-old Theodore Dehon Jervey, who enlisted as a private.[89] Jervey, who resided at 113 Wentworth Street, was involved with the importing and exporting firm of W. C. Bee & Company[90] and also in blockade running during the war. Following the war, he held the post of Collector of the Port of Charleston from 1885 to 1889, and at the time of his death he was president of the Miner's and Merchant's Bank of Charleston.[91]

Indeed, while the officer corps of the Charleston Battalion contained politicians, commercial and shipping merchants, factors, accountants, physicians, planters, and many lawyers, it has been demonstrated that a goodly number of enlisted men came from the same social and occupational strata. General Hagood remembered that, because of education and culture, their "discipline and character were peculiar" and that the unit had "too much intelligence and too little rigidity of discipline in its ranks for men without force of character to command it successfully."[92] Traditionally, years of study are required to become well educated, and time is also consumed in gaining success in business and making social connections, all of which are characteristic of men on average older than most Confederate soldiers. From forty-nine-year-old lieutenant colonel Peter Gaillard down to twenty-one-year-old lieutenant George Brown, Jr., the average age of the battalion's officer corps was thirty-five, mature yet not past their prime. Having officers of this maturity was not unusual in Civil War battalions or regiments, but if, as General Hagood states, the ranks were filled with the intellectual and social peers of these officers, then perhaps this battalion as a whole was older.

It was remembered that many of the men in the Irish Volunteers "had long passed the meridian of life when they entered Confederate service, and their furrowed brows and whitened locks formed a striking contrast to the ruddy cheeks and beaming eyes of their younger and stronger comrades."[93] With the secession of South Carolina from the Union, several German citizens organized a company of the younger German Fusiliers into the "German Volunteers," a light artillery company that served in Virginia for much of the war. However, the older members of the Fusiliers remained behind in defense of their adopted city, joining the Charleston Battalion.[94] Consequently, the Fusiliers had too few men of sufficient youth and strength to take the field and had to be combined with the Union Light Infantry in order to form Company F.

On one occasion, a detachment from Company A, the Charleston Riflemen, marched through the city and an admiring onlooker noted, "Conspicuous in the ranks was the venerable Reeves, whose bent form and silvery locks gave evidence of at least three score and ten years. . . . What an earnest of the feeling of our people when the gray-haired old men . . . shoulder their rifles, knapsacks and blankets to join with the young in the cause of their native State."[95] Reeves was just one of the many soldiers in the battalion with silvery locks. Fifty-year-old A. J. Champlin of the Calhoun Guards and fifty-two-year-old George W. Lawton of the Union Light Infantry mustered into the Charleston Battalion in the spring of 1862 and served side by side with their younger comrades until Champlin was killed and Lawton mortally wounded in Petersburg, Virginia two years later.

Granted, probably not every soldier in the battalion was gray of hair and bent of form, but the ranks were filled with men more mature than the traditional eighteen-year-old Confederate soldier. Prof. Bell Irvin Wiley, in his 1943 study entitled *The Life of Johnny Reb*, sampled 11,000 infantry privates from eleven states, ninety-four regiments, and 141 companies endeavoring to determine the average age of the Confederate soldier. Wiley's numbers—which remain the authority on the subject—indicate that the age most represented was indeed eighteen and that the percentages decreased rapidly after age twenty-three. Only one-sixth of these men were in their thirties, and one-twenty-fifth were in their forties.[96] A tabulation of ages of the 118,000 Union soldiers from the state of Indiana supports Professor Wiley's research that even in the North the age most represented was eighteen, with over 20,000 Indiana soldiers in that column. The number dropped by half at age nineteen, with 10,519 men represented, and continued to drop steadily as the ages increased.[97]

Relative to the Charleston Battalion, only Companies C and F provide the men's ages in their compiled service records, and only for those who enlisted in the spring of 1862, when the battalion was formed. Out of sixty-nine men in Company C whose ages were provided, only fifteen soldiers were between eighteen and twenty-three years old, eighteen men were between twenty-four and twenty-nine years old, while thirty-six men were thirty or older, eleven of them being in their forties. The service records of eighty-five men from Company F reveal twenty-one soldiers between the ages of eighteen and twenty-three, another twenty-six men between twenty-four and twenty-nine years old, and thirty-six men in their thirties and forties. Two soldiers from this company, George Lawton and Peter Davis, were over fifty years old.

In a similar comparison, a compiled casualty list of the Sumter Guards records fifty-six deaths between 1863 and 1865, of which forty-six of the men's ages are provided. Fifteen men out of the forty-six were between eighteen and twenty-three years old, and one soldier, Pvt. T. B. Garrett, was sixteen years old. On the other hand, twenty-two of the forty-six men were between thirty and forty years old and two were over forty.[98]

Based on the available ages of the men of the Twenty-fifth South Carolina, which included the Charlestonians of the Washington Light Infantry, the average age in that regiment was twenty-five years old. The average age of the officers of that regiment was thirty years old, as opposed to the thirty-five-year-old average found in the Charleston Battalion.[99] Collectively, these samples suggest that the battalion contained a higher concentration of mature soldiers than the average Confederate unit, excluding of course "Reserves" and "Home Guards," which often contained the elderly.

A classic example of the Home Guard unit, North or South, was the Thirty-seventh Iowa, or "Graybeard Regiment," known as "a remarkable command . . . organized under General Order 89, State of Iowa, August 25, 1862, which specified that the regiment should be 'composed of active and vigorous men, *over the age of 45*, and be assigned to garrison duty . . . the average age of the men thus recruited was 57 years.'" A number of these men, however, were in their seventies and eighties. Though they performed guard and garrison duty throughout the war, it was boasted, "Had occasion demanded they would undoubtedly have gone into action cheerfully and acquitted themselves honorably."[100]

Whether its men were older than most soldiers or not, the Charleston Battalion was not intended to be a garrison or detail unit, and so the men earnestly pitched into the task of drill throughout the spring of 1862, preparing to meet their ultimate charge: the defense of Charleston. Though most of them had been in active militia service since December 1860, none of them had yet engaged the enemy face to face. In May, the whole battalion was placed on James Island, where they encamped near the fortification on the Secessionville peninsula.[101] After viewing the battalion on dress parade, fellow Charlestonian and lieutenant colonel of the Twenty-fourth South Carolina Infantry, Ellison Capers, wrote that he was "highly gratified with the performance of their evolutions." He added, "The Battalion is admirably drilled and disciplined, and will doubtless make their mark on the enemy; and do honor to their mother city, if the chances of war shall afford them an opportunity."[102] The battalion would not have long to wait before "chance" afforded them an opportunity.

CHAPTER 5

"All Did Their Duty": Secessionville

The coming of spring revived the seemingly lethargic Union Army at Hilton Head as they finally commenced the long anticipated advance up the coast to operate against Charleston. By May 21, John's Island and Wadmalaw Island south of the city had been evacuated by all Confederate troops, save for a small cavalry force that remained to keep an eye on the enemy gunboats sitting in the Stono River.[1] For the last ten days of May, these boats plied the Stono, shelling the Southern defenses on James Island as far away as the work on the Secessionville peninsula.[2]

An assault on Charleston seemed imminent. Gen. John Pemberton, Lee's successor as commander of the Department of South Carolina, Georgia and Florida headquartered in Charleston, ordered that the troops on James Island be issued forty rounds of ammunition, fill their canteens, and be ready to meet the enemy whenever he left the cover of his gunboats. Pemberton then wired Savannah and Richmond informing them of the threat and requesting reinforcements.[3] Making use of all available forces, Pemberton even called out the Citadel Corps of Cadets with their eight pieces of artillery to report to James Island.[4]

Gen. S. R. Gist, Confederate commander of James Island, had approximately thirteen thousand troops with which to meet the advancing Federals. Among them were the men of the Charleston Battalion.[5] To harass the menacing Federal gunboats, General Gist ordered Capt. C. E. Chichester to take

seventy artillerists and four forty-two-pounder cannon of the
Gist Guards out to Sol Legare Island. As ordered, Chichester
erected a small earthwork on the island on Sunday, June 1,
and that evening took his guns out to await the enemy. During
the crossing from the mainland to Legare via River's Causeway, however, the second gun in line fell off the causeway
bridge into the mud, where it stuck fast. Unable to pry the
gun out, Chichester sent the rest of his cannon on to the
earthwork, where they dueled with the Federal gunboats for a
solid hour the next morning. Five o'clock that afternoon
Chichester received the order to pull back to the mainland
after dark, but unfortunately, disaster struck again. His train
of weapons now numbered three instead of four guns, and
while recrossing the causeway the first and third gun in line
also fell off into the muck near the piece from the day before.
Enlisting more help, but still unable to retrieve the guns,
Chichester headed back to James Island with the disappoint-
ing news.[6]

At about 3:00 P.M. on Monday, June 2, the Seventy-ninth
New York Highlanders landed on Battery Island, followed
later by the Twenty-eighth Massachusetts and four companies
of the 100th Pennsylvania. These troops were the vanguard of
Union brigadier general Henry Benham's 7,000-man force
brought up from Hilton Head and Port Royal to assault
Charleston. Before dark, the Federals made a reconnaissance
on neighboring Sol Legare Island, and though Confederate
pickets were clearly visible across the marsh on James Island,
there was no exchange of fire.[7] Among the Confederate pickets observing the blue-clad interlopers were members of the
Charleston Riflemen, Company A of the Charleston Battalion.

The next day a more forceful probe was made by the Federals, designed to sweep Sol Legare Island clear of any Rebels.
This reconnaissance resulted instead in a contest over the possession of Chichester's three Southern cannon stuck in the
mud off River's Causeway. The expedition, consisting of elements of the Seventy-ninth New York, 100th Pennsylvania, and
Twenty-eighth Massachusetts, moved east down the length of

the island, reaching the Legare plantation house and its out-buildings, where it halted.

To the left across a cotton field was a wooded area, and beyond that was River's Causeway and James Island. The Twenty-eighth Massachusetts was sent out to investigate the woods and what they might conceal, finding shortly that they hid Confederate pickets. Hearing that a brisk firefight was under way, Capt. James Cline swung his detachment of the 100th Pennsylvania to the left and formed line of battle to meet whatever Southern force came out of the woods.

Half an hour later, the battered remnants of the Twenty-eighth Massachusetts came scrambling back with Rebels hot on their heels. Though they tried to regain their composure, after another Rebel volley the Twenty-eighth continued their retreat, leaving exposed Captain Cline and his 160 Pennsylvanians. Cline stated, "In a few minutes the action became quite warm, and several were killed or wounded."

Cline was soon ordered to send twenty men farther to the east past the Legare slave quarters to protect the Federal right flank, which he promptly did. As the action intensified, Cline personally went back for reinforcements, and upon his return to his exposed position the Confederates in the woods broke forward in a charge.[8] Capt. Hazard Stevens, son of Brig. Gen. Isaac I. Stevens, the commander of General Benham's second division, recorded the Confederate charge years later in a biography of his father. Captain Stevens wrote that the Confederates were in a wood just across a large cotton field from the Federal position and here the firing began. "Soon afterward a column of the enemy, apparently a regiment, which was in fact the Charleston Battalion, the crack corps of the city, emerged from the woods and advanced by the flank in columns of four *headed by a mounted officer*. In this order they charged down the road and across the field at the double quick."[9]

Captain Stevens had it correct, except that not all of the Confederates in the charge were of the Charleston Battalion. The mounted officer was Lt. Col. Ellison Capers, at the head of a portion of his Twenty-fourth South Carolina Infantry.[10] In the ensuing fight, Cline and his small detachment were isolated by the Charleston Battalion and captured. Sgt. Robert Moffatt of the 100th Pennsylvania remembered Captain Cline shouting to his men to cut their way out, as the Confederates "kept pouring volley after volley on us till within 10 paces of us."[11] These were the first of many Union prisoners taken in their first campaign to capture Charleston.

The weather was not favorable during the first few days of June, and the conditions on the day of the skirmish were "unsuited for military operations of any kind; from nine o'clock in the morning until late at night the rain poured down in continuous showers, the roads and fields were transformed into miry bogs."[12] These were the miry bogs that held fast to Chichester's guns.

As Lieutenant Colonel Capers remembered it, "[I] was sent before day on June 3, with part of the Twenty-fourth and a big rope, to pull the guns out of the bog, and had no idea of a fight until I got to Lamar's fort. There Lamar told me if I got the guns I would have to fight for them. *I did fight for them.*"[13]

According to Capers' official report of the skirmish, he arrived at River's Causeway and found the advance Southern pickets, consisting of the Beauregard Light Infantry and Charleston Riflemen, close to the enemy, in particular the Twenty-eighth Massachusetts, who had halted in the woods to their front. These two companies were ordered to join Capers' command, and using the Marion Rifles as skirmishers, the plan was to drive the Twenty-eighth out of the woods. Upon reaching the opposite side of the causeway, Capers formed his companies to the right of it and after a half-hour's work drove the enemy across Legare's fields and back to the Legare house and its outbuildings.

Despite the risk of being exposed to Union shellfire from the gunboats in the Stono River, Capers resolved to make an assault on these buildings so as to isolate Cline's smaller force.

Capers planned to use the remaining five companies of the Charleston Battalion under Lt. Col. Peter Gaillard, who had just reached the field, to surround and capture Cline and his men. Capers estimated the total strength of Gaillard's five companies, excluding Company A, at only "about 124 strong," a much lower figure than previously estimated. Four of the battalion's six companies were designated to take part in the charge. These were: Company A, the Charleston Riflemen under Lieutenant Lynch; Company C, Irish Volunteers under Captain Ryan; Company D, Sumter Guards under Lieutenant Hopkins; and Company E, Calhoun Guards under Captain Miles. Lieutenant Colonel Gaillard "took command of the center and left as a reserve."[14] According to Capers, the charge was "well and nobly performed," capturing twenty-two prisoners of the 100th Pennsylvania. Taken under fire from Federals hidden behind the Legare slave quarters, as well as Union gunboats, Capers withdrew his force under cover of a fire provided by the Charleston Light Infantry and the Union Light Infantry/German Fusiliers, which were the remaining companies B and F of the Charleston Battalion, along with three of his own from the Twenty-fourth.[15]

Gaillard reported that he hurried to the scene of action when he was informed that Capers was engaged with a larger force than his own and, upon receiving his orders, sent his companies into line. Gaillard stated that "by some misapprehension" a part of the Union Light Infantry and German Fusiliers was somehow caught up in the charge but never got into the action. Though his command behaved admirably in their first fight, Gaillard felt it necessary to mention in his report that most of his men had been either on picket duty or performing labor during the twenty-four-hour period prior to the action and were, therefore, not at their best.[16]

The chief results of this engagement were twofold: (1) the capture of enemy prisoners who would provide information as to the strength and intent of the Union landing force and (2) valuable combat experience for troops who had yet to see any real fighting. Though all of the companies belonging to the Charleston Battalion played a part in the fight at the Legare plantation, the god of war—"Chance"—shed its grace on a company that was to prove itself on many battlefields as particularly anxious to fight. It had been Company C, the Irish Volunteers, who isolated Cline's detachment of the 100th Pennsylvania near the Legare house, ultimately forcing them to surrender. In the final rush on the Federal position, Captain Ryan grabbed the Pennsylvanian Cline by the throat and, with his sword raised in the air, demanded his surrender. One of Cline's men, "a strapping Pennsylvanian," charged Ryan, intending to run him through with a bayonet, until Confederate Irishman Rody Whelan bounded forward. "[Whelan] locked bayonets with his Captain's assailant. . . . The bayonets twisted like wire, when by a quick twist of the wrist elevating the guns, Whelan . . . laid his opponent sprawling on the ground—saving his Captain's life."[17]

The Charleston Battalion's casualties in the skirmish were as follows. Lt. Henry Walker, adjutant of the battalion and a member of Company F, was wounded and captured. Although his fellow soldiers thought that he recovered while a prisoner of war, twenty-one-year-old Walker died of his wounds on July 4, 1862.[18] Walker's peacetime business partner and member of Company A, Lt. J. C. Saltus, was slightly wounded. Also of Company A, Sergeant Patterson was slightly wounded, as were Privates Chaney and Carstens, and Pvt. J. A. Kelly was missing. In Company C, twenty-six-year-old third corporal Edward Lannigan and twenty-one-year-old private Edward Lee were wounded, as was Pvt. Roddy Whelan, who had saved Captain Ryan from being bayoneted. Twenty-year-old private Thomas Bresman was also among the Irish Volunteers wounded but his injuries proved to be fatal.[19, 20] Also listed as wounded from this company but yet not found on its rolls was Pvt. M. Hartwell.[21] In Company D, Lt. J. Ward Hopkins was "seriously, but not dangerously wounded," along with Pvt.

William MacBeth.[22] The *Charleston Daily Courier* reported an additional soldier in Company D, one of two brothers, Isaac and Hertz Valentine, as being slightly wounded,[23] though neither of the compiled service records for these brothers indicates that they were wounded in the skirmish.

With a foothold thus gained, Brig. Gen. Henry Benham landed the balance of his two divisions on the southern tip of James Island, where they further established their base camps and erected batteries used to engage nearby Confederate works, with special attention paid to the "Tower Battery" on the Secessionville peninsula. To his superior at Hilton Head, Gen. David Hunter, General Benham reported it "indispensable that we should destroy or capture the fort and floating battery of the enemy at Secessionville." These Confederate positions with their heavy guns quickly became a nuisance threatening the security of Benham's camps; therefore, he ordered a reconnaissance in force to capture the battery, scheduled to take place in the predawn darkness of June 16, 1862. Brigadier General Stevens' second division, amounting to 3,000 men with four guns in tow, led the Federal advance, while the 3,100 men of Brig. Gen. Horatio Wright's first division supported them.[24]

General Stevens' division was in position by 3:30 a.m. on June 16 and advanced half an hour later, capturing a handful of Southern pickets before pushing out into the cotton fields that lay before the Confederate position at Secessionville. Other Confederate pickets from the Charleston Battalion's Company B, the Charleston Light Infantry, under the command of Captain Simons, managed to escape and scrambled back to their battery with the enemy following closely.[25] The assaulting Union column consisted of eight companies of the Eighth Michigan, the entire Seventh Connecticut, and the Twenty-eighth Massachusetts, preceded at a short distance by the remaining companies C and F of the Eighth Michigan, acting as a storming party. Swiftly, the Federal host moved forward to within 100 yards of the Confederate work, when a violent burst of canister and grapeshot split their line in two. Stunned but no less determined, the left companies scrambled to the left and the right companies to the right.[26] The battle of Secessionville was on.

Geography played a critical role, favoring Confederate defense in the ensuing battle. The cotton fields over which the Federal forces advanced narrowed sharply from 200 yards wide, where the charge began, down to hardly more than 50 yards wide just in front of the Confederate battery, offering little space for maneuver. The fortification itself was advantageously placed, lying in the shape of a giant *M* astride the narrow isthmus of the Secessionville peninsula, with each leg resting on an impassible marsh and tidal creek. Its walls of hard-packed earth, which rose nine feet high, were crowned with artillery. Immediately in front of the work, felled timber and a ditch seven feet deep created obstacles. Yet despite such formidable defenses, the three companies of the Eighth Michigan moving to the right managed to gain the parapet, where they grappled with the Confederate artillerists. At this point the Michiganders overwhelmed the gunners and more and more Northern troops entered the fort.

A second blast of canister had struck the Union column before it could find shelter along the marsh. This round had been administered by the Tower Battery's commander, Lt. Col. T. G. Lamar, who was laboring frantically—and with some success—to break the enemy attack using his guns since few infantry were on hand. Lamar's small infantry force amounted to a few pickets from Captain Simons' Charleston Light Infantry, Captain Miles with his Calhoun Guards, who had spent the night at the battery,[27] and a 100-man fatigue party from the Twenty-second South Carolina Infantry arrived from James Island. Expecting only to perform labor on the fortification that day, these men had slogged for three hours through the predawn darkness, a trek made worse by a coastal thundershower, with the result that they were nearly exhausted on their arrival. Adrenaline revived them, however, and Lamar quickly threw them into line adding to the Confederate defense. Knowing that his force would soon be overwhelmed by the Federal reinforcements gathering in the cotton fields before him, Lamar ordered Captain Simons to hurry back to the camps, eight hundred or so yards in rear of the fortification, and bring up the Charleston Battalion and the Pee Dee Battalion.[28] Simons quickly returned with the 125 men of the Pee Dee Battalion, followed closely by the Charleston Battalion. The Pee Dee Battalion entered the fort to find Union troops to their left pouring into the battery. Halting only to form a battle line and receive orders, these men rushed forward and swept the invaders back over the parapet and out of the fort. As the Pee Dees reached the crest, they halted in the face of a withering musketry fire delivered by a Union line formed in the brush and weeds along the base of the fort's nine-foot-high wall. Here the two sides locked into a close-range duel.[29]

Though the Federals had not gained the parapet on the Confederate right, they were poised to do so, having reduced the gun crew defending that flank to only one lieutenant and two privates. Before they could exploit their advantage, however, Lamar directed Miles and the Calhoun Guards to the threatened right angle, and the rest of the Charleston Battalion rushing into the fort formed alongside.[30]

About this time Lamar was struck in the neck by an enemy ball and he soon placed Gaillard in charge of the right angle and flank. Not long afterward Gaillard was also wounded, but he continued to command his men until the engagement neared its close. An eyewitness remembered Gaillard's "heroic conduct" as he held his men to their work. Here on the right as on the left the battle now settled down to a duel, with both sides loading and firing as fast as they could at point-blank range. On both flanks the Southerners were atop the walls of the fort and the Northerners were huddled behind the thin fringe of myrtle bushes and trees skirting the marshes at the base of the fort's walls.

Each of the battalion's companies arriving quickly found a place in line and added its fire. The Sumter Guards were led by Capt. Henry King, who insisted on joining his men in the fight even though he was suffering from a serious illness. Courageous though he was, King was soon felled by a bullet in the chest, becoming perhaps the first member of the Charleston Battalion to fall. More casualties in his Sumter Guards quickly followed his wounding. Thirty-four-year-old Samuel F. Edgerton was shot through the left hip and died the next day. Twenty-nine-year-old corporal Isaac Valentine, born and educated in Charleston, was killed by enemy fire upon reaching the parapet. Valentine, whose twin brother, Hertz, was severely wounded in the arm during the battle, was a bookkeeper for Gibbes & Company.[31]

Other companies were also feeling the effects of the Federal fire. Captain Miles of the Calhoun Guards was a notable Charleston physician, and as he assisted a wounded comrade, he was severely wounded in the thigh by a Federal volley. Though the papers listed Miles as being killed in action, he rapidly recovered.[32] Thirty-year-old private Thomas Parker of the Calhoun Guards was killed instantly when a bullet drilled into his brain, entering behind his left ear. Parker was raised and educated in Charleston, where he had become a wealthy commercial merchant and partner in the firm Robert Adger & Company. J. B. N. Hammett, an established attorney and a private in Company B, the Charleston Light Infantry, also died along this portion of the line, leaving behind a wife and two children. Nineteen-year-old private Gustavus Poznanski, who had been living with his parents in Canada prior to the outbreak of hostilities, became one of the youngest members of the Charleston Light Infantry—and the whole battalion, for that matter—to be killed in the battle on the right of Lamar's Tower Battery.[33]

Among the Federal regiments forming for another assault in the fields in front of the Confederate position was the

Seventy-ninth New York Infantry, nicknamed the "Highlanders" because of their predominantly Scottish composition. In their ranks was Alexander Campbell, who with his brother James had been born in Scotland and immigrated with the family to the United States just before the war. Alexander chose to settle in the North and fight for the Union, while James Campbell, twenty-six years old, had settled in Charleston and at the moment was a member of the Charleston Battalion's Scottish Union Light Infantry. Unbeknownst to each other, they were on the same field of battle, Alexander preparing with his comrades to mount a second charge against the Confederate left, and James rushing to support the Confederate right. Upon reaching the parapet with his company, James personally repulsed a group of Union attackers by rolling a log over them, and he then fended off several more with the handspike of a nearby cannon until he was able to secure a rifle.[34] Miraculously both James and Alexander survived the battle. Thirty-six-year-old sergeant Robert Joseph Henry, also of the Union Light Infantry, was not as fortunate as James Campbell. Born and raised in Charleston, Henry was killed early in the engagement on the very same stretch of parapet by a Union bullet that bored into his skull under his left ear. He left behind a wife and four-month-old child.[35]

The Pee Dee Battalion had stabilized the situation on the work's left angle and flank, and the bulk of the Charleston Battalion had accomplished the same on the right, but the left center of the position was literally undefended, as Capt. Samuel Reed and most of his gunners of the First South Carolina Artillery had been shot down. Just as the Charleston Battalion arrived on the scene, Col. Thomas Wagner of the First called out for volunteers to operate and support Reed's gun at the left center. Eagerly responding to Wagner's call, no doubt to sustain the reputation won in the skirmish of June 3, Capt. William H. Ryan and his Irish Volunteers veered off from their comrades and rushed to the threatened position. Thirty-year-old private William Shelton acted as gunner and, aided by others, poured a steady fire on the enemy to their front, right, and left.[36]

The entire battle thus far had consumed probably no more than half an hour, but in spite of its brevity it had been a very dynamic and deadly thirty minutes, the results so far being only that the initial Federal assault had been checked. Union troops remained grounded on each flank but managed to fire on the Confederate defenders. Long-range Federal artillery shells screaming in from faraway Sol Legare Island were now in play against the Confederate defenders as well. Meanwhile, Federal reinforcements in the form of the Seventy-ninth New York were rushing forward through the cotton fields out front, launching the day's second charge against the Confederate position. Forming in support for a third charge was the 100th Pennsylvania, a portion of which had been captured by the Charleston Battalion on June 3.

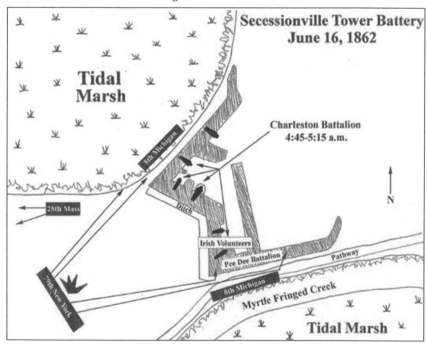

Map by author.

Onward came the brave Scotsmen of the Seventy-ninth New York, undeterred by the sight of the wreckage-strewn battlefield over which they passed. As they approached the fort, they received blast after blast of artillery similar to those administered to the Eighth Michigan that preceded them, yet still they rushed forward. Manning Reed's gun, the Irish Volunteers poured an effective fire of both artillery and musketry into the charging New Yorkers with the result that, like the Michiganders, the left companies of the regiment went to the left of the battery and the right companies went to the right. There they joined the wearied Michiganders who had been driven back by the Pee Dees. On this front the Seventy-ninth successfully pushed farther around the Confederate left flank, where they quickly mounted the parapet and renewed the hand-to-hand struggle with the South Carolinians.[37] Federal infantry also gained the parapet at the left angle amongst the Irish Volunteers and poured a serious enfilading fire across the interior of the battery. Daniel Howard, a twenty-five-year-old private in the Irish Volunteers, grappled with a Union attacker in what was described as "a desperate hand to hand combat." Howard struggled with his attacker but was overpowered, losing his life near Reed's cannon.[38] This second assault was ambitious, had momentum, and might have won the day but for want of adequate support from the 100th Pennsylvania. As their charge began, these "Round Heads" coming up behind the Highlanders were practically atomized by the well-served guns of Lamar's battery, and those who survived clung to the ground. Ere long the decision was made by the Union high command to break off the contest altogether and withdraw what survivors they could from the battlefield. After forty-five minutes of fighting, the Union frontal assaults against Lamar's Tower Battery had been met and repulsed. There was, however, still some fighting to be done.

One hundred and twenty-five yards across the marsh protecting the Confederate right flank, the rattle of musketry was heard followed in a split second by a shower of bullets and booming artillery fire from an undetected Federal force. The exhausted men of the Charleston Battalion had just begun to relax after their fight when they were rudely jolted by this fire. These fresh Union troops, namely the Third New Hampshire Infantry and Third Rhode Island Heavy Artillery, were pouring a "continuous and deadly fire," witnesses reported. "The gun carriages were perforated and torn by many balls. Many of our men fell at the guns and along the line formed to the rearward of the battery on its right flank."[39] These New Englanders had managed to reach a point behind the Confederate right flank where they could fire into the unprotected rear of the battery, and resultantly the few remaining Confederate artillerists were compelled to abandon their guns and take cover while the infantry desperately returned the enemy fire.

Due to loss of blood from his neck wound, Lieutenant Colonel Lamar now passed command of the entire battery to Lieutenant Colonel Gaillard, who was himself severely wounded in the knee. Without hesitation, Gaillard moved some of his men down the bank of the marsh, where they stood opposite their foe and exchanged rifle shot for rifle shot in a slugging match of endurance. Regarding this affair in his official report of the engagement, Lamar—who remained on the field even after he had passed command to Gaillard—simply stated that the enemy "made a flank movement on my right . . . where they were gallantly met by the Charleston Battalion." The exhausted Charlestonians tore cartridges and rammed home round after round to the point of giving out, when on the field arrived reinforcements in the form of the Fourth Louisiana Battalion, who according to Lamar "gallantly met [the Federals] with a cheer."[40] The *Charleston Mercury* reported, "This reinforcement and its galling fire disheartened the foe."[41] In addition to the arrival of the Louisianans at the battery, playing on the rear of the Federal flank movement and hastening their flight were the

Twenty-fourth South Carolina Infantry and Eutaw Battalion, who both rapidly advanced from their camps several miles from the battlefield to aid in the Union defeat.

The battle of Secessionville was over as far as the actual fighting was concerned, though Federal guns kept up an annoying fire that lasted for some time. The weary Charlestonians hunkered down to endure the shellfire, most of which became embedded in the battery walls or harmlessly overshot the position, though a few shells did burst above the work, and their fragments caused the final casualties of the engagement. Capt. Julius Blake of Company A, the Charleston Riflemen, was wounded at this time by a piece of shell. Lt. John J. Edwards of Company D, the Sumter Guards, rushed to assist the fallen Blake when a second shell exploded, killing Edwards instantly with a fragment through his brain.[42] Edwards was, perhaps, the final casualty of the battle.[43]

When the Confederate killed and wounded were tallied up, unquestionably the First South Carolina Artillery had seen the worst of it. These unarmed artillerists had been shot down like cattle in the opening moments of the battle when the Eighth Michigan charged over the parapet on the Confederate left. As far as the infantry was concerned, a quick scan of the casualty list suggests that the Charleston Battalion bore the brunt of the Union attack against the Secessionville battery, with a total loss of forty-nine officers and men killed, wounded, or captured. This was almost half of the battalion's total force engaged. The battalion had sustained an astonishing loss to its officer corps—far more than any other unit in the fight—with ten officers killed or wounded. In fact, the Charleston Battalion accounted for nearly half the total number of Confederate officers killed and fully three-quarters of the Confederate officers wounded in the battle, out of the ten commands that participated in the action in some capacity. The second-longest infantry casualty list belonged to the Pee

Dee Battalion, which lost one officer and twenty-eight men killed or wounded.[44]

Casualties in the Charleston Battalion, June 16, 1862

Lt. Col. Peter C. Gaillard wounded in knee.

Co. A: Capt. Julius Blake and Lts. Francis R. Lynch and J. C. Saltus wounded. Cpl. J. W. Guy and Pvts. Samuel F. Collins, James Barkley, and E. N. Jeanerette captured on picket duty June 8, 1862.

Co. B: Pvts. P. Gilhooly, J. B. N. Hammett, and Gustavus Poznanski killed. Pvt. John Andrews killed in camp at Secessionville when shell burst near his tent.[45] Pvts. M. Lacy and W. H. Sutcliffe wounded. Pvts. J. R. Gibbes and P. J. Johnson wounded and captured.

Co. C: Pvt. Dan Howard killed. 1st Sgt. John Burke, Pvts. Edward Lannigan, John May, and John Murphy, and Q.M. R. P. Smith wounded. Edward Lee wounded and missing.

Co. D: Capt. Henry C. King, Lt. John J. Edwards, and Pvts. S. F. Edgerton and Isaac Valentine killed. Pvts. G. W. Dingle, R. C. Evans, W. W. Johnson, T. P. Lockwood, A. J. Roumilat, E. S. Tennant, Hertz Valentine, and J. T. Wells wounded.

Co. E: Pvt. T. Parker killed. Capt. Francis T. Miles, Lt. J. Waring Axson, 5th Sgt. S. C. Black, and Pvts. C. P. Brown, C. B. Buist, H. E. Choate, Isaac Holmes, and J. E. J. Smith wounded.

Co. F: Sgt. R. S. Henry killed. Lt. George Brown and Pvts. James Davis and William Comans wounded.[46]

As the list of casualties indicates, a number of men from the battalion were no longer alive to share in the glory. Two of the most lamented of all the Confederate dead were the battalion's Capt. Henry C. King and Lt. John J. Edwards, both of the Sumter Guards. Charlestonian William Grayson wrote in his diary that Secessionville had "cost the Confederates a number of valuable lives, among these are some of my old and valued acquaintances, Henry King, John Edwards and others . . . the cause cannot fail which is consecrated by such sacrifices."[47] The *Charleston Mercury* eulogized Henry King as "kindly and genial, and adverse from quarrel," adding that "he came slowly and reluctantly to the issue of disunion, to which, with unfaltering and steady zeal, he devoted himself, for life and death."[48] Prior to the battle, the question was raised as to why at his age and ill health he did not resign from service. To a brother officer, King had answered that "his honor was involved in the struggle, and he could not quit the field."[49] Of John Edwards, the *Mercury* wrote, "There were not many men amongst us who had so universally won the warm regard of all around him. . . . He was a noble, high-toned gentleman; and, being very wealthy, could have easily screened himself from military duty, but his honor   dictated his path of duty."[50] Lt. J. Ward Hopkins rose to captain of the Sumter Guards. Peter J. Barbot was elevated to lieutenant, though he would resign his commission just a few months later, on September 25, 1862.[51]

As the battle had neared its close, Gaillard succumbed to his wound and passed command of the Tower Battery to Lieutenant Colonel McEnery, who commanded the recently arrived Louisiana Battalion. Command of the Charleston Battalion passed to Maj. David Ramsay, as did responsibility for writing the official postbattle report of the battalion's role in the engagement. Once things settled down, with the enemy chased back to their camps along the Stono and the wounded tended to, Ramsay's report, less than a page in length, was turned in on June 21, 1862.

Penned by one of Charleston's leading attorneys, the body of this brief document opened frankly with: "All did their duty, and the list of dead and wounded will testify with what devotion." Unable to list every act of gallantry "simply because it would be to furnish a roll of those engaged," Ramsay first remarked on the "distinguished conduct and skill of Lieutenant Colonel Gaillard." The major next recounted the log-rolling and handspike episode of Lt. James Campbell of Company F and also how "Mr. Josiah Tennant, of the Calhoun Guard, . . . felled no less than six of the enemy." The Charleston papers ran with these two larger-than-life displays of courage, and local gossip embellished the feats of Campbell and Tennant even further, particularly in the case of the latter. Some time later, prominent Confederate diarist Mary Chestnut recorded, "Tennant proved himself a crack shot at Secessionville. They handed him rifles loaded in rapid succession. And at the point he aimed were found thirty dead men."[52] In his report, Major Ramsay further sustained the reputation rightly won on June 3 by Capt. William Ryan, noting his handling of Reed's twenty-four-pounder gun. Ramsay honored Lt. George Brown and Sgt. Henry Hendricks of Company F and Lt. Alexander Allemong of Company C for their bravery in bringing up ammunition time and again through a heavy volume of enemy musketry.[53] Thirty-five-year-old Sergeant Hendricks, a peacetime deputy sheriff, was also dispatched under a heavy fire to direct the movements of the Louisiana Battalion as they approached the scene of battle "without receiving the slightest injury, and resumed his place at the battery . . . it was a gallant and daring feat, eliciting the admiration of both officers and men."[54]

On up the chain of command, the reports rang with praise for the Charleston Battalion and its defense of the Tower Battery. Lieutenant Colonel Lamar thanked foremost among the infantry Capt. Francis Miles and his Calhoun Guards, who were the first troops to be placed in line. According to Lamar, Miles "and his men fought like heroes and did all that men could do." Lamar also praised Lieutenant Colonel Gaillard and Major Ramsay, who "conducted themselves with the utmost coolness as gallant as officers could be." Finally he spoke of the whole battalion, whose men "acted with commendable courage and determination and deserve the thanks of the country."[55] Again ranked chief among the infantry, this time by Gen. Nathan Evans, commander of James Island, was the

Charleston Battalion. Evans echoed the sentiment of his subordinate, Lamar, that "the country, and South Carolina in particular, owe a debt of gratitude and thanks which I know a grateful people will acknowledge."[56]

Shortly after the battle, Brig. Gen. William Duncan Smith was placed in command of James Island. On June 22, 1862, Smith issued an order, directed to Major Ramsay but read aloud to the whole battalion, that stated, "Allow me to express to you, Col. Gaillard being absent, my appreciation of your gallant services and of the distinguished conduct of your Battalion in the defence of Secessionville."[57]

Two and a half weeks before the battle of Secessionville, the Charleston Battalion's rank and file numbered (on paper at least) 558 men, but Lt. Col. Ellison Capers of the Twenty-fourth South Carolina Infantry had estimated five companies of the battalion at "about 124 strong" on June 3, 1862. In his postbattle report of Secessionville, the Charleston Battalion's Maj. David Ramsay stated that he had only 100 men in the fight, all six companies being represented. Chiefly sickness was responsible for such small numbers, especially considering the low-country fevers of June, but also many battalion soldiers were older, and for many of the men the transition from urban life to soldiering had been taxing. Other factors also contributed to the battalion's poor show of strength. From the beginning, subtract the more than 30 cooks and musicians from the firing line. Nativity played a key role as well. Being Charlestonians of social, economic, and political clout, a considerable number of men from this hometown unit managed to gain detached duty to less arduous service in the Confederate shops and hospitals or to supervise engineering and civilian operations. Several men had transferred to different units by June of 1862, several more men had died of disease or by accident, some men were on furlough, and lastly a few more had outright deserted or were otherwise AWOL. It is believed that these factors helped cut the battalion's effective strength by as much as two-thirds, leaving perhaps fewer than 176 men available to fight the battle of Secessionville. Doubtless, on the morning of battle, each of the six companies left a detachment behind to guard their camps and form a reserve force as well. These battlefield and other reductions account for the smallness of force presented by the battalion at Secessionville.

The basis for the theory that sickness played a major role in the battalion's low effective strength is the surviving muster and pay rolls of Company E, the Calhoun Guards. For the initial muster period extending from March 24, 1862, through April 30, 1862—before strenuous campaigning began—there were present for duty in the Calhoun Guards one captain, one first lieutenant, one second lieutenant, one brevet second lieutenant, four sergeants, and thirty-two privates, for a total of only forty men. This does not include absentees but the company total, once it included absentees, was raised to sixty-seven. For the period ending on June 30, 1862—well into the low country's disease season and after their first battle—this company counted only seventeen privates, two sergeants, two corporals, and one lieutenant present for duty: twenty-two men total. Nine casualties were sustained at Secessionville, but a staggering twenty-two officers and men were absent from Company E due to sickness. Another officer and seven privates were on furlough.[58] Clearly the fighting strength of the Calhoun Guards was reduced by half due to sickness and nearly two-thirds when other absentees are included. Historically, sickness was the largest killer in all nineteenth-century warfare; it is therefore probable that similar percentages held true for each of the battalion's companies in the summer of 1862.

CHAPTER 6

Recruitment and Resupply

On July 8, 1862, the Charleston Battalion was ordered to "encamp near Saint Stephen's Railroad Station," nearly forty miles up the Northeastern Railroad from Charleston.[1] St. Stephen's was a sleepy little village where the railroad crossed the Santee River in a region long ago settled by French Huguenot immigrants come to Carolina in search of religious tolerance. Though these Frenchmen had initially quarreled with the Anglicans over political control of the early colony, almost two centuries later, by 1860, the Huguenot progeny were counted among the most prosperous planters in South Carolina and the wealthiest lawyers and businessmen in Charleston.

With 170 years of naturalization behind them, many Huguenots patriotically answered the call of their state in 1860, and a few of them, as soldiers in the Charleston Battalion, were headed to visit relatives in the second week of July 1862, riding the rails up the Northeastern Railroad to St. Stephen's. Awaiting the battalion's arrival at St. Stephen's was their wounded lieutenant colonel Gaillard, who was born in the neighborhood and whose family had fled to St. Stephen's as the Union Army approached Charleston. According to a newspaper correspondent at St. Stephen's, Gaillard was "in the bosom of his family, rapidly recovering from his wound."[2] The casualty list after Secessionville clearly shows that the battalion had sustained the greatest loss among the infantry and was certainly in need of rest and relaxation. No doubt that fact coupled with Gaillard's presence were the chief reasons the battalion had been sent up to St. Stephen's, but a more suitable place of retirement couldn't have been found. St. Stephen's Depot was as far away from the fighting as you could get, while at the same time being directly linked by rail to Charleston—no more than a few hours' travel time away—if the battalion was summoned back.

It is also possible that the battalion was sent to St. Stephen's to coincide with a Federal raid up the Santee. On Monday July 7, 1862, one day before the battalion was ordered to St. Stephen's, two Federal gunboats ascended the Santee with the presumed intention of destroying the Northeastern Railroad Bridge. Confederate batteries along the river attacked both boats, and when they turned to flee, one boat grounded on a sandbar and was captured along with its crew. The Union loss was reported to be at 100 killed and wounded.[3]

Another major attraction of this region was that the country along the Santee afforded more food than the burdened farmland around Charleston, which supported the city's inhabitants as well as its defenders. On July 9 a Charleston paper recorded that in St. Stephen's "the most extensive corn crops of the entire district promise to be unusually abundant, say from thirty-five to fifty bushels an acre."[4] It was not unusual for Confederate troops to be deployed in a certain locale simply to assist in the harvesting of crops, so perhaps the men of the Charleston Battalion were sent to trade combat for some good old-fashioned farm work.

Peace and quiet abounded at St. Stephen's and food was plentiful too, but little was accomplished in the way of recouping the losses sustained during the fighting June 3-16. Only six new recruits joined the battalion while it was away in St. Stephen's. Credited to Company B were Thomas Hughes, a fruiterer who lived at 28 State Street, and Nassau Street resident W. Taylor, both of whom joined in August. Also joining in August, but going to Company C, were Patrick Dailey and Spring Street laborer Thomas Connelly. Lastly, credited to Company D were J.Cheek and Henry Poyas Foster. Cheek was from Charleston, like the other men, and he enlisted on July 21 as a transfer from the Sixth South Carolina Cavalry. Foster was from nearby Summerville but had been educated in Charleston and was preparing to attend the College of Charleston at the time of his enlistment on July 27, 1862.[5]

Well rested and with their wounds healed, the battalion had returned to Charleston by late August or early September, where they encamped throughout the city at locations like Citadel Square, the Race Course, and Camps Limehouse, Simons, Magnolia, and Gaillard. Martial law, which had reigned over Charleston since before Secessionville, was repealed on August 19, but the men for the most part still remained confined to their camps. It is hard to imagine being a soldier on duty in your own city, encamped perhaps just a few blocks away from your home or businesses, yet lacking the total freedom to pop in and say hello to family and co-workers. The officers, on the other hand, had considerable freedom, and some even chose to quarter themselves in their private residences. The officers, like many in the ranks, were prominent men of the city and enjoyed easy access to the commanding general. From time to time they could be found visiting with General Beauregard at his quarters in the Mills House Hotel.[6] Drill, fatigue duty, and dress parade, however, became routine for the men in the ranks to keep them from growing idle. What free time they had they spent largely in camp.

Martial law had been abolished owing to the fact that the Federals had officially broken their stranglehold on the city and returned to Hilton Head. Coinciding with the repeal of martial law and the withdrawal of the enemy, Charlestonians witnessed for several nights a comet in the sky just west of the North Star. It was faint enough, as comets go, that it might have gone unnoticed but for the fact that many considered it a good omen.

Martial law or no, a military force was still needed to patrol the streets, and Lt. Col. Peter Gaillard was detailed as provost marshal over the city. Naturally the Charleston Battalion, posted in the city, was the provost guard and Maj. David Ramsay commanded. Capt. Thomas Y. Simons of Company B was detached as acting judge advocate of the department.[7]

Falling under Gaillard's authority were two unfortunate fatalities, which occurred in December. Twenty-one-year-old 3d Sgt. Lawrence Maddigan of Company C was killed when Pvt. James Edmonds, also of Company C, accidentally discharged his gun. Maddigan died at Roper Hospital on December 5 and was buried the next day.[8] It is presumed that the shooting was accidental, as there is little evidence to the contrary, though eight months later, in August of 1863, Edmonds' service record ends with him "in confinement under sentence." In June, he had been on detached duty at the gas works, so his confinement may have been unrelated to the shooting.[9]

On Christmas Eve night, Pvt. Samuel F. Collins of Company A was murdered on King Street "by some person or persons unknown."[10] Collins and three others from his company had been captured by Union troops while on picket duty a week before the battle of Secessionville and had just been exchanged in October. Collins had survived being captured by the enemy, along with the rigors of imprisonment at Fort Delaware, Delaware, and Fort Columbus, New York, only to be murdered on Christmas Eve in his own city.[11] Such deaths, though unfortunate, might well be expected in a wartime environment, with thousands of men bearing weapons, many of them having been exposed to combat and somewhat desensitized to violence. With the revocation of martial law, however, came a resurgence of crime and vice, as the soldiers in the city had more latitude to roam about. Often soldiers committed crimes against other soldiers as well as against the civilian populace. On one occasion in late 1862, nine drunken sailors ransacked a local bar. In another violent episode a crowd of soldiers threw bricks at a young naval officer.[12] Such violence stemmed in large part from the alcohol distilled and sold in bars on virtually every street near the city's waterfront, and such raucous behavior spilled over into the multitude of brothels that accommodated the physical needs of the intoxicated soldiers and sailors.

Replacing battlefield losses now that the battalion had returned to Charleston was not difficult. Being *the* "distinctive City Battalion" had a number of advantages when billeted in its own city, not the least of which was the ability to attract new recruits. From late August 1862 to December 31, 1862, over sixty men joined the Charleston Battalion, replacing their battle and other losses. Most of these men were from Charleston, like forty-five-year old John Cassidy, an Irish-born policeman who joined Company F. Virtually all these men were victims of the Confederacy's April 1862 conscription act; however, it is curious that fully half of the new recruits were credited in particular to Company B, the Charleston Light Infantry. In September, Company B counted forty-nine privates, noncommissioned officers, cooks, and musicians and four officers. By the end of December Captain Simons received uniform coats, shirts, drawers, socks, and shoes for eighty-seven men.[13]

The whole battalion received new uniforms as presents that Christmas but gone were the elaborate dress parade uniforms of 1860-61. The drab Confederate gray or greenish-tan "butternut" uniform was the standard issue. New clothes were new clothes nonetheless, and at a formal muster held on December 31 at Citadel Square, one witness recorded that the battalion "wore their new uniforms and presented a remarkably fine appearance . . . they were invariably praised by the spectators." Following the review, Major Ramsay paraded his men down Meeting Street to Confederate Headquarters, where they gave a salute to General Beauregard.[14]

The Charleston Battalion remained posted in the city throughout the winter, sharing the city's parks and squares with the South Carolina Siege Train, Twenty-first Battalion of Georgia Cavalry, and Forty-sixth Georgia Infantry, though some of the officers managed to sleep in their own beds at their peacetime homes.[15] On January 22, Company E, the Calhoun Guards, was ordered by Gen. Roswell Ripley, commander of Charleston's defenses, to move from its camp at Colums Lumber Yard to White Point Garden "for the purpose of taking charge of the guns stationed there and drilling as heavy artillery." Three days later, on January 25, 1863, Company E effectively became an artillery company and would serve as such for the next seven months.[16] As mentioned earlier, due to the nature of Charleston's defenses, several of the Charleston Battalion's companies had advertised in February of 1862 as organizing for the artillery—Company E, however, was not one of them.

Only the Charleston Battalion and South Carolina Siege Train remained posted in the city by May.[17] The *Charleston Mercury* declared, "The dress parades of the Charleston Battalion . . . are daily witnessed by a large number of spectators." These parades, which occurred each afternoon at 5:30 on Union Wharf, were one of the few social highlights in a city enduring the hardships of war. The *Mercury* went on to say, "The maneuvers of the battalion are most complete and expert, and a visit to Union Wharf in the afternoon will be amply repaid."[18] Dress parades served as a recruiting stimulus as well, and throughout the spring and summer more and more men flocked to the banner of the Charleston Battalion. As was the case during the previous fall, not all were from Charleston. Indeed, due to conscription, men from the midlands and upstate now entered the battalion's ranks. Thirty-two-year-old Josiah Newton and thirty-seven-year-old H. H. Martin, both farmers from Laurens County, joined the battalion during this time. Unaccustomed to the coastal climate, Newton was hospitalized due to fevers in July of 1863 and Martin died of typhoid on August 9, 1863, leaving behind a wife and several children.[19] Thirty-six-year-old Aaron Arnold from Spartanburg enlisted in Company B a short time later and, like Martin, was soon afflicted with typhoid fever. He died on August 9, 1863, in Summerville, South Carolina, a retreat twenty miles northwest of Charleston considered to be a healthier location.[20] This was the fate of many a soldier from the higher elevations who came to Charleston only to die from sickness before ever firing a shot in defense of their state and country.

Many of the new men, however, were hometown soldiers selecting their hometown battalion, thereby maintaining the unit's Charlestonian integrity. True to form, these men represented every race, class, and occupation found in their diverse city, from Company A's B. L. Groverman, a cabinetmaker who lived on Bogard Street, to Middle Street grocer D. Hines, who enlisted in Company B. Spring Street gardener Edward Hanley and James O'Neill, an eighteen-year-old orphan employed as a blacksmith, both Irishmen, joined Company C, the Irish Volunteers. Likewise, Charlestonians of German descent like carpenter Frederick Seibert of Sires Alley joined Company F—in part the German Fusiliers. E. T. Hughes, a bookkeeper at the Planters & Mechanical Bank, joined Company E, as did Thomas Cole, a free black drayman residing on Line Street who joined as a drummer. Also during this season, policeman William Cleary, who lived on Linguard Street, and bank treasurer S. W. Fisher, who resided on Smith Street, both joined Company D.[21]

Two complete anomalies in the influx of new soldiers were Irishmen John Cronin and William Mullins. Forty-seven-year-old private Cronin was a Virginia resident who had emigrated from Ireland. He had not been in the Palmetto State very long and was perhaps not as motivated as other South Carolinian soldiers. By the end of the summer he had deserted to the Union Army and taken the Oath of Allegiance.[22]

Mullins on the other hand appears to have been simply caught up in the American Civil War, trying desperately to return to his family. He was an Irish immigrant who lived with his wife and children in New York, though "at the commencement of hostilities [he] was at Memphis, Tenn. where he had been in the habit of going every Winter," most probably for employment. Unable to pass through the lines to return to his family, Mullins traveled to Charleston, where he appealed in vain to the British Consul for a passport to New York. Failing to obtain one and thus stranded in Charleston, he bought a small boat and endeavored to earn a living as a fisherman until June of 1862, when he was thrown in jail on suspicion of dealing with the nearby enemy. He remained there until January of 1863, when he was released after consenting to join "Rebel service" as a private in Company F of the Charleston Battalion. Though not an enthusiastic supporter of the Confederacy, Mullins served faithfully until June 24, 1864, when during the siege of Petersburg, Virginia he "offered himself" to the enemy. His strange circumstances were recorded in red ink by the Union provost marshal at Fortress Monroe, presumably so his unique situation would be made known and his return to New York hastened. Mullins was returned to New York, all right, but not New York City, where his family awaited. He was delivered rather to the Union prisoner-of-war camp at Elmira, one of the worst such camps North or South during the war. Fortunately Mullins survived imprisonment and was finally released at war's end on May 19, 1865.[23]

In six months, January 1 through July 1, the battalion gained over 350 men, nearly six times the number of men who joined the previous autumn. Added to those 120 or so original members still in the field, the Charleston Battalion again resembled an actual battalion, with approximately 500 men. Company A gained 28 men, Company C 55, Company D 85, and Company F 73. Company E received the fewest with only 16, and Company B again gained the most new members with 94 men. Remarkably, by March 1, 1863, Company B had tripled in size and Captain Simons was hard pressed to fully outfit with clothing and equipment the nearly 150 men in his company.[24] The fact that Confederate regulations allowed no more than 125 men in a single company was an issue to be sorted out later.

Why more men were in the ranks than the year before and

why the company distribution was so uneven is no mystery, however. The need for troops had become severe, so the mechanics of conscription were being refined in order to reach more of the South's male populace. Hoping to bring more good men into the army, at the beginning of the new year General Beauregard acted without government authorization and issued General Orders No. 7, which allowed all men eligible for conscription to "join any particular Company or Regiment" that needed recruits provided that they "offer themselves for service." Those who came forward promptly would be permitted to volunteer and "receive all benefits secured by law to volunteers" as long as they joined units that had been in service since the spring of 1862. By volunteering, new men avoided the stigma of conscription. They also skipped weeks of instruction at camps and went instead directly to the unit in the field. This is why men from the city were able to choose the Charleston Battalion rather than risk being assigned to another South Carolina unit. The mystery remains, however: why Company B over the other battalion companies? The answer lies somewhere in the fact that throughout the spring this company's first lieutenant William Clarkson was detached to the state's Board of Conscription. While on this duty, Clarkson spent weeks away from his company, scouring the upper counties of the state for recruits, which doubtless explains the influx of men from that region. In any event, for now at least the Charleston Battalion was brimming full.

New uniforms, new recruits—what more was needed? The answer is new weapons. It would seem that with Charleston being the principal blockade-running port for the Confederacy, and with so many of the Charleston Battalion's rank and file having connections in commercial and shipping affairs, that the unit would surely have carried the best weapons available.

In the old militia system, the Charleston Riflemen had been the flanking company of the Seventeenth Regiment,

which meant that they carried rifles in order to effectively protect the flanks of the regiment. As mentioned in chapter 1,
though the Seventeenth Regiment had a "beat" or "line" organization it contained only volunteer companies. Yet regardless
of status, the other companies aside from the Charleston
Riflemen probably carried smoothbores.

Once in Confederate service the Charleston Battalion was
at the mercy of the government and its sketchy supply system.
In other words, the battalion took what it could get. From req-
uisitions made in the first three months of 1863 it looks as
though the best the battalion could obtain was the 1851, .69-
caliber U.S. Springfield smoothbore musket. One Confederate historian wrote of this weapon, "At close range the musket
was formidable, but a Yank more than 100 yards away was
comparatively safe."[25] From the accounts of Secessionville, a
close-range battle, this weapon proved very effective. Of all
the battalion's companies, early in 1863 Company D received
the largest issue, with ninety-three of these muskets, the same
number of bayonets, and 3,200 buck and ball cartridges.[26]
"B&B" cartridges, as they were called, contained three buck-
shot wrapped in their paper housing with the .69-caliber ball.
When fired, this "spread" would hopefully make up for the
gun's lack of accuracy. Company E received the fewest with
only thirty-three of these weapons, while Company C received
four actual rifles but 800 buck and ball cartridges for smoothbores.[27] This inconsistency suggests that the battalion, like
many Confederate units, may have carried a variety of
weapons.

On February 17, 1863, General Beauregard issued a proclamation that all noncombatants be removed from Charleston
and Savannah, stating, "The movements of enemy's fleet indicate an early land and naval attack on one or both of these
cities." True to the general's "Napoleonic" style, he made a
patriotic appeal: "Carolinians and Georgians! the hour is at
hand to prove your devotion to your country's cause! Let all

able-bodied men from the seaboard to the mountains rush to arms!"[28]

The battle of Secessionville helped purchase a year of relative peace on the Charleston front. Convinced that the James Island approach to Charleston was too heavily defended, though not yet prepared to launch a large-scale naval assault against the city's harbor entrance, the Federal forces sixty miles to the south spent the winter of 1862-63 strengthening the positions they had gained thus far. The Confederate triumphs in Virginia during the spring and summer of 1862— General Jackson's Valley campaign and General Lee's repulse of the Union Army from the gates of Richmond—helped reduce the pressure on Charleston, and coupled with the results of Secessionville they had breathed new life in the Confederate war effort. In reality the victories in Virginia did more to alleviate the Union pressure on Charleston than the results of Secessionville. The Northern government was prohibited from dispatching from the Virginia theatre the large number of troops necessary to overwhelm Charleston's defenses.

With the coming of spring 1863, however, a new Federal campaign against Charleston materialized. By March 1863 the Union war machine had hit full stride, and because battlefield success was not forthcoming in Virginia, Northern public opinion—all important for the upcoming 1864 presidential election—demanded a morale-building victory, for example, the capture of Charleston, where Northerners felt all the trouble had begun. The new and improved Union Navy was to be the star player in the renewed contest for Charleston. Very much an old wooden navy in 1862, the South Atlantic Squadron now counted seven single-turreted ironclad monitors, one double-turreted ironclad known as the *Keokuk*, which somewhat resembled the monitors, and the sixteen-gunned *New Ironsides*, the most powerful warship afloat. This was the largest fleet of ironclads ever assembled and it was commanded by Adm. Samuel DuPont, who, in the first week of April 1863, acting under pressure from his superiors in Washington, brought his vessels up from Port Royal intending nothing less than to bully his way into Charleston Harbor. DuPont was a true sailor of the old wooden navy and in that fashion had stormed into Port Royal in November of 1861. Being an old sailor, however, he doubted the invincibility of the new iron warships. Aside from his concerns over the ironclads themselves, to his superiors DuPont expressed his concern that even if his vessels made it past Forts Sumter and Moultrie at the entrance of the harbor, they would then enter one of the most concentrated fields of artillery fire in the history of warfare: a veritable porcupine turned inside out.

Preceding DuPont's naval advance up the coast was the Federal army, marching under the command of Maj. Gen. David Hunter. On March 30, 1863, news of the Federal advance reached Charleston by the Savannah train, which informed the local papers that Union troops had landed on Seabrook Island and John's Island, driving in the Confederate pickets.[29] By all accounts it looked as though the Federal army was again going to land on James Island, this time in a larger effort coordinated with the navy. Despite the fact that a bigger, stronger enemy was at the gates of Charleston, the city, its citizens, and its defenders were, according to the *Mercury*, "ready, in every respect, for whatever may occur."[30]

The Union blow was delivered about midafternoon April 7, 1863, in the form of the largest naval assault of the war. Col. Alfred Rhett, commanding at Fort Sumter during the action, gave a concise timeline of the attack in his official report.

> At 2 o'clock p.m., April 7 instant, the whole iron-clad fleet advanced to the attack in the following order, viz: Four monitors were in advance, led by the Passaic. The Ironsides came next, followed by three other single-turreted monitors, and the Keokuk, a double-turreted monitor bringing up the rear. At thirty minutes past 2 p.m. the long roll was beaten and every disposition made for action. At fifty-five minutes past 2

p.m. the garrison, regimental, and Palmetto flags were hoisted and saluted by thirteen guns, the band playing the national air. At 3 o'clock p.m. the action was opened by a shot from Fort Moultrie.[31]

For two and a half hours the battle raged in full view of hundreds of spectators lining Charleston's High Battery wall. Each Union vessel that came within range of the Confederate forts received a pounding, the worst struck being the USS *Keokuk*, which came within 900 yards of Sumter and received no less than ninety direct hits. The riddled *Keokuk* sank near the harbor entrance the next morning, and acting under the advice of his subordinates, Admiral DuPont decided that his battered ships should not renew the contest. The Union juggernaut had been stopped cold at the gates of Charleston.

Though the results were thus far favorable for the Confederates, Charleston braced for a renewed enemy attack because thousands of Federal troops remained poised to land on James Island. The Confederate high command anticipated that the Union Army would now attack in concert with the navy, and accordingly every available soldier was placed on James Island and at the entrance of the harbor. Most of the Charleston Battalion remained in the city as a central reserve force, save a twenty-five-man detachment from the fattened Company B, which was positioned in the second-tier casemates of Fort Sumter as sharpshooters. These men, under their lieutenant William Clarkson, were in Sumter during DuPont's ironclad assault and were the only infantrymen in and around Charleston to participate in the naval action of April 7.[32] A new assault had not yet materialized three days following the repulse of DuPont, and defiantly the *Charleston Daily Courier* printed, "We are ready for them. Officers, gunners and people are eagerly expectant of their coming."

They, meaning the Union forces, never came. A disheartened DuPont withdrew his ironclads within a week of his defeat, and as he led his column down the main ship channel past Morris Island (with several vessels so battered that they had to be towed), he could see the smokestack and tops of the gun turrets of the ill-fated *Keokuk*. What he could not see, however, was that a portion of the Union naval signal book carelessly left behind on the *Keokuk* was riding the current, would soon reach shore, and would eventually find its way into the hands of General Beauregard.

In the end the Union Army under General Hunter made no effort to land on James Island. In his defense Hunter had never been issued explicit orders to cooperate with the navy let alone make an independent assault, and so he withdrew from Charleston shortly after DuPont. Unlike the Federal withdrawal following the battle of Secessionville, however, this time Federal troops remained in the neighborhood, occupying Folly Island and Coles Island, guarding the entrance to the Stono River, and occupying Seabrook Island further to the south. This chain of coastal barrier islands afforded a highway of sorts to Charleston.

The Union brigade on Folly Island was under the command of Brig. Gen. Israel Vodges, who kept his men busy for the next two months fortifying their positions on the island's southern end, while they simultaneously erected hidden artillery batteries on the island's northern end with an eye to future Union operations. Indeed, a new assault was on the drawing board, and this time it was to be a truly *cooperative* effort between the Union army and navy. Folly would serve as a springboard for a landing on Morris Island to the north across Lighthouse Inlet. Morris Island's northern tip was barely a half-mile distant from Fort Sumter and within eyesight of Charleston. If Union troops could drive the Confederates from Morris Island, heavy-rifled artillery batteries could then be established within easy range of Sumter. Fort Sumter could be reduced by these guns within a few days' time, giving the Union Navy a better chance at entering the harbor and forcing the city's evacuation.

New, more energetic leadership was needed in order to accomplish such an ambitious undertaking, and necessarily General Hunter was replaced by Brig. Gen. Quincy Gillmore, perhaps the North's foremost authority on rifled artillery and engineering operations.[33] As a captain, Gillmore had accomplished a similar and no less spectacular feat with his reduction of Fort Pulaski in the Savannah River in April of 1862. In addition, the gun-shy Admiral DuPont was replaced by Adm. John Dahlgren, the navy's chief of ordnance and a friend of President Lincoln.[34]

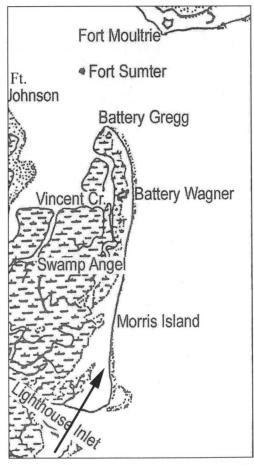

Union approach to Battery Wagner. Courtesy South Carolina Historical Society.

CHAPTER 7

"A Sad Day in Charleston": Battery Wagner

At 11:10 on the morning of Thursday July 9, 1863, Confederate signalmen on Morris Island flashed a frantic message back to Charleston: "Heavy works unmasked on Little Folly last night. Enemy strongly reinforced on Big Folly . . . I think an attack on this island imminent."[1] Early the next morning, July 10, a massive artillery barrage preceded the rowboat assault of over five thousand Federal troops of Gen. Truman Seymour's division, who made a spectacular landing on the southern end of Morris Island. Though Confederate balloon and other reconnaissance of Folly Island revealed a substantial enemy presence, they failed to detect General Vodges' masked artillery batteries, which were vital to the success of any assault launched from Folly. The Confederates were ill prepared to defend against the waterborne host that rowed across Lighthouse Inlet and stormed the beaches of Morris Island that sultry July morning.

General Beauregard had 5,841 troops with which to defend James Island, Morris Island, Sullivan's Island, the harbor fortifications, and the city itself. Again, due to the nature of Charleston's defense, 2,819 of these men were artillerists, leaving only 2,462 infantrymen and 560 cavalrymen to meet the invader head on.[2] On Morris Island, under the command of Col. Robert F. Graham, there were 330 artillerymen and 612 infantrymen to engage the enemy. Of Graham's force, 212 men of the Twenty-first South Carolina infantry were at Battery Wagner and the remaining 400 men of this regiment under Maj. George W. McKiver were guarding the point of attack—the beach at Lighthouse Inlet.[3] Confederate resistance proved determined but ineffective against the overwhelming Federal numbers, supported as they were by the Union batteries on Folly Island and the guns of Admiral Dahlgren's fleet, which enfiladed their positions from the Atlantic. By nine o'clock that morning General Gillmore's troops had driven the Confederate survivors three-quarters of the way up the island, where they sought protection inside Battery Wagner. Thus far the Union attack had gone far better than anticipated.

The *Charleston Daily Courier* warned the city's inhabitants, "The hour of trial we say is at hand or is rapidly approaching. . . . Let us do our duty as if the fate of the city rested with each one of us." Charleston's mayor, Charles MacBeth, meanwhile issued a series of proclamations requesting "all women and children, and other non-combatants to leave the city as soon as possible" and all business to cease "until the safety of the city is assured."[4] There were many Charlestonians scattered amongst the Confederate cavalry, artillery, and infantry stretched taut in defense of their city, one of whom was the mayor's son, Capt. J. Ravenel MacBeth, captured in the fighting on Morris Island that very morning.

One historian of the Morris Island campaign succinctly summed up Beauregard's plan: "By set strategy, the forces guarding Charleston were to stall and slow the enemy attack. The Charleston Battalion, with any other units that could be spared from other areas, would be quickly sent to the threatened sector."[5] Thus, the battalion defending hearth and home was to be used as shock troops. In the meantime Beauregard wired Gen. W. H. C. Whiting in Wilmington and Gen. Hugh Mercer in Savannah to send all available troops as soon as possible.[6]

Though Beauregard—as departmental commander—situated himself in Charleston and was in charge of the city's defense, Charleston's immediate commander was Brig. Gen. Roswell S. Ripley. On July 10, Ripley hurried to Morris Island to aid in its defense. While en route he sent a wire back to the city from Fort Sumter requesting the immediate dispatch of three companies of the Charleston Battalion to Morris, holding the remaining two companies in town as reserves.[7] Company E remained on duty as heavy artillery in the city and therefore was not included in the shuffle.

General Gillmore was under the impression, and with good reason, that few Confederates opposed him on Morris Island. Convinced of quick success, in the gray dawn hours of July 11 he launched a frontal assault against Battery Wagner. Much to his surprise, however, the battery had been reinforced during the night. The 1,200 blue-clad assaulting men were soundly repulsed, and they stumbled back to their own lines, bloodied and minus one-third of their number. Gillmore wisely decided to mass his troops and erect heavy batteries to pound Wagner before launching another assault against the battery.

Though Morris Island was the main Union objective, it was not the only scene of action. To ensure success, the Federal plan called for a large diversion on James Island to draw Confederate troops from the real attack against Morris. By July 10, three brigades numbering 5,260 Union troops under Gen. Alfred Terry had landed on James Island.[8] Terry, however, was under orders not to provoke a battle, and accordingly he engaged only in a show of force.[9]

Col. Charles H. Simonton, the Charlestonian commander of the Twenty-fifth South Carolina, was in charge of the James Island defenses. On July 11, with Terry's bristling division lodged on his island, Simonton wired back to the city for reinforcements. General Ripley, who had ordered the Charleston Battalion to Morris Island, now authorized that the battalion be diverted to James Island. Simonton was told, "Hold on and give the enemy a warm reception. The Charleston Battalion is ordered over. Where do you want them to report?"[10] The situation remained fluid, however, and the battalion never actually joined Simonton, though three companies did arrive at Fort Johnson on James Island, where they were held in reserve. North Carolinians and Georgians coming to aid in

Charleston's defense were instead sent piecemeal to Simonton as they arrived. Between July 10 and July 14 approximately six thousand reinforcements from Wilmington and Savannah arrived, swelling the Confederate force on James Island enough that it could lash out at Terry, which it did on July 16, resulting in Terry's abandonment of James Island altogether. Among the Confederates on James Island responsible for dislodging Terry's force was Pvt. William Henry Sinkler, Colonel Gaillard's future son-in-law. Young Sinkler, who also happened to be the nephew of Lt. William Sinkler of the Charleston Light Infantry, was a gunner in Park's company of the Marion Light Artillery. These guns supported the Twenty-fifth South Carolina on July 15 and 16.

On the afternoon of July 14 Col. Robert Graham was relieved from command of Morris Island and placed in command of Fort Johnson. Graham's successor was Brig. Gen. William Booth Taliaferro, a Virginian and one of "Stonewall" Jackson's hardened veterans.[11] The next day the two companies of the Charleston Battalion remaining in the city were summoned across to Fort Johnson to join their comrades, and from there the whole battalion was ferried to Morris Island to relieve the wearied garrison of Battery Wagner.[12] As the companies made their way from Battery Gregg down the island to Wagner, they were greeted by shellfire from Admiral Dahlgren's ironclads. Defending Wagner with the battalion were the recently arrived Thirty-first and Fifty-first North Carolina infantries, two companies of the First South Carolina Regulars serving as artillery, two companies of the Sixty-third Georgia heavy artillery, and one company from the First South Carolina Artillery.

JULY 18, 1863

Maj. John Johnson, Confederate engineer at Fort Sumter, remembered, "At length came the 18th day of July, made memorable by a land and naval bombardment of uncommon severity . . . followed by the second assault of Wagner."[13] At

Wagner, General Taliaferro recorded that Federal batteries on land and at sea formed a ring of fire around him and "poured for eleven hours, without cessation or intermission, a storm of shot and shell upon Fort Wagner which is perhaps unequaled in history." The general estimated that at least nine thousand projectiles had been thrown at his battery that day. A soldier two miles across the marsh on James Island, in the act of writing a letter to his wife during the bombardment, recorded, "While I am writing the very earth trembles with the incessant roar of heavy guns."[14] Fortunately, few men died from the effects of the shells due to Wagner's enormous bombproof shelter, which, though crowded and hot, afforded considerable protection. Despite this shelter, the Charleston Battalion opted to remain outside along the parapet. Moved by such bravery, Taliaferro reported to General Beauregard that the battalion, "with heroic intrepidity never surpassed, animated by the splendid example of their field officers, had no protection except such as the parapet afforded them, yet maintained their position without flinching during the entire day."[15] After the battle, Lt. Col. Peter Gaillard boasted, "My command was exposed . . . the whole day, never having left its position, and it is with pride I say it was not demoralized in consequence of its exposure."[16] So memorable was their conduct that thirty years later at a veteran's reunion in Georgia one aging witness of July 18, 1863, recounted, "In all the flight of time and the records of valor, no example ever transcended their splendid heroism. All honor to the glorious name and deathless fame of 'Gaillard's Charleston Battalion.'"[17]

The officers of the battalion had indeed set a splendid example that day. While Lieutenant Colonel Gaillard moved from position to position through the bursting shells to steady his men, himself once or twice half-buried in sand from nearby explosions, Major Ramsay calmly seated himself in a chair in the middle of the battery's parade ground and perused a newspaper. The major rose occasionally to assist in carrying a wounded soldier to a place of safety, taking care each time to fold his paper. It was remembered that Ramsay's "imperturbable coolness and encouraging example . . . contributed not a little in keeping up the esprit de corps" of the garrison.[18] About two o'clock that afternoon a Union shell cut the flag from the flagstaff, blowing it into the battery. Without a moment's hesitation Major Ramsay, Sgt. William Shelton of Company C, Pvt. John Flynn of Company F, and Lt. William Readick of the Sixty-third Georgia artillery rushed up to the parapet, exposing themselves to artillery and sharpshooter fire, and calmly refastened the flag to the flagstaff. Caught up in the moment, Capt. R. H. Barnwell of the engineers dashed out and planted a battle flag alongside the garrison flag. Later that afternoon, another shell knocked down the battle flag, and Pvt. A. Gilliland of the battalion's Company D ran out and set it back up.[19]

Companies A and B of the Charleston Battalion, detached under Capt. Julius Blake, were posted outside the battery, guarding the left gorge and sally port along its rear wall. At one point during the afternoon, one of Admiral Dahlgren's ironclads moved up the channel and began to enfilade the rear of the battery. Captain Blake reported that this fire killed one man in Company B and wounded Lt. William Clarkson. Several others in both companies were struck only "lightly" by shell fragments, though their position was "soon after completely torn up by shell." Blake was then issued orders from Gaillard to "seek the best protection they could find," and he moved most his men to the left curtain of the battery, while others moved to the sand dunes in rear.[20]

THE BIG ASSAULT

The daylong bombardment was evidence enough to the private soldier that a major attack was to follow, but the higher-ups knew the morning of July 18 of the Union plan, through intercepted signals sent from General Gillmore to General Seymour. The big assault came at dusk, about 7:30 or 8:00 on Saturday July 18, 1863. The job was assigned to Seymour's

7,000-man division. Seymour afterward explained, "That moment was chosen for moving forward when the dusk of the evening still permitted the troops to see plainly the way . . . but was yet sufficiently indistinct to prevent accurate firing by the enemy. Our troops were to use the bayonet alone." Seymour decided that his First Brigade under Brig. Gen. George C. Strong, numbering 2,950 men, would spearhead the assault. Of the regiments in this brigade—the Forty-eighth New York, Seventy-sixth Pennsylvania, Third New Hampshire, Sixth Connecticut, Ninth Maine, and temporarily the Fifty-fourth Massachusetts (Colored)—only the 650-man Fifty-fourth could be regarded as a full regiment. Just arrived from their debut fight on James Island on July 16, the Fifty-fourth was selected to lead the charge. Seymour described the Fifty-fourth as "a colored regiment of excellent character, well officered, with full ranks," which had "conducted itself commendably a few days previously on James Island." In support of Strong's brigade was the Second Brigade, under Col. Halderman S. Putnam, and the Third Brigade, under Brigadier General Stevenson.[21]

It was remembered that before the Fifty-fourth began its assault, "General Strong presented himself to the regiment and informed the men of the contemplated assault upon Fort Wagner and asked them if they would lead it . . . they answered in the affirmative."[22] Then Strong pointed to the regiment's color bearer and asked the black soldiers, "If this man should fall, who will lift the flag and carry it?" The regiment's white colonel, Robert Gould Shaw, stepped forward, removed the cigar from his lips, and answered, "I will."[23] The regiment was then formed by battalion in two columns, Colonel Shaw commanding the right column and Lt. Col. E. N. Hallowell the left as they moved up the beach toward Wagner, barely visible in the twilight. As the columns advanced, "the enemy opened upon us a brisk fire; our pace now gradually increased till it became a run," Hallowell remembered. "Soon canister and musketry begun to tell upon us. With

Colonel Shaw leading, the assault was commenced."[24] One Union observer noted that the black regiment had not gone far when Wagner "opened with rapid discharges of grape and canister, and its parapet was lit by a living line of musketry."[25] However, a Confederate defender remembered that the attackers were within 100 yards of the battery before they were allowed to open fire. He reported, "The stillness was ominous and oppressive. Then came a few stirring words, addressed by the Federal officers to the troops; they responded with loud prolonged huzzas, and breaking into a full run they rushed gallantly upon the fort."[26]

Geography had favored the Confederate defense of the Tower Battery at Secessionville, and so too did it favor the Confederates inside Battery Wagner. Located as Wagner was astride the narrowest point of Morris Island, the battery's right rested against a tidal creek and its left against the ocean, while in front a marsh pinched in from the creek, which funneled the attacking column into a compact field of fire.

The garrison of Wagner numbered approximately 1,600 men, including about 250 artillerymen and a little more than 300 men from companies A, B, C, D, and F of the Charleston Battalion. The battalion's Company E was still serving as heavy artillery and consequently not with the battalion at Wagner on July 18. As previously stated, throughout the day the Charleston Battalion had remained outside of the bombproof shelter during the Federal bombardment, and as a result they were the first body of troops to reach their positions once the Fifty-fourth began its advance up the beach.

Lieutenant Colonel Gaillard, with Major Ramsay, had command of companies C, D, and F, which were placed on the right front of Battery Wagner, extending from the sally port on Vincent's Creek to near the middle of the battery's face, where the line was picked up by the Fifty-first North Carolina. Companies A and B of the battalion, under Capt. Julius Blake, were posted on the beach guarding the battery's left curtain, which included two howitzer field pieces of the First South

Carolina Regulars (Third Artillery).[27] From his position along the wall, General Taliaferro could see that as the Massachusetts men came within range "they were met by a shower of grape and canister from our guns, and a terrible fire of musketry from the Charleston Battalion and the Fifty-first North Carolina."[28] Not within Gaillard or Taliaferro's sight, Captain Blake's position on the left with the Charleston Riflemen and the Charleston Light Infantry "was a very advantageous one," enabling these companies "to enfilade the ditch and parapet of the work proper, as well as to fire upon the column advancing upon the beach." Blake felt that "the right attacking column was, . . . by our fire and that of the splendidly-served howitzers, made to oblique to their left . . . subjecting them to a severe cross-fire."[29]

Blunted by this fire, the black soldiers did indeed veer to their left, where they struggled across the ditch fronting the battery and fell under the crossfire of the Fifty-first North Carolina above them and the Charleston Battalion farther to their left. General Taliaferro remembered, "These two commands gallantly maintained their position and drove the enemy back quickly from their front, with immense slaughter."[30] Lieutenant Colonel Gaillard recalled that his men "met the infantry assault with great coolness and deliberation" and that, on his front at least, the attack was "repulsed in a short time, when I directed my men to cease firing."[31] The Union assault and repulse was probably a little more violent than Gaillard let on in his report. An eyewitness remembered that the colonel had exhibited "coolness and efficiency in keeping his men well in hand, and restraining or directing their fire according to circumstances." As he had at Secessionville, Gaillard was seen "passing up and down the line," holding his men to their task. At one point, "to stop their fire and save ammunition, [Gaillard] mounted the parapet and moved along the length of his command, at the risk of being shot both by the enemy and by cross fire of Confederate troops."[32] Another witness remembered that while Gaillard strode the parapet, a number of Federal bullets perforated his coat pockets, narrowly missing their mark.[33]

Things were not as clearly decided 150 yards down the line toward the ocean, where the landward side of the battery's southeast salient was scaled by a strong contingent of the Fifty-fourth, led by their twenty-six-year-old colonel Shaw. Much of the Massachusetts line that crested the western side of the salient was met hand to hand and viciously repulsed by the Fifty-first North Carolina. One member of the Massachusetts regiment who encountered the North Carolinians remembered, "Upon leaving the ditch for the parapet, [the Confederates] obstinately contested with the bayonet our advance. Notwithstanding these difficulties, the men succeeded in driving the enemy from most of their guns, many following the enemy into the fort. It was here, upon the crest of the parapet, that Colonel Shaw fell. . . . Hand-grenades were now added to the missiles directed against the men."[34]

A small Federal lodgment was gained beyond the left of the Fifty-first North Carolina, however, on a section of the line, which mounted several cannon. Assigned to support these artillerists were the 425 men of the Thirty-first North Carolina regiment. Unlike the ferocious Fifty-first, these men from the "Old North State" remained neutralized in the bombproof shelter, unable to regain their nerves after the daylong bombardment. As the helpless artillerists swung their sponges and rammers without adequate infantry support, more Federals ascended the salient in their sector. Taliaferro immediately spotted this danger and ordered Gaillard and Col. H. McKethan of the Fifty-first to direct their fire to the left so as to rake the face of the battery and prevent the enemy from being reinforced or withdrawn.[35] The remainder of Strong's brigade followed in the wake of the Fifty-fourth and consequently passed through this deadly enfilading fire. Seymour stated in his official report, "General Strong had urged his command on with great spirit and gallantry, but his losses had been so severe that his regiments were much shaken. . . . Fragments of each regiment, however—brave men, bravely led—went eagerly over the ditch, mounted the parapet and struggled with the foe inside." Unfortunately Seymour had to order and reorder in vain the Second Brigade, under Colonel Putnam, to advance to Strong's aid. Due to this lack of support, Strong's assault evaporated, "although detached portions, principally from the Forty-eighth New York and Sixth Connecticut, with the colors of those regiments, still clung to the fort." Members of the Fifty-fourth also still remained in the battery.[36]

The tardy Putnam did not live to file an official report. Though he was slow to advance that evening, it was not due to cowardice but rather a misinterpretation of orders. When he finally did move, he and his men pushed down the beach, pausing only to allow the remnants of Strong's brigade, including much of the Fifty-fourth Massachusetts, to pass to the rear. A New Yorker advancing in Putnam's brigade remembered, "The grape and canister from the enemy's guns dealt death and destruction in our ranks."[37] The Seventh Connecticut led the brigade onward through the Confederate fire toward Wagner's left, where they swept over both the landward and seaward parapets of the southeast salient. Once again, the portion of the attacking line that scaled the salient to the west was quickly destroyed by the Fifty-first North Carolina, but the portion to the seaward side met little resistance. Here one Union observer remembered, "By a combined and determined rush over the southeast angle of the fort, the enemy was driven from that portion of the work. Some hundred men were now inside, with Colonel Putnam at their head." After a short time, however, Putnam and his band became isolated when much of his brigade, stunned by the withering crossfire, withdrew out of range of the fight. This was the final phase of the battle. By the fates of war, the portion of the parapet held by Putnam was the roof of Wagner's large bombproof shelter, which formed somewhat of a natural fortification within the fortification. From this perch, Putnam and his men were temporarily able to hold their own, because their rifle fire "commanded the interior of the fort."[38] Ironically this was the section of line assigned to the Thirty-first North Carolina, some of whom still remained in the shelter just yards beneath the Federal invaders.

Realizing that he must at once unseat the enemy contingent before they were reinforced, General Taliaferro called for a scout to reconnoiter the Federal position. The first person to volunteer was Lt. James Campbell, the Scotsman from the Charleston Battalion's Union Light Infantry who had distinguished himself along a similar parapet at Fort Lamar a year before. Campbell managed to reach a position from which he could observe the Federal mass on the salient and, apparently caught up in the excitement, he boldly called on them to surrender, whereby he was grabbed and taken prisoner.[39] Once a

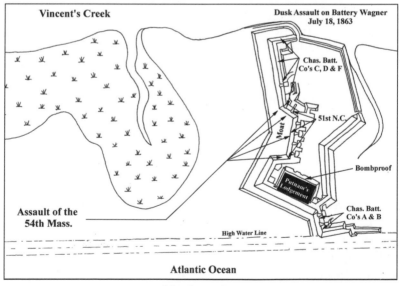

Map by author.

Lt. James Campbell of the Scottish Union Light Infantry.
Courtesy South Carolina Department of Archives and
History, Campbell Family Papers.

prisoner, Campbell found himself amongst fellow Scotsmen serving in the Union Army, and according to one Northern witness, Campbell exclaimed, "Had I known I was to have been taken prisoner, I would have worn my kilt!" Campbell would spend the remainder of the war in various Northern prison camps, beginning with Johnson's Island, Ohio, then Point Lookout, Maryland, and finally Fort Delaware, Delaware, where he was released in June of 1865.[40]

Unaware of Campbell's fate, Taliaferro called on Gaillard to furnish a body of men to charge the position.[41] Gaillard—who about this time narrowly avoided death when another bullet passed through his coat pocket, striking a soldier next to him[42]—issued the general's challenge. The challenge was accepted by Maj. David Ramsay, who, with Capt. Ward Hopkins, Lieutenant Cay, Sergeant Smith, and a portion of Company D, moved off in the darkness across the parade of the fortification.[43] Major Ramsay placed himself in front as the advance got under way, but he had not gone far when he and his men were delivered a brutal volley of musketry from the direction of the bombproof shelter. Ramsay was in the act of turning to give a command when he was struck by one of these bullets in the back—a wound that would prove mortal. This blast sadly enough proved to be friendly fire from one of the North Carolina regiments who had been unable to distinguish friend from foe in the darkness, and worse still, it effectively checked altogether Ramsay's attempt at retaking the shelter.[44]

Once more, General Taliaferro called for volunteers to attack the salient. This time, Maj. J. R. McDonald of the Fifty-first North Carolina quickly responded, as did Capt. William H. Ryan, the intrepid commander of the Charleston Battalion's Company C—the Irish Volunteers. Probably because the Fifty-first was very much engaged on their left, maintaining a fire on Putnam's invaders and otherwise holding the situation in check, the general selected Captain Ryan instead of Major McDonald.[45] Captain Ryan picked twenty men from his company and another twenty or so from the Union Light Infantry to make the assault. Lt. A. E. Allemong, of the Irish Volunteers, ran to enlist a portion of Company D, but he returned to find that Ryan had already begun the charge.

Defending one's hearth and home transcended self-preservation, and as it had at Secessionville, the scythe of destruction swept once more through the command structure of the Charleston Battalion. Upon nearing the bombproof shelter, Captain Ryan and his party were struck by a devastating volley, this time delivered by Putnam and his stalwarts atop the shelter. First to fall was, of course, Captain Ryan, who was killed by a plunging enemy Minié ball that entered under his left collarbone, passed through his body, and exited just above his right hip.[46] General Taliaferro reported that Ryan and his men had "advanced with great spirit," but upon the death of their captain the men "hesitated and the opportunity was lost."[47] The general now ordered that the howitzers on the beach along with Captain Blake's two companies of the Charleston Battalion sweep the seaward face of the salient with grape and musket fire, which ultimately had a favorable effect.

Cut off from reinforcements and surrounded, Putnam and his men, hard pressed as they were, held fast to their position. Determination was fading fast, however, and as Putnam tried to rally his men a Confederate bullet killed him. Command fell to the only regimental commander left standing, Maj. Lewis Butler of the Sixty-seventh Ohio, who did what he could to extract his men from the bombproof shelter and lead the survivors back down to the beach.[48] A number of Federals preferred the uncertainty of the shelter to the risks inherent in passing back through the Confederate fire. Those who remained, however, were soon captured when Confederate reinforcements arrived in the form of Gen. Johnson Hagood and the Thirty-second Georgia. Two companies of this regiment were sent along the left of the parapet, while Captain Blake, with his two companies of the Charleston Battalion, "deployed along the Western face," encircling the salient and forcing the surrender of what Union troops remained.[49] Lt. Iredell Jones of the First South Carolina Regulars (Third Artillery) joined in this last undertaking and remembered that he and his fellows "charged them at the point of the bayonet, and either killed, wounded, or took possession of the whole party."[50] With their capture, the battle was effectively over.

The Union high command had wrongly calculated that after such a pounding as Wagner's garrison had received all day from artillery fire, there would be few Confederates alive to contest their assault. This belief was smashed once the battle got under way, and as with the Union assault against Secessionville, when it became clear that the Unionists had bitten off more than they could chew, no more troops were committed and the battle was broken off. In his report. General Gillmore summed up the battle in one small paragraph: "On the 18th, an attack was made on Fort Wagner by land and naval forces, commencing about noon in a combined cannonade and bombardment, and terminating in an assault of the army about sunset. We gained and held for more than one hour the southeast salient or half bastion of the work, but finding it isolated from and commanded by the main body of the work, we were obliged to abandon it."[51] When the sun rose the next morning, the scene in front of the battery and along its seaward walls was horrifying. Mangled bodies and parts of bodies lay strewn everywhere. In the ditch before the battery the dead and wounded were piled in some places three or four deep. General Seymour's division had suffered greatly, having lost 1,515 of the 7,000 men committed to the assault.

Aside from preparing for another attack, when the battle ended that night the paramount job for the Confederates at Wagner was to tend to the wounded and get them back to

Charleston as quickly as possible, where they could be treated. The business of burying the dead commenced the next morning. All day of the 18th, the citizens of Charleston, ignoring the pleas of the governor and commanding general to evacuate the city, watched the bombardment of Wagner from every vantage point available, and as the battle raged that night, they remained glued to their positions. One spectator remembered, "The battery, house-tops and steeples were crowded with anxious spectators. Hundreds of fair women were there with hands clasped in silent prayer for the success of their gallant defenders."[52] That night and the next day, throngs of citizens crowded the wharves as the steamers brought boatload after boatload of wounded back to Charleston. The anxious citizens watched as Charlestonians and brave North Carolinians were offloaded along with many Yankees, black and white. Alternate cries of grief and excitement were heard as—mixed in amongst these unfamiliar faces—husbands, sons, brothers, and neighbors were recognized. On Sunday July 19 an artilleryman on James Island wrote to his mother, "Truly it must be a sad day in Charleston. I understand the Charleston Battalion was on Morris Island. If so the dead and wounded arriving must cast a gloom over the city."[53]

All told, the Confederate loss at Wagner was 226 killed, wounded, and missing. Of the seven commands that participated in the battery's defense, only the Fifty-first North Carolina (68 casualties), who grappled hand to hand with the enemy, suffered greater casualties than the Charleston Battalion. The battalion lost 58 men on July 18, 1863, plus 2 on July 17 and 2 more on the 19th—of approximately 320 in the action. Most of these casualties occurred when Major Ramsay and Captain Ryan charged the southeastern salient. At a later date, Capt. Ward Hopkins of Company D, a participant in Ramsay's charge, wrote that his company "suffered severely in repelling the enemy." At Wagner, as at Secessionville, Hopkins' Sumter Guards lost more men than any other company in the battalion, with 21 killed and wounded.[54]

Casualties in the Charleston Battalion, July 18, 1863

Co. A:

Killed: Sgt. J. F. Lamberts.

Wounded: Pvts. L. R. Spiesenger, F. L. Larovins, H. U. Grover-man, S. Ham, J. D. Cheney, J. M. Wilder, Hunt, Jr., and Harvey.

Missing: Pvt. J. M. Hurst, Jr.—prisoner.

Total: 11*

Co. B:

Killed: Pvts. John C. Edwards and S. J. Nesbit.

Wounded: 1st Lt. William Clarkson, 2d Lt. William Sinkler, and Pvts. T. D. Eskew, William Hill, Jr., T. M. Hendricks, H. R. Fowler, B. H. Turner, and R.M. Wood.

Missing: Pvts. J. Cronin, D. McLean, and G. Phelan.

Total: 14*

Co. C:

Killed: Capt. William H. Ryan and Pvts. M. Toole and James Callahan.

Wounded: Cpl. John F. Preston and Pvts. L. H. Hill, Patrick Manion, and Samuel Reynolds.

Total: 7

Co. D:

Killed: 1st Sgt. William K. Smith and Pvt. S. T. Hyde.

Wounded: 1st Lt. J. A. Cay, Cpl. H. E. Saylor, and Pvts. T. W. Atkinson, J. J. Ball, W. A. Bailey, J. P. Ballentine, A. Bumpus, W. W. Fowler, W. W. Hamlin, J. F. Harrison, J. H. Sosbee, W. L. Macbeth, J. A. Madden, R. Owens, M. Stone, J. M. Timmons, E. F. Walker, and W. A. J. Ware.

Total: 21**

Co. F:

Wounded: Maj. David Ramsay, 1st Lt. George Brown, and Pvts. J. W. Glenn, J. Brown Barry, H. Schroder, J. D. Ashcroft, and A. Slant.

Missing: Lt. James Campbell—prisoner.
Total: 8

*Wounded on July 17, 1863: 2d Sgt. J. B. Gardner, Co. B; Pvt. C. A. Speissenger, Co. A.
**Wounded on July 19, 1863: Lt. J. T. Wells, Co. D; Lt. William Dove Walter, Adjutant, Charleston Battalion.[55]

As these men arrived on the steamers they were sent to Roper Hospital on Queen Street, the Trapmann Street Hospital, and Citadel Square Hospital. Major Ramsay was taken to his residence.

The Battalion's Wounded at Roper Hospital

Pvt. W. Hill, Co. B, left shoulder, severe; Private Callaghan, Co. C, left knee, dangerous; Private Fowler, Co. D, throat, left arm, and chest, mortal, since dead; Pvt. J. H. Sosbee, Co. D, contusion, slight; Private Stone, Co. D, left thigh and lung, since dead; Pvt. J. M. Timmons, Co. D, arm amputated, doing well; Pvt. W. A. J. Ware, Co. D, left thigh, since dead; Private Barry, Co. F, left ankle, slight; Private Glenn, Co. F, contusion of hip, slight.

Trapmann Street Hospital

J. Fork, Co. A; J. D. Wilder, Co. A; B. H. Turner, Co. B, leg wound; R. M. Wood, Co. B; L. H. Hill, Co. C, head; Samuel Reynolds, Co. C, neck; J. J. Ball, Co. D, arm; J. P. Ballentine, Co. D, wrist; A. Bumpus, Co. D, foot; J. F. Harrison, Co. D; E. F. Walker, Co. D, thigh; H. R. Fowler, Co. F.

It is believed that these men from Co. B, Charleston Battalion, were also taken to the Trapmann Street Hospital: Pvt. S. J. Nesbit, dead; Lts. William Clarkson and William Sinkler and Sgt. J. B. Gardner, slightly wounded from the effects of shells;

Pvts. H. R. Fowler, W. Hill, Jr., H. H. Turner, and R. M. Wood. The company's captain, Thomas Simons, "had a slight contusion on the right breast and was somewhat stunned, by the close explosion of a shell." On the day of the attack Simons was detailed at Wagner as "Officer of the Day" and was not with his company.

Citadel Square Hospital

Pvt. T. W. Atkinson, shot through right thigh.

Though Charleston families mourned their dead and feared for the lives of their wounded, they were nonetheless thrilled over the part their soldiers played in the defense of Battery Wagner. One Charlestonian soldier in the "Eutaw Regiment" wrote to his wife describing the Federal lodgment inside the battery, adding, "Fortunately the Charleston Battalion was there in time, and our brave Charleston boys ever true, and always to be relied on . . . pitched in, and after an hour's hard fighting, hand to hand, drove the enemy out."[56] The *Charleston Mercury* proudly proclaimed that the battalion's conduct was "the theme of general praise amongst all who witnessed their gallantry and steadfast courage" and that "these gallant men behaved in a manner worthy the fame their organization had so dearly won at Secessionville."[57]

CHAPTER 8

"Resolute Men": Siege Warfare

At ten o'clock on the evening of Tuesday, August 4, 1863, David Ramsay died at his home on Broad Street from the mortal wound he received at Battery Wagner. His funeral took place the next evening at Central Presbyterian Church (Circular Congregational) on Meeting Street, where his body was laid to rest next to that of his grandfather, Dr. David Ramsay. A gathering of Master Masons, to whom Ramsay belonged, was held at the Grand Lodge of Ancient Freemasons an hour before the funeral.[1] Just as the social fabric of Charleston had torn when Henry King and John Edwards died at Secessionville, so too the city now mourned the loss of David Ramsay: "One of the 'bright, peculiar stars' of South Carolina was this scholar, statesman, soldier, gentleman . . . unsurpassed in intellect . . . at heart a lover of the Union he fought to destroy, but a martyr to the State to which he deemed his allegiance was due."[2]

No less mourned by Charlestonians was William H. Ryan. Five days after his death at Wagner, the *Charleston Mercury* wrote, "Few men have fallen more universally lamented in our community than Capt. William H. Ryan. . . . Of a handsome mien, unobtrusive and kind manner, his acquaintance was large and his friends all who knew him. . . . No nobler soldier fell that bloody day."[3] Ryan was born and raised in Charleston in a large family like many of the Irish Volunteers, and like them he was willing to risk all in his city's defense. In the battalion's very first fight—Sol Legare Island, June 3, 1862—he

Grave of David Ramsay, Circular Congregational
Church, Charleston. Photograph by author.

had raised his sword and grabbed Pennsylvania captain James Cline by the throat demanding that officer's surrender, resulting in the capture of valuable prisoners. On the morning of June 16, 1862, without hesitation Ryan led his company to the point of danger near Reed's guns in the left angle of the Tower Battery at Secessionville. Instinctively he volunteered to lead an all-or-nothing assault on Putnam's salient that night at Wagner. Ryan's body was laid to rest in St. Lawrence Cemetery just north of the city along the Cooper River.

For the dead and wounded the fight was over, but for the living the campaign had only just begun. The enemy was at the gates, battle was to be a daily affair, and the death of Ramsay and Ryan created three command vacancies that needed to be filled. With Ramsay dead the battalion needed a worthy lieutenant to Gaillard, and the senior company officer, thirty-one-year-old commercial merchant Capt. Julius Blake of Company A, got the job. Filling Blake's vacancy in the Charleston Riflemen was Capt. William Dove Walter, then serving as the battalion's adjutant. Lastly, it would take a stout Irishman to fill the shoes of Company C's William H. Ryan, and equal to the task was thirty-seven-year-old policeman Lt. James M. Mulvaney.

There was little time, however, to stop and think about who was killed or wounded or who was elevated to what command. The enemy was still within earshot of the city, and accordingly, fresh Southern troops were cycled to the front to meet the next attack. The day after the battle, the Charleston Battalion was ordered to Fort Johnson,[4] from which point each company was ferried back to the city, where they returned to their respective campgrounds by July 21.[5] The worst kind of fighting lay ahead—siege warfare—and the Charleston Battalion was to have its fair share of it. Siege warfare meant exposure to the elements; round-the-clock enemy shellfire; midnight picket duty; labor, labor, labor; and sniper fire that might just as well kill a man for heeding the calls of nature as for going into battle.

Convinced of the immense casualties he would incur by

storming Battery Wagner a third time, General Gillmore decided to pursue an engineering operation. Over the next month and a half, Gillmore's men established a series of fortifications parallel to Wagner and connected to the rear with zigzagged trenches. Artillery batteries were built at each parallel, and as each new line was established closer to Wagner, their range increased and became more effective. Ere long the Union artillery on Morris Island could pound Battery Wagner, Fort Sumter, Fort Moultrie, James Island, and eventually even the city itself—five miles away—at their leisure. The objective was to someday get the Federal trenches close enough that an infantry assault could leap forward and overwhelm Wagner's garrison, eliminating that annoying obstacle and allowing the Federals to get on with the real business of destroying Sumter.

On the last day of July, the battalion's missing Company E, Calhoun Guards, numbering forty-six officers and men, was ordered to Battery Wagner for its first tour of duty on Morris Island.[6] The company had been serving as heavy artillery in charge of the White Point Battery in the city, a battery whose name was soon changed to "Battery Ramsay" in honor of the Charleston Battalion's fallen major. On August 1, after almost two weeks of rest, the battalion was reunited with Company E when they arrived for their second tour at Wagner, which was now commanded by Charlestonian colonel Lawrence M. Keitt.[7] All told, the battalion, except for Company E, served three tours of duty on the island at Batteries Gregg and Wagner—July 15-19, August 1-7, and August 17-27—during the fifty-eight-day Union siege. Company E performed two tours of duty on Morris Island as heavy artillery.[8]

As fate would have it, the battalion returned to Morris Island for its third tour of duty coinciding with much of what became known as the "First Great Bombardment of Fort Sumter," a merciless close-range bombardment that lasted from August 17 to September 2. The Union objective since the beginning of the campaign was the destruction of Fort Sumter. General Gillmore had by mid-August advanced his heavy batteries close enough to Wagner that an accurate and effective fire could be maintained on Fort Sumter by throwing shells over the battery. Regardless of how well this worked, ultimately to achieve the Union objective Morris Island had to be cleared of Rebels. While Gillmore's land batteries threw 6,878 rounds at Sumter during this First Great Bombardment, some of these batteries, supplemented by Admiral Dahlgren's ironclads, gave a daily and nightly pounding to Batteries Wagner and Gregg to reduce the offensive power of those installations.[9] All the while Union sappers dug their trenches closer to Wagner's walls.

Brig. Gen. Johnson Hagood took command of Morris Island on August 20, and in his report of infantry strength on the island, he showed the Charleston Battalion at 227 men in the five infantry companies.[10] Prior to the battle of July 18, the battalion's aggregate strength was approximately 500 men, including a considerable number of men who were hospitalized from seasonal fevers or otherwise not available for action. Subtract those absentees, along with the 46 men of Company E posted in the city, and the battalion had just over 300 men in the battle. The battalion lost 2 men on July 17, another 58 men in the battle on July 18, 2 more men the day after, plus 15 more from August 1 to 20. The subtractions account for General Hagood's figure.

On August 23 the battalion suffered perhaps its most important casualty. Lieutenant Colonel Gaillard and his men were in advance of Wagner and exposed to the effects of an intense enemy bombardment. To alleviate the suffering of his command, Gaillard dispatched a courier to request permission to withdraw from the exposed position. Recognizing that the courier would have to pass through a deadly fire moving up the beach from Battery Wagner to Battery Gregg and back again, at the last minute, the fifty-year-old Gaillard recalled the courier and took his place on the mission. On Gaillard's return to Wagner, he rode through a severe fire in which his left hand and wrist were shattered by a nearby shell burst.

The damage might have been worse but for the fact that he had removed his uniform coat in the sweltering August heat and draped it over his left forearm as he rode. The garment was much torn by the fragments but it succeeded in reducing the damage.[11] Gaillard was loaded on the next available steamer and brought back to Charleston, where surgeons amputated his left hand above the wrist. In his report of the day's fighting, General Hagood stated, "I regret to report among the wounded the gallant Lieutenant-Colonel Gaillard, of the Charleston Battalion. His hand and wrist were so shattered by a shell as to render amputation necessary. The loss of the services of so efficient and brave a man at this crisis is a serious calamity."[12] Two days later the Richmond newspapers mistakenly reported, "On Sunday, the brave Colonel Gaillard lost his life."[13]

Not many lieutenant colonels in Confederate service fit into Gaillard's category of age and social station, let alone would have—at that age—insisted on enduring the hardships of active campaigning with their men. Many a younger man had died from the effects of amputation, and now Gaillard was to be put to the physical challenge of nineteenth-century surgery and recovery, a recovery made somewhat easier by the fact that it would take place in Charleston. Because it pleased the gods of war, Lt. Julius Blake was now the commander of the Charleston Battalion. A little more than a month ago, Blake was merely the captain of the battalion's Company A, and then upon the death of Major Ramsay he ascended to the battalion's second highest command, and now Blake took Gaillard's place while that officer recovered.

About the same time that Gaillard was wounded, Pvts. Cameron Smith and B. O. Turner were wounded by the shell-fire, and enemy sharpshooters wounded Lt. S. B. Gardner and killed Pvt. Newman Edwards. Strangely enough, these men belonged to the Charleston Battalion's "Company G." Heretofore the battalion had only six companies (seven if you divide Company F between the Union Light Infantry and German

Fusiliers), but as of August 14, 1863, a new Company G was carved out of Capt. Thomas Simons' Company B, Charleston Light Infantry.

COMPANY G

When the Charleston Light Infantry returned from its second tour of duty on Morris Island, an issue long since brewing was finally resolved. As mentioned in a previous chapter, this company numbered well more than the maximum allowed to one company by Confederate law, which was 125 men. On August 10, 1863, Captain Simons wrote the following letter to Brig. Gen. Thomas Jordan, General Beauregard's chief of staff:

Camp Gaillard
Charleston, August 10, 1863
Brig. Genl. Thomas Jordan
Chief of Staff

Genl.,

I have the honor to request your attention to the following state of fact—my company has now an aggregate of 170 men besides some 15 more who will report by the end of the week. It has been found impracticable for one set of infantry officers to take charge of the interests and welfare and discipline of so many men. We have now six companies in the [Charleston] Battalion and it is proposed to divide my command into two companies, which it is believed will materially lend to the better care of [the men,] their accoutrements, arms, etc. and to promote their officer's efficiency and discipline. . . . It is suggested that the present officers rise one grade and that the vacancies be filled as has been the habit of the Battalion by election.[14]

With heavy fighting in front of Charleston, no time was wasted in accommodating Captain Simons' request to form a new company, especially since it would promote efficiency. On the very same day that Simons wrote his letter, Company B was divided, with the surplus going to form a new Company G, per Special Order No. 155 from General Beauregard's headquarters. Four days later, on August 14, the new company officially mustered into service and was sent to Morris Island to join the rest of the battalion.

Captain Simons' brother-in-law, Lt. William Clarkson—who during May and June had spent five weeks scouring the interior of South Carolina for the state's Conscription Board—became *Captain* Clarkson of Company G. Clarkson's service on the board is significant, because more than half of the men in the new Company G were from upstate South Carolina, in particular Spartanburg, where Clarkson had focused his recruiting efforts. The remainder of the new company was a mixture of city and country men who joined Company B in the early months of 1863. In short, Company B had to be divided in order to alleviate the burdens of an oversized command in any case, and it proved a convenient vehicle for removing many of the outsiders from the veteran Charlestonians in Simons' command. One piece of supporting evidence for this theory lies in the fact that Charlestonian Clarkson was not the first choice to command the new company. The command was first offered to 2d Lt. Alfred H. Masterman, an original member of Company B who declined the position on account of the fact that his father and a number of relatives and friends were in Company B. Also, two Masterman family slaves served as cooks in the company. He didn't want to be amongst strangers even if he were their captain. In the August 1863 letter in which Masterman declines the offer of command, he also states that he had known Captain Simons for many years and wished to remain under his command for better or worse. On August 25 Company G returned to Charleston from Morris Island, ahead of the other battalion companies, after completing its first tour of duty as an independent company.

The next day, Col. George P. Harrison, Jr., of the Thirty-second Georgia Infantry, took command of Morris Island, and in a report he estimated the Charleston Battalion's strength—

without Companies E or G—at 208 officers and men. Harrison also gave an idea of what the daily conditions were like at Wagner. "About the middle of this afternoon, the enemy's fire on this place and Battery Gregg became quite warm, and about an hour before sunset they concentrated their whole fire on this work and our rifle-pits in front. This fire was not only exceedingly rapid, but very accurate, the enemy using every variety of projectiles."[15] By the evening of August 27, Companies A, B, C, D, and F had also made their way back to the city for a brief respite.

The long, hot month of August 1863 finally faded out and September was ushered in by intensified Union artillery fire. Union sappers were now within yards of Wagner's ditch, close enough that they could hear the Confederates inside the battery. With victory in sight, General Gillmore slackened his fire against Sumter and directed nearly all of his artillery against Wagner for the final knockout punch in preparation for rushing it with infantry.

Across the harbor, General Beauregard concluded that, though the fall of Morris Island was now a certainty, a strong infantry force might still hold Fort Sumter. To this end, Beauregard had striven throughout Gillmore's siege to remove Sumter's heavy guns so as not to lose them to the enemy and use them instead to bolster the inner harbor batteries; all were removed save three, which bore on the main ship channel. In anticipation of the pounding that must follow the Confederate evacuation of Morris Island, as each gun was removed from Sumter, its empty chamber was stuffed to the gills with saturated cotton bales surrounded by wet sand. Beauregard began to change out Sumter's garrison from artillery to infantry during the night of August 25, when all but one company of the First South Carolina Artillery was removed from the fort and 150 Georgians of Colquitt's infantry were brought in.[16] As long as the Confederacy possessed the two-acre "island" of Fort Sumter, it could maintain the booms, mines, and other obstructions that stretched across the main ship channel to Fort Moultrie, with a fair chance at holding back the Union Navy. The mines in particular struck terror in the hearts of all Union sailors, even Admiral Dahlgren, owing to the established doctrine that when struck by a mine an ironclad tended to sink to the bottom in mere seconds, leaving few if any survivors.

Fort Sumter officially became an infantry post on the night of September 4, when Charlestonian major Stephen Elliott relieved Col. Alfred Rhett, also a native of the city and long the proud commander of the post. Fresh from its brief rest, the Charleston Battalion officially took over as Sumter's garrison with *all seven* companies—Company E now restored to infantry—numbering 320 strong and commanded by newly commissioned *major* Julius Blake.[17] The symbol of the Rebellion, the military keystone to the Confederacy's supporting arch that was the Southeast, was now entirely entrusted to the will, determination, and fighting ability of Charlestonians.

So cognizant was Major Elliott of the paramount importance of holding Sumter at all costs—and likewise of the probability of a Union amphibious assault against the weakened fort—that he immediately issued orders to defend against such an attack. Each night a fifty-man detachment, fully equipped with loaded weapons and fixed bayonets, under the command of one officer was to man the gorge wall, which faced Morris Island. Similar precautions were taken on the north face, where the gun embrasures were more or less open to intruders. If an attack by barges was spotted, the long roll was to be sounded and all companies were to form in the parade ground, where they would be assigned to threatened positions.[18]

Two nights into the battalion's tour at Fort Sumter, the elaborately choreographed evacuation of Morris Island took place. Col. Lawrence Keitt was again in command of the island, and with the assistance of several steamers covered by the Confederate ironclads *Charleston* and *Chicora*, he removed the Twenty-seventh and Twenty-eighth Georgia and Twenty-fifth South Carolina regiments, along with his remaining artillerymen. At dawn, September 7, the Union troops of the Third New Hampshire swept up the island and captured a few tardy Confederate launches attempting to escape. In the lot were six men from the Charleston Battalion, most likely sent from Fort Sumter by Major Elliott to assist in the evacuation.

BOAT ATTACK

The jubilant Federals, at long last the sole occupants of Morris Island, now stood on solid ground less than a half-mile from the battered Fort Sumter. According to plan, General Gillmore had finally taken Morris Island and reduced Fort Sumter to a harmless pile of brick and dirt with no offensive capabilities. From here on out the Union general would "cooperate with the fleet by a heavy artillery fire when it was ready to move in." In Gillmore's words, it was now up to the navy to "enter, remove the channel obstructions, run by the batteries on James and Sullivan's Islands, and reach the city."[19]

Neither General Gillmore nor Admiral Dahlgren was fully convinced, however, that Sumter ceased to constitute a threat, and even if they did, the fort still had to be occupied by Federal troops in order to remove the channel obstructions in preparation of a full-scale naval assault. Before storming the fort outright, at ten o'clock in the morning of September 7 Admiral Dahlgren sent, under flag of truce, a note to Major Elliott demanding Sumter's surrender, which the major sent back to Charleston for a reply from General Beauregard. The general's response was returned immediately: "Inform Admiral Dahlgren that he may have Fort Sumter when he can take and hold it."[20]

This the admiral resolved to do, but unknown to Dahlgren, Gillmore planned his own amphibious assault against the fort on the exact same night. When the two officers learned of each other's intentions, they were unable to come to an agreement over who should command the assault. Both commanders pushed ahead with their plans, but the interservice race was narrowly won by the navy, whose force of well more than six hundred marines and sailors was towed within rowing distance of Sumter shortly after midnight on the morning of September 8.[21]

> Major Stephen Elliott, commanding at Fort Sumter, had nightly expected an assault and following Dahlgren's note demanding the fort's surrender, the major beefed up his usual dispositions. On the night of September 7-8, Elliott had the Charleston Battalion placed according to the following: Captain [J. W.] Hopkins' company (D), 43 men, lay on their arms on the parapet of the gorge and Captain [F. T.] Miles' Company (E), 12 men, at the breach in the northwest face. The guards, excepting the sentinels on post, were to defend the sally-port. Captain [T. Y.] Simons' Company (B), 28 men, lay at the entrance on the west face. In case of an alarm, Captain [S.] Lord's Company (F), 42 men, was to occupy the southwest angle and support Captain Hopkins on the right. Lieutenant [J. C.] Saltus' Company (A), 12 men, at the southeast, was to support him on the left. Lieutenant [J. O.] Harris' Company (G), 25 men, was to occupy the northeast angle. Captain [J. M.] Mulvaney, Company C, 43 men, was to support Captain Miles.[22]

In the event of attack, the remaining 115 men of the battalion were to be formed on the parade ground as a reserve force to be directed by Major Elliott to the most threatened sector. Elliott had also managed to obtain from Charleston a supply of fireballs and hand grenades, and he nightly placed detachments of men at three points along the fort's parapet to hurl the curious weapons down on any attacker.[23] Elliott's heightened state of alert was due in part to a signal from Dahlgren's flagship ordering such an attack that was intercepted and decoded by a Confederate signalman on the deck of the ironclad *Chicora* stationed just inside Charleston Harbor.

Around one o'clock in the morning on September 8, the

ever-vigilant Major Elliott personally observed two columns of Federal rowboats heading toward Sumter in the darkness. Immediately the alarm was sounded and the better part of three companies were ordered into supporting positions as Elliott cautioned his men to hold their fire until the enemy had begun their landing.[24] One witness remembered that Federal sailors and marines, who had been told to expect only a corporal's guard defending Sumter, "sprang to the assault with vigor and determination . . . they were met, however, by resolute men," who poured on them a "rapid and spirited fire of musketry."[25] Not wanting to waste precious seconds reloading their weapons, after their initial volley the men of the battalion hurled grenades and fireballs down on their attackers. When these were exhausted, they threw brickbats and other debris. "This storm of miscellaneous missiles was too much for the storming party, and the forlorn hope fled in confusion."[26] A German Fusilier in Company F remembered that after this

The boat attack on Fort Sumter. Courtesy South Carolina Historical Society.

fight the Charleston Battalion was often heralded as the "Brickbat Battalion."[27]

One line of boats was steered toward the southeastern angle and the gorge wall, where a more negotiable "beach" allowed the easiest access for the Federals, while the other line headed toward the northeastern angle of the fort. Consequently the men of Company D, Sumter Guards, and the newly organized Company G did much of the fighting.[28] According to Major Elliott, "[The enemy] were received with a well directed fire of musketry and hand-grenades. Fragments of the epaulements were also thrown down upon them. The crews near shore sought refuge in the recesses of the foot of scarp, those farther off in flight. The repulse was decided, and the assault was not renewed."[29]

Confederate batteries on James and Sullivan's islands along with the guns from the ironclad *Chicora* smothered the approaches to Sumter, thereby eliminating the possibility of further support. Only a few enemy boats managed to land at Sumter, while the remainder turned and fled seaward to avoid certain destruction. Captured paperwork indicated that 870 men were involved in the attack, though probably no more than 600 came within firing of the fort, while at least 127 were killed, wounded, or captured during the affair. In addition, several enemy barges were captured, along with a number of Federal battle flags. One in particular was said to have been Major Anderson's 1861 garrison flag, brought along to be triumphantly hoisted over Sumter once it had been retaken by United States forces. Major Elliott had suffered no casualties in the 104 men of the battalion that he committed to the battle.[30]

Theodore A. Honor, a Charlestonian of the Twenty-fifth South Carolina, wrote in a letter to his wife, "On Tuesday night about 2 o'clock our Camp [on James Island] was startled out of their slumber by the loud roar of cannon, and the quick rattle of musketry. . . . By the flashes of the guns we soon found out that the firing was in the direction of Fort Sumter." When after a short time the musketry ceased and the artillery died off, Honor and his comrades knew "that our brave boys, the Charleston Battalion, who are now garrisoning the fort, had repulsed and driven them back." Near the close of his letter, he proclaimed, "All honor to The Charleston Battalion. It seems as if it is the Charleston boys that is to save the old city."[31]

Once again the enemy's attacking column had been defeated, just as it had at Secessionville, at this same approach to Charleston Harbor made by Admiral DuPont almost five months before to the day, and at Battery Wagner. The common denominator of all four Confederate victories was the Charleston Battalion. Praise echoed from the lips of everyone who heard of the spirited defense of the decrepit Fort Sumter. In his preliminary report of the engagement, Major Elliott proudly stated, "The garrison, consisting of the Charleston Battalion, behaved admirably. All praise is due to Major Blake, his officers and men, for the promptness and gallantry displayed in the defense."[32] In his official report, which he submitted to General Beauregard, Elliott stated, "The Charleston Battalion fully sustained its well-earned reputation by cheerfully enduring the hardships of their position and moving forward with energy in the moment of danger."[33] In turn Beauregard wired Richmond of the victory, stating, "Garrison behaved with gallantry and coolness."[34] Back in their city, the *Charleston Mercury* wrote, "The men of the Charleston Battalion . . . repelled the foe with a gallantry worthy the name which the Battalion won so dearly at Secessionville, and afterwards at Battery Wagner."[35]

Casualties in the Charleston Battalion, Morris Island Campaign[36]

At Wagner, August 17, 1863
Co. B:
Killed: Pvt. Edward Burns.
Wounded: Pvt. E. Williams, seriously.

Co. D:
Wounded: Pvts. R. Owens and J. R. Pinson, slightly.

Co. E:
Killed: Pvts. Eugene Baker and Ogier Martin, both had their legs shot off.
Wounded: Capt. Francis T. Miles, stunned by concussion; Lt. Waring Axson, very slightly in right knee; Sgt. D. C. Webb, stunned; Pvt. E. F. Randall, stunned by concussion and hit in back; Pvt. W. S. Mellichamp, slightly in thighs; Pvts. C. P. Brown, J. S. Westendorf, Campbell King, and R. A. Britton, stunned by concussion.

At Morris Island, August 20, to evacuation, September 6, 1863
Lt. Col. Peter C. Gaillard, wounded left hand 8/23/63, amputated.

Co. B:
Wounded: Pvts. H. R. Fowler, chest slightly; A. M. Kerrigan, severely in body 8/23/63; and W. R. Malloy, head and shoulder.

Co. C:
Wounded: Pvts. Patrick Lee, slightly in hand 8/22/63; Patrick Culleton, slightly in hand; and Patrick Costlee, wounded in back and captured.

Co. D:
Wounded: Pvts. John Walker, slightly; J. F. Fowler, seriously in hip and arm; W. A. Davis, slightly in right hand; and J. T. Saxon, forefinger left hand 8/23/63.

Co. F:
Wounded: Capt. Samuel Lord, contusion in side by shell explosion; and Pvt. James Pringle, thigh and back 8/20/63.

Co. G:
Killed: Lt. J. B. Gardner, at Wagner 8/23/63; and Pvt. N. Edwards, on picket 8/23/63.
Wounded: B. O. Turner, at Wagner 8/20/63, severely in head.

Captured during evacuation of Morris Island, September 6-7, 1863
Co. B: Pvts. Andrew Doyle, musician; and Benjamin Hernandez, musician.

Co. C: Pvts. Thomas King, musician; and James Richardson, musician.*

Co. F: Pvts. Patrick O'Brien and W. Thompson (not listed in compiled service records).

*It is interesting, if not amusing, to note that four of the six men captured were musicians.

CHAPTER 9

"Gaillard's Regiment": The Twenty-seventh South Carolina Infantry

In the first two years of the war, winter usually brought a cessation of hostilities as the opposing armies went into winter quarters. The war was changing, however; it was intensifying, especially in the major theatres of Virginia, where General Lee's army remained locked in eternal combat with the Union Army of the Potomac, and along the Georgia-Tennessee border, where the Federals were preparing to invade the southeastern Confederacy through its back door at Chattanooga. Along the south Atlantic coast, the situation was deadlocked, as General Gillmore and Admiral Dahlgren—in a cruel twist of fate—had gained enough ground that they could actually see their objective just a few miles away across Charleston Harbor, yet only their shells and their prisoners of war allowed to enter the beleaguered city.

In September of 1860, the men of the Charleston Battalion had been civilians, many of wealth and prominence, anticipating with boiling blood the outcome of the election of that year. By September of 1861, they were militiamen who looked with pride at the events they helped to bring about—secession and war—hoping that they would get their chance to kill a Yankee before the show ended. September of 1862 found them in the uniforms of their national army, enlisted, whether they liked it now or not, for the duration of the conflict, with ranks thinned by disease and battle. The conflict had not ended in 1862, nor had it ended a year later in 1863, and with the enemy at the gates of their beloved city, the men of the Charleston Battalion could see no end in sight.

As the seasons changed, so too had the battalion gone through changes. Lt. Col. Peter Gaillard was recovering from the amputation of his left hand, and the battalion's much-admired major David Ramsay was dead, leaving the men under the command of Maj. Julius Blake, late captain of Company A. Gone forever too were Henry Campbell King, John Edwards, and William H. Ryan, all three promising officers who commanded the respect of their men—a hard thing in a unit where, as General Hagood stated, "there was too much intelligence in the ranks . . . for men without force of character to command it successfully."[1]

Changes in the command structure were more obvious than the changes that had taken place in the ranks, where the new recruits now outnumbered the original militiamen of 1860. When estimating the strength of the Charleston Battalion, one must always take into consideration the phenomenon that with this particular unit there were an inordinate number of men who, through social connections, were able to secure detached duty far from combat. Always add to those absentees the standard one-fourth to one-third who were sick, then—following a battle—the wounded, dead, or those otherwise unavailable for service. By this formula the battalion had been reduced to barely 120 effectives in September of 1862. Recruitment and conscription had brought in more Charlestonians but also many men from the midlands and upper counties of the state, which swelled the battalion to more than 500 men by July of 1863. Due to the above-mentioned formula—especially the casualties at Wagner and the effects of coastal fevers on those inland newcomers—the battalion's effective strength was no more than 320 officers and men in the wee morning hours of September 8 when they crushed Admiral Dahlgren's boat attack. Presently on their way to join the battalion were 63 new men who had volunteered under a recent presidential proclamation that allowed them to choose in which branch and unit to serve.[2]

On September 20, 1863, section two of Special Order No. 188 from General Beauregard's headquarters signaled the birth a new brigade to be commanded by Brig. Gen. Johnson Hagood. A native of Barnwell, South Carolina, Hagood was born on February 21, 1829, and graduated from the South Carolina Military Academy (the Citadel) at Charleston in 1847. Like many South Carolinians, he pursued a legal career and was admitted to the state bar in 1850.

Prior to the war, Hagood held the rank of brigadier general in the state militia, and upon secession he became colonel of the First South Carolina Volunteers, which traveled to Charleston in January of 1861 to assist in the reduction of Fort Sumter. Following Sumter, Hagood took his regiment to Virginia, where he was present during the first major clash of arms at Manassas. Colonel Hagood held a command on James Island in June of 1862 and participated in the repulse of the Federal flanking movement at Secessionville, after which he was promoted to brigadier general on July 21, 1862. A year later Brigadier General Hagood was again on James Island and participated in the skirmish of July 16, 1863, before he was ordered to relieve General Taliaferro at Wagner on July 19. Hagood served several tours as commander of Morris Island during the ensuing siege.[3]

In 1862 General Beauregard had promised Hagood that when an opportunity arose that officer would be given "a good brigade with which to take the field." Upon reflection of the creation of Hagood's brigade, General Beauregard said, "I gave him the best troops I had."[4] These troops—the best in the entire department of South Carolina, Georgia, and eastern Florida—were the Eleventh, Twenty-first, and Twenty-fifth South Carolina regiments, the Seventh Battalion of South Carolina Volunteers, and the Charleston Battalion.[5] Of these five commands, the Charleston Battalion had by far the most combat experience, and only this battalion could boast having played a conspicuous role in every major Federal assault against Charleston: Secessionville, DuPont's iron-clad assault, July 18 at Battery Wagner, the Morris Island Campaign and lastly the nighttime boat attack against Fort Sumter. This was an enviable record unmatched by any other South Carolina infantry unit in the defense of Charleston.

Ten days after the creation of Hagood's brigade, Special Order No. 198 ordered that the Charleston Battalion be increased to a full regiment by the addition of the three companies of the First Battalion South Carolina Sharpshooters.[6] This battalion was more of a regular Confederate organization as opposed to a volunteer organization, and though a handful of its men claimed Charleston as their home, its ranks had been filled predominantly with men from every other corner of the state: Edgefield, Lexington, Marion, Newberry, Orangeburg, Pickens, Sumter, and Yorkville. One soldier, Pvt. J. R. Holsenback, was enlisted on April 6, 1863, by Capt. Robert Chisholm in Macon, Georgia. Holsenback deserted the Sharpshooters on May 11, 1863.[7] In addition, unlike the Charleston Battalion, the Sharpshooters' officers were almost to the man not from Charleston. The Sharpshooters' commander, Maj. Joseph Abney, hailed from Edgefield, while Company A's Chisholm was from Beaufort. Company B's captain, Joseph Blythe Allston, was from Georgetown, as was Lt. J. G. Huguenin.[8] Only Company C's captain, Henry Buist, was from Charleston, where he was a partner in the legal firm of MacBeth & Buist and resided on Bull Street near Coming Street.[9] Buist's subordinate, Lt. E. H. Holman, was from Orangeburg.[10]

The issue of adding the Sharpshooter companies to the Charleston Battalion had come up once before in December of 1862 and was not met with enthusiasm by the men of the latter unit. Speaking on behalf of the men, Captain Blake wrote a letter to Major Ramsay that month expressing that many of the men rejected being consolidated with the Sharpshooters because they desired to remain "a distinctive City Battalion." Blake went on to remind Ramsay that for the same reason these Charlestonians had earlier "objected . . . to form a part of the 24th [Regiment]." In the same letter, Blake urged Ramsay to consider the wishes of the men on this issue, because "though they be in the ranks . . . many of them are intelligent gentlemen and holding in civil life social position equal to the officers."[11]

There were even objections to the consolidation on the side of the Sharpshooters. On December 2, 1862, Capt. Joseph Blythe Allston protested the proposed consolidation in a letter to Gen. Thomas Jordan, General Beauregard's chief of staff. In his letter, Allston admitted that while his relationship with Lieutenant Colonel Gaillard and some of the other officers was "personally pleasant & agreeable, the original organization of the [Charleston] Battalion is of an entirely opposite character." This last was a reference to the Charlestonians' dislike of the idea of consolidation with outsiders. Furthermore, from a more practical standpoint, Allston was concerned that because the officers in the Charleston Battalion were elected while those in the Sharpshooter Battalion were appointed, future difficulties would arise in filling vacancies. To this end he implored, "To combine the two in the same organization would lead to dissatisfaction when perfect harmony now exists."[12]

Despite such protests, the new regiment came into existence and was officially designated as the Twenty-seventh South Carolina Infantry. Under the assumption that he would fully recover from the amputation of his left hand, Lieutenant Colonel Gaillard was promoted to full colonel to lead the new unit, and Major Blake was promoted to lieutenant colonel. Third in the chain of command was Maj. Joseph Abney, commander of the Sharpshooters and veteran of the Palmetto Regiment during the Mexican War, in which regiment he had been second lieutenant of Company D from Edgefield, the "Old 96 Boys."[13]

Joseph Abney was born in Edgefield District on December 2, 1819, near Lorick's Ferry. Though he received little in the way of formal education, he became somewhat of a classical scholar, proficient in mathematics and highly skilled as an orator. Early on Abney taught school in his rural district, but eventually he traveled to Abbeville, South Carolina, where he studied law, and then to Columbia, where he was admitted to the bar in 1842. He returned to Edgefield to practice law, but soon the United States annexed Texas and war with Mexico erupted. His service in this war as second lieutenant in the Palmetto Regiment nearly brought him death, when he was severely wounded at the battle of Churubusco and later in Mexico City, where he was stricken with dysentery. Over a decade of peace followed the Mexican War, allowing Abney to develop his legal career before the Civil War broke out. In February of 1862, he was elected colonel of the Twenty-second South Carolina Volunteer Infantry, but five months later he was appointed by General Pemberton as major in the regular Confederate Army, commanding the newly organized Sharp-shooter Battalion.[14]

Thus far, only Company B of Abney's battalion had seen combat. This was at the battle of Pocotaligo, South Carolina, October 22-23, 1862, where they supported a section of the Beaufort Volunteer Artillery and assisted in covering a with-drawal movement. During the action, Allston's company suf-fered ten casualties. Brig. Gen. W. S. Walker, commander of the forces at Pocotaligo, in his report thanked "Captain All-ston's sharpshooters . . . [for] covering our retreat and behav-ing for the most part, with great spirit."[15]]

ORGANIZATION OF THE
NEW TWENTY-SEVENTH REGIMENT

Co. A: Formerly Co. E, Calhoun Guards
    Capt. Francis T. Miles, Lt. B. W. Palmer, 2d Lt. J. Waring Axson

Co. B: Formerly Co. B, Charleston Light Infantry
Capt. Thomas Y. Simons, Lt. William Sinkler, 2d Lt. Alfred H. Masterman

Co. C: Formerly Co. F, Union Light Infantry/German Fusiliers
Capt. Samuel Lord, Lt. George Brown

Co. D: Formerly Co. D, Sumter Guards
Capt. J. Ward Hopkins, Lt. J. A. Cay, 2d Lt. A. St. John Lance

Co. E: Formerly Co. A, Sharpshooters
Capt. Robert Chisholm, Lt. S. R. Proctor

Co. F: Formerly Co. B, Sharpshooters
Capt. Joseph Blythe Allston, Lt. J. G. Huguenin

Co. G: Formerly Co. C, Sharpshooters
Capt. Henry Buist, Lt. E. H. Holman

Co. H: Formerly Co. C, Irish Volunteers
Capt. James M. Mulvaney, Lt. A. A. Allemong

Co. I: Formerly Co. A, Charleston Riflemen
Capt. William Dove Walter, Lt. F. C. Lynch, 2d Lt. J. C. Saltus

Co. K: Formerly Co. G, offshoot of the Charleston Light Infantry
Capt. William Clarkson

So the Charleston Battalion was reborn through its new identity, the Twenty-seventh regiment, and through Hagood's new brigade, in which it served. Throughout the fall and winter of 1863-64, the units of Hagood's brigade stood watch over the

approaches to Charleston, ever vigilant of the movements of
the nearby enemy. The end of September found the men of
the Charleston Battalion posted in Fort Sumter, but throughout October, November, and December, the new Twenty-seventh regiment was shuffled back and forth among that
bastion, the city, and James Island. During the first few
months of 1864 the regiment was often encamped on James
Island, where its officers were doggedly drilled and redrilled
in regimental evolutions and campaigning procedures. Also
while on James Island the men were issued new clothing and
new weapons—the .577-caliber Enfield rifle.[16] Rejuvenated,
and well equipped, the "Charlestonians' Regiment" was a formidable fighting force. Despite its new identity, old habits
died hard, and many citizens and military men still referred to
the new regiment and the Charleston Battalion as one and
the same. "[The] sharpshooters were . . . attached to the
Charleston Battalion," wrote Lt. Col. John G. Pressley of the
Twenty-fifth South Carolina, for example. "That battalion
thereafter became the Twenty-seventh South Carolina Volunteers."[17] More commonly, though, as the months went by, officers and civilians alike began to refer to the unit simply as
"Gaillard's Regiment," as they once had "Gaillard's Battalion."

Soon to be lived out by the men of the old Charleston Battalion was a second lifetime of triumphs and defeats con-
densed into a twelve-month period far more intense than
their previous three years' service. The final act of the drama
would test beyond reason the courage and determination of
these Charlestonians by taking them far from home to the
seat of war in Virginia and North Carolina. Only a handful of
these men would be present at war's end.

The spring of 1864 marked the beginning of the end of the
war, as Union general Ulysses Grant, now commanding all the
Union forces east and west, unleashed a three-pronged assault
in Virginia against General Lee and the Confederate capital of
Richmond. As usual, the Army of the Potomac would march
south head to head against General Lee, but simultaneously a

new Northern army, designated as the Army of the James, under Gen. Ben ("Beast") Butler, was to advance west from Hampton Roads along the line of the James River, which ultimately led to Richmond. The third element of Grant's movement was a back-door invasion of the vital breadbasket that was the Shenandoah Valley, destroying "everything that could possibly be used to plant, reap, or store crops, thereby eliminating Lee's source of food."[18] In April of 1864, with the military situation stalled out in front of Charleston, both Generals Beauregard and Gillmore were summoned north to Virginia by their respective governments—Beauregard to defend the south side of Richmond against Butler's advance up the James River, and Gillmore to add weight to Butler's thrust.

Curiously, the same two opponents who had spent the last nine months slugging away at each other at Charleston would face each other in a different theatre of operations 400 miles away, almost without ever disengaging one another in combat. They did not travel north alone, however. Each commander brought a substantial portion of the troops he was familiar with from Charleston. General Gillmore brought nearly twenty thousand men from his department to Virginia, leaving only enough troops around Charleston to maintain possession of the coastal islands and to continue the shelling of the city. Principal among the Confederates defending Charleston who were ordered to Virginia was Hagood's brigade, containing the Twenty-seventh South Carolina. Colonel Gaillard, recovered from his amputation, was once again in command and traveling with his men.

George Alexander, a French teacher who lived on Bull Street, had been a private in the Calhoun Guards back in April of 1861 when Major Anderson surrendered Fort Sumter. On Sullivan's Island in 1861, "there were many a hero in embryo, no doubt bumbling about the sands at the Myrtles and chasing Sand Crabs to their holes," Alexander reflected years after the war. "Our Chances for immortality were still in the dim future." Many chances had been afforded up through 1863, and the

Calhoun Guards' service record and casualty list attested to that fact. In April of 1864, however, Alexander was a sergeant in Company A (Calhoun Guards) of the new Twenty-seventh regiment bound for the Old Dominion, where many more chances at heroism and immortality were to present themselves.

VIRGINIA

Gaillard's regiment departed Charleston with the rest of Hagood's brigade on April 28, 1864. The brigade numbered 4,246 men on paper, but as was always the case, according to the general, "the majority of these men never got into the field," rightly or wrongly, because they possessed skills needed to keep the production side of the Confederacy in operation or social connections that kept them out of the fighting.[19] A report filed in April before their departure stated that Gaillard's regiment numbered 526 men present for duty.[20] The first leg of the journey took the men from Charleston by rail to Wilmington, North Carolina, at which place the entire brigade had arrived by May 4. On May 5, portions of the brigade began moving by rail to Petersburg. Gaillard's regiment, accompanied by General Hagood and a few companies of the Twenty-fifth regiment, departed Wilmington the next day, arriving in Petersburg during the night of May 6-7.[21]

Quite literally upon stepping off the train in Virginia on May 7, the Charlestonians' Regiment, as Hagood so famously named Gaillard's command—many of whom were older and unused to constant marching and fighting—were thrust into battle at Port Walthall, where they helped check a Union attempt to cut the line of the Richmond & Petersburg Railroad. In this engagement the regiment suffered six killed, thirty wounded, and nine missing, for a total of forty-five casualties.[22] Five of the six dead from the regiment were from the Charleston Light Infantry, including 2d Lt. Alfred H. Masterman. This company also accounted for two of the thirty men wounded.

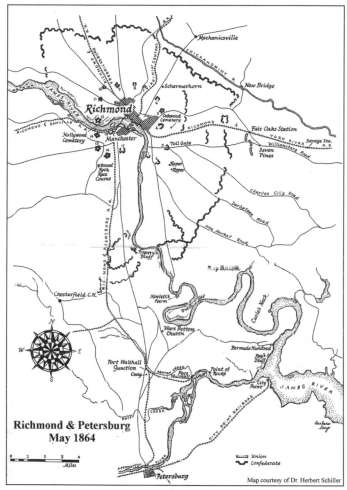

Courtesy Herbert Schiller.

Two days later, and two miles to the south, on May 9, Hagood's brigade was engaged in a fight along Swift Creek to protect the vital railroad and turnpike bridges that crossed that stream and connected Richmond with its supply depot of Petersburg to the south. Owing to the large numbers of casualties sustained at Port Walthall, and the fact that it was one of

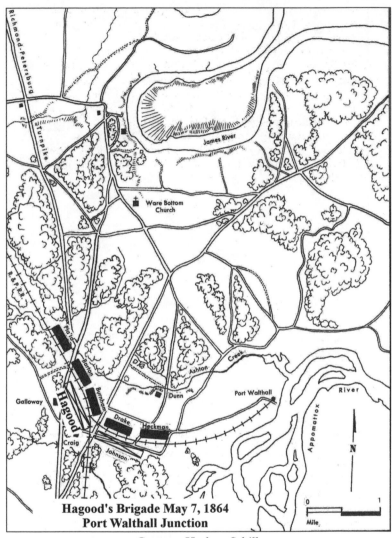

**Hagood's Brigade May 7, 1864
Port Walthall Junction**

Courtesy Herbert Schiller.

the smaller commands in Hagood's brigade, the Twenty-seventh was held in reserve at Swift Creek, yet it did participate in covering the withdrawal of the Twenty-first, Twenty-fifth, and Eleventh South Carolina after they drove back the enemy. According to Hagood's report, the Twenty-seventh lost one man killed, and Lieutenant Colonel Blake was slightly wounded in this action.[23] Other sources, however, indicate that two men from the Twenty-seventh were killed at Swift Creek: twenty-one-year-old William Edward Bee of the Sumter Guards and William Bryan of the Charleston Light Infantry.[24]

With only a few days of rest in between, these men were rushed a few miles north, where they skirmished with the enemy at Drewry's Bluff on May 14 and fought an engagement on May 16 that helped turn back yet another Union attempt to cut the Richmond & Petersburg Railroad.[25] Though there is

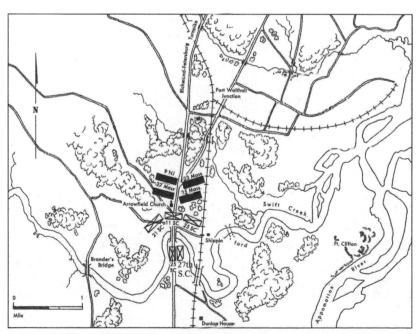

Hagood's attack north of Swift Creek, May 9, 1864.
Courtesy Herbert Schiller.

At left, the Richmond-Petersburg Turnpike Bridge (Route 301) crosses Swift Creek. Gaillard's regiment held the south side of the creek near this battle marker, while other portions of Hagood's brigade attacked the enemy north of the creek. Photograph by author.

Swift Creek today. Photograph by author.

no individual unit breakdown of casualties for the Twenty-seventh in these battles, Hagood reports that his brigade numbered 2,235 men on May 15 and that he lost 433 men in the battle of the following day.[26] The Charleston Battalion portion lost at least 14 killed and an unknown number wounded between May 14 and 16. Among the dead was thirty-eight-year-old Rial Seay, a veteran of the Mexican War who died on May 15 of a stroke. He was one of the many recruits enlisted into the new Company G at his hometown of Spartanburg, South Carolina by Lieutenant Clarkson. Unlike many new recruits, however, Seay had much previous military experience. Aside from his service in Mexico, he had organized a company in the Fifth South Carolina Infantry, was elected captain, and

Rial Seay. Courtesy Ronald S. Giamongo.

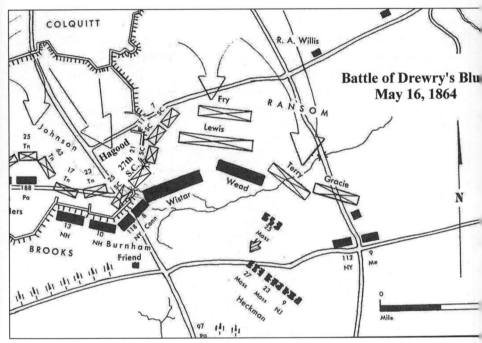

Courtesy Herbert Schiller.

Drewry's Bluff defenses at Fort Darling looking south along the James River. The battle of Drewry's Bluff was fought approximately one and a half miles to the southwest. Photograph by author.

Looking south along the Richmond-Petersburg Turnpike (Route 301). To the left of the turnpike, in the trees beyond the 7-Eleven sign (site of the Bellwood Drive-in Theater), Gaillard's regiment charged the Federals on May 16, 1864. Photograph by author.

traveled to Virginia in the war's early stages, where he was wounded at Seven Pines near the gates of Richmond in 1862.

Another battalion fatality was Charles Pinckney Brown, a signer of the Ordinance of Secession.[27] Maj. Joseph Abney from the Sharpshooters was also severely wounded during the fighting.

These three battles and intervening skirmishes resulted in a series of Confederate victories that effectively bottled up Union general Ben Butler in the oddly shaped peninsula formed by the James and Appomattox rivers known as Bermuda Hundred. Much to the chagrin of Grant, who expected Butler to vigorously maneuver in cooperation with his own operations against Lee north of the James River, Butler instead sat down and consolidated his position. This proved to be of serious consequence for Grant, for Butler's inactivity allowed the transfer of nearly half of Beauregard's force south of the James—including Hagood's brigade—to Lee's army northeast of Richmond, just in time to participate in the three days of battle around Cold Harbor June 1-3, 1864.

Cold Harbor was almost entirely a defensive battle for the Confederates, fought for the most part from behind well-laid fortifications. The result was that only three deaths were reported from the ranks of Gaillard's command: 1st Lt. William Mason Smith, adjutant of the Twenty-seventh; Pvt. Thomas Atkinson, of the Sumter Guards; and thirty-one-year-old Jacob Staubs, from Allston's company of sharpshooters.[28] Lt. William Sinkler from the Charleston Light Infantry was wounded in the calf. The Federal casualties, however, were staggering, with the loss of some seven thousand men shot down in the first half-hour of their attack. One Union soldier remembered that the Confederate volleys seemed like volcanic blasts and that his comrades were killed so quickly that they fell "like rows of blocks or bricks pushed over by striking against one another."[29] Indeed, the Confederate repulse of General Grant's army was so quick and decisive that General Hagood reminisced, "It may sound incredible, but it is nevertheless strictly true, that the writer of these Memoirs, situated near the center of the line along which this murderous repulse was given, and awake and vigilant of the progress of events, was not aware at the time of any serious assault having been given."[30]

Brutally defeated at Cold Harbor, General Grant paused to regain his composure and reorganize his forces. Then he sidled southeast and crossed the James River for a dash against Petersburg—Richmond's vital supply hub. For the first time in more than a month of continuous combat, Grant outmaneuvered Lee, and his lead elements arrived in front of Petersburg's eastern lines before noon on June 15. Lee had not anticipated such a bold maneuver, and consequently Petersburg lay virtually helpless, the bulk of its defenders having been attached to Lee's army north of the James River. Like a powerful tempest, the Union host easily swept aside successive lines of Beauregard's skeleton force. As night fell, the victorious Federals halted to await reinforcements, a decision that proved fateful. The recent slaughter at Cold Harbor had taught the blue-clad soldiers to be wary of frontal assaults against Confederate entrenchments that *appeared* to be thinly defended, and though they had managed to overrun and capture the outer defenses of Petersburg, they gained the impression that they were being lured into a trap. The unexpected reprieve bought enough time for Hagood's brigade to hustle back down to the Petersburg lines, where they filed into the trenches after dark on June 15, 1864, to participate in the next three days of fighting collectively known as the Battle of Petersburg. This timely Confederate arrival saved the day, prolonging the war and resulting in the Siege of Petersburg, during which Gaillard's regiment endured sixty-seven consecutive days and nights in the trenches.

The day of June 24, shortly after the siege began, proved to be a devastating day for Gaillard's command when it charged the enemy's works, only to be overwhelmed by a spirited counterattack resulting in the loss of 143 of their number. Eight men had been killed, 22 were wounded, and an astounding 113 counted as missing, presumed captured or dead.[31]

Daily losses became the norm during more than two months of grueling trench warfare, until the men of Hagood brigade were withdrawn from the Petersburg lines and marched south and west to fight the disastrous battle of Weldon railroad on August 21, 1864. This battle proved to be a slaughter ground for the South Carolinians. During the offensive action, Hagood's men swept over a portion of the Union line, only to find themselves trapped in a reentering angle, nearly surrounded, and subjected to a severe crossfire.

According to Hagood's report, in one of the war's most surreal battlefield scenes, a Union officer rode out, grabbed up a flag from Gaillard's regiment, and told the men to surrender. An awkward silence descended over the field as both sides ceased firing and many of the men began to surrender. Union soldiers immediately advanced to gather prisoners, with the result that the field was crowded with Federals and Confederates, some of the latter surrendering while others refused. The silence was broken, however, when Hagood pushed his way through the crowd, ordered his men not to surrender, and demanded that the Union officer drop the flag and return to his lines. When the officer protested, Hagood gave him one final chance to drop the flag and go. Obviously ignorant of the temperament of the Southern general before him, the Union officer continued to debate the subject, whereupon Hagood drew his revolver and shot the man from his horse. In one fluid movement, Hagood had shot the Union officer, grabbed the flag, mounted that officer's horse, and then, handing the recaptured flag to Pvt. Isaac Dwight Stoney of the Sumter Guards (an orderly in his staff), he led the survivors back through a hailstorm of Federal rifle fire. In his report, Hagood singled out Private Stoney for gallantry and recommended his promotion.[32] Subsequently, Pvt. Dwight Stoney became 2d Lt. Dwight Stoney, Company D, Sumter Guards, Twenty-seventh South Carolina Infantry. Interestingly enough, though Stoney was of English lineage, his family had intermarried with French Huguenots, and his father was named Peter Gaillard Stoney.

Of the action at Weldon, Union major general G. K. Warren reported, "General Hagood's brigade struck a part of our line where the troops were in echelon and they found themselves almost surrounded, and everyone thinking they had surrendered, ceased firing. Troops immediately advanced to bring them in when their officers commenced firing, and Captain Dailey, provost-marshal of the Fourth Division, was shot by General Hagood." During Hagood's retreat, the enemy advanced and managed to capture at least three other flags from his brigade.[33] Years later, Hagood admitted that he had confused the flags, and the flag he saved from the Federal officer was actually that of the Eleventh South Carolina, not the Twenty-seventh. However, one of Gaillard's battle flags was captured during the retreat. This flag, now on display at Pamplin Historical Park near Petersburg, was returned to South Carolina in 1905 courtesy of the United States War Department.[34]

Six hundred eighty-one men—all who were present for duty in Hagood's brigade—went into the fight at Weldon railroad and only 292 came out unhurt.[35] A survivor from the Twenty-fifth regiment remembered that after the battle the brigade was somewhat re-formed, and he witnessed that General Hagood's "eyes welled up with tears as he moved about among this pitiful remnant of his once magnificent brigade."[36] Gaillard's share of the butcher's bill came to 2 killed, 22 wounded, and 71 missing but presumed killed or captured.[37]

This now exhausted skeleton of a brigade was allowed to encamp in a rearward place of safety—the Dunlap family farm along Swift Creek, ironically the same piece of ground these men had defended three months earlier. During this season, however, the fighting had shifted far to the south and the environment along Swift Creek was peaceful and rejuvenating. The men enjoyed unlimited bathing in the creek, vegetables brought in to improve their diet, and new clothing and

Battle flag of Gaillard's regiment captured at Weldon railroad.
Courtesy Pamplin Historical Park and National Museum of the Civil
War Soldier, Petersburg, Virginia. Photograph by Jill Pascoe.

shoes. After a few weeks, hundreds of sick and wounded men
returned to the ranks. Along Swift Creek, all things considered, the men of Gaillard's regiment spent a pleasant September—the fourth September in military service for some of
them—resting and recuperating from five months of solid
marching and fighting. November, however, found them in
action once again, this time fighting along the Richmond
lines north of the James River at New Market Road, Duff's Hill
Farm, and Fort Harrison. They remained on the Richmond
front until December 21, 1864, when, quite abruptly, the men
were loaded onto railroad cars for a circuitous Christmas journey to Wilmington, North Carolina via Danville, Virginia and
Greensboro, North Carolina.[38]

NORTH CAROLINA

When Hagood's command arrived at Wilmington, it gave the appearance of a slim brigade with 1,391 officers and men, only a fraction of the men who had rolled out of Charleston eight months earlier.[39] In January of 1865 part of Hagood's brigade fought at the second battle of Fort Fisher, where on January 15, nearly 500 men—including the better part the Twenty-first and Twenty-fifth regiments—were lost to the enemy.[40] The Twenty-seventh had not been dispatched to the fort and therefore managed to escape capture.

On February 20, Hagood's remnant, now numbering 900 men, fought at the Battle of Town Creek, south of Wilmington and across the Cape Fear River from Fort Fisher, where almost half their number, serving as a rearguard, was cut off and captured. At Town Creek the movements of Hagood's brigade had been directed by Col. Charles Simonton of the Twenty-fifth South Carolina. Simonton's conduct in the face of the overwhelming Federal assault was no less than gallant yet highly criticized by Hagood, who claimed that Simonton had waited too late to extract his troops, resulting in such a large contingent being captured.

By Simonton's account, no less than 150 men from the Twenty-seventh were lost to the enemy at Town Creek.[41] Some survivors managed to make their way through the marshy wooded country to rejoin their units, but as Hagood asserts in his memoirs, others from his command discreetly made their way back to South Carolina and out of the war altogether. He had suffered the same problem after the battle of Fort Fisher, as Gen. Braxton Bragg reported from Wilmington in a January 25 letter to Hagood's division commander, Gen. Robert Hoke. Bragg complained, "Large numbers of Hagood's brigade are represented as straggling off home, plundering indiscriminately as they go."[42]

On February 23, the brigade moved inland to Rockfish Creek. There it remained until March, when it was absorbed into Gen. Joseph Johnston's Army of the Tennessee. Around

March 8, Hagood's brigade was reinforced by one company of the Second North Carolina, the survivors of the Tenth, Thirty-sixth, and Fortieth North Carolina, and Adam's Light Artillery Battery.[43] Though Hagood's memoirs state that these additions raised his strength to just over 1,100 men, the official returns show no more than 898 officers and men available to fight.[44]

In the neighborhood of Bentonville, North Carolina, General Johnston consolidated every Confederate still in the field for a last-ditch attack against General Sherman, who, having marched through Georgia and South Carolina, had now entered North Carolina. Sherman was marching northeast, bent on uniting his column with the victorious Union forces moving inland from Wilmington at the railroad hub of Goldsboro. Outnumbered at least three to one by Sherman's column alone, Johnston's only hope was to defeat Sherman and then turn about and strike the Federals marching from the coast, to prevent their concentration. The Battle of Bentonville, as it came to be known, lasted for three days, from March 19 to 21, and was the last offensive operation of the Army of the Tennessee. Hagood's brigade was placed near the right center of General Hoke's division, which constituted the left wing of the Confederate line. Though the Federals were driven from their positions, unfortunately they were not kept from Sherman's desired concentration, and following the battle, Johnston consolidated his commands and retreated east toward Raleigh. There are no surviving records that break down the casualties in the Twenty-seventh, but on March 19, the first day of battle, Hagood's brigade (of which the original South Carolina components accounted for approximately 500 muskets) lost 270 men. On the 20th the brigade lost 8 more and on the 21st another 18.[45] These losses were predominantly in the North Carolina elements of the brigade.

General Johnston, now hopelessly outnumbered, came to the realization that he could accomplish nothing more than to simply "annoy" Sherman's army. Johnston's ragged band evacuated the state capital at Raleigh and moved west until he entered into negotiations with Sherman, which ultimately led to surrender on April 26, 1865, near Greensboro, North Carolina. General Lee had surrendered to General Grant at Appomattox, Virginia on April 9, making Johnston's army the last major Confederate army east of the Appalachian Mountains.

CHAPTER 10

Attrition

In the final year of the war, the Charleston Battalion had lost virtually all of its men and all but one of its original officers through fatigue, wounds, death, imprisonment in Yankee camps, and—truth be told—a small amount of desertion. On October 20, 1863, Lt. F. C. Lynch of the Charleston Riflemen died of "consumption," the nineteenth-century term for tuberculosis.[1] On April 1, 1864, even before the battalion left for Virginia, its Company G—now Company K of the Twenty-seventh—was officially disbanded per Special Order No. 77.[2] It will be remembered that the August 14, 1863, division of the oversized Company B, Charleston Light Infantry, had created this company. In September of 1863, General Order No. 125 issued by the Confederate government stated that "no authority exists for organizing new companies out of companies now in service," a statement aimed at General Beauregard, who had taken advantage of loose terminology in the 1862 General Order No. 82 to create several such new companies throughout his department. By the spring of 1864, the final official word had come down from the Confederate War Department and these new companies were disbanded.[3] Capt. William Clarkson reverted back to First Lieutenant Clarkson of the Charleston Light Infantry. As for the men of the disbanded company, some records indicate that they were distributed throughout the regiment, though eighteen men belonging to "Company K, 27th regiment" are listed as killed in action or died in Northern prisons throughout the Virginia and Carolinas campaign. Others still are recorded as serving through to the first months of 1865 in "Company K."[4]

Aside from Lieutenant Lynch, who died, two other original officers left the battalion before it departed for Virginia. Samuel Lord, the captain of the Union Light Infantry/German Fusiliers, resigned his commission on January 1, 1864, due to health problems. Throughout November and December of 1863, he had been on sick furlough and was admitted to the Soldiers Relief Hospital in Charleston. On December 13, he was declared unfit to attend to his duties due to "congestion of the liver," and the surgeon in charge felt he needed to remain in the hospital for at least an additional month. His condition may have been related to the contusion he had received in his side by an exploding shell while serving on Morris Island in August of 1863. Following his resignation, Lord, a peacetime lawyer, was assigned to duty in Charleston as Confederate military district attorney.[5] Capt. George W. Brown took command of the company.

The Calhoun Guards' captain Francis T. Miles was assigned to special duty in Branchville, South Carolina in January of 1864, most probably to tend to Federal prisoners captured around Richmond who were being detained at Branchville en route to Georgia. During this period, several detachments from Ward Hopkins' Sumter Guards had been sent to Branchville to guard these prisoners. Miles resigned from command on April 18, 1864, when he was placed on the Medical Examining Board.[6] Lt. Barnwell W. Palmer was promoted to fill Miles' position as company commander. Under Palmer was Lt. John M. Easterby, an aged veteran of the Mexican War. Easterby fell ill in the autumn of 1863 and was hospitalized first in Charleston, then later in Columbia, the shift in climate likely indicating that he was stricken with fever. He eventually rejoined the command at Petersburg in 1864 but remained sick and was admitted to the Episcopal Church Hospital in Williamsburg, Virginia. He was finally transferred homeward to recuperate near Charleston, in Summerville,

South Carolina. Easterby resigned his commission in July of 1864.[7]

The rest of the original March 1862 officer corps was whittled away in Virginia and North Carolina beginning June 3, 1864, at Cold Harbor, when Lt. William Sinkler, the wealthy planter from the Charleston Light Infantry, was shot through his left calf. The wound failed to heal and Sinkler was assigned to light duty at home as provost marshal of Charleston, where on January 2, 1865, he was retired to the invalid corps.[8]

On June 15, 1864, the Charleston Battalion had entered the Petersburg lines just after sundown to the right of the City Point Road near Hare's Hill, a slight eminence west of Harrison's Creek. Darkness concealed the fact that Gaillard's regiment was in an exposed position. There were two Hare's Hills, named after a father and son with that last name; the battalion's position was at the hill named after the younger Hare, which was very near the Appomattox River, present-day site of the Petersburg city landfill. Before the sun rose the next morning—June 16, the two-year anniversary of the battle of Secessionville— a Federal artillery barrage opened on their position. The very first shell burst wounded a number of men of the battalion and killed Capt. Ward Hopkins of the Sumter Guards and Capt. Barnwell W. Palmer of the Calhoun Guards.[9] Later that day the enemy assailed the battalion's position and Lt. A. A. Allemong of the Irish Volunteers was mortally wounded. He died on June 22 in Petersburg.[10] All three men had been present at Secessionville, where Hopkins had been promoted to captain due to the death of his superior, Henry King, and Allemong had been commended for gallantry. General Hagood lamented in a later report, "Captains Hopkins and Palmer . . . were killed by the same shell. . . . Lieutenant Allemong was wounded and has since died. . . . In short the best and bravest of my command have been laid beneath the soil of Virginia."[11] Also during the three-day Battle of Petersburg, Lt. J. C. Saltus of the Charleston Riflemen was captured in a fight on June 18, 1864.[12]

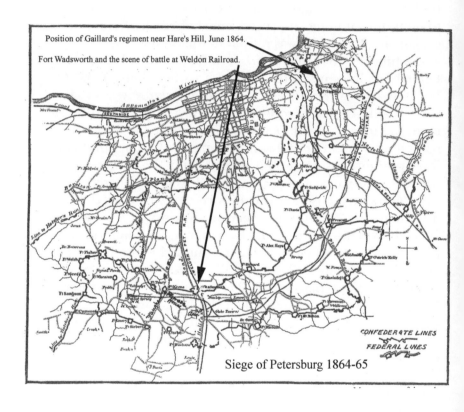

Position of Gaillard's regiment near Hare's Hill, June 1864.

Fort Wadsworth and the scene of battle at Weldon Railroad.

CONFEDERATE LINES

FEDERAL LINES

Siege of Petersburg 1864-65

Shortly after the Siege of Petersburg began, Gaillard's men took part in an assault on the enemy's trenches to their front on June 22 and then again on June 24, 1864. On the 22nd the Union Light Infantry's captain George Brown was killed.[13] During the second assault on the 24th, the Federal position was carried but the charge was not supported properly, and the enemy eventually regained their position, though only after hard fighting. During this struggle, Lt. J. Waring Axson—in command of the Calhoun Guards after Captain Palmer's death—was killed at the head of his company early in the assault, and Capt. James M. Mulvaney of the Irish Volunteers was captured while standing on the enemy works, emboldening his men by waving his cap in the air.[14] Unrelated to the Charleston Battalion but damaging to the Twenty-seventh as a whole, more than half of Company G from Abney's Sharpshooter Battalion was captured inside the enemy works on this occasion, including the company's Charlestonian commander, Capt. Henry Buist.[15]

The battle of Weldon railroad on August 21, 1864, resulted in the decimation of Hagood's entire brigade, when it penetrated a portion of the Federal line only to find itself surrounded and completely unsupported. Though many were killed or wounded, a large number of men—among them nearly all that remained of the Irish Volunteers—were captured, including Gaillard's second in command, Lt. Col. Julius Blake. Captured along with Blake were Lt. A. W. Muckenfuss of the Charleston Light Infantry and Lt. H. W. Hendricks of the Union Light Infantry. Both Muckenfuss and Hendricks had entered service with the battalion as sergeants in the spring of 1862. Through daring action, Hagood managed to lead a remnant of his brigade back to safety.[16] Not quite 700 men went into the fight, and only 292 officers and men remained fit for duty when it was over. Fifty-nine officers went into the battle of Weldon railroad but only 18 survived unhurt. Counted among these fortunate few were the one-handed, fifty-one-year-old colonel Peter C. Gaillard and Capt.

Thomas Y. Simons of the Charleston Light Infantry.[17]

Due to the loss of his hand, Gaillard had been legally exempt from service, but still he insisted on sharing the hardships of war with his men. On June 8, 1864, the brigade surgeons ordered that Gaillard, emaciated from illness and wounds, "leave the trenches for a few weeks." This he was forced to do, "but still he remained near his men, watching and waiting for the moment when he could again take the field." He returned just in time for Weldon railroad.[18] Just after that fight, Gaillard was detached from his regiment to command the post of Weldon, North Carolina. Though he would never lead his Charlestonians in battle again, he fought near them at Wilmington in February of 1865, where he commanded Company D of the Thirteenth North Carolina, Company C of the Sixty-eighth North Carolina, and a naval detachment manning a series of river batteries along the Cape Fear three miles south of the city.[19] After the fall of Wilmington, he was retired to the invalid corps on March 6, 1865.

With Gaillard gone, command of the "Charlestonians' Regiment" passed to Captain Simons, the regiment's senior company commander.[20] Maj. Joseph Abney, of the Sharpshooter Battalion, would have ascended to command the regiment but he had been wounded at Drewry's Bluff and never returned to the regiment. Ultimately Abney was retired to the invalid corps on March 6, 1865.[21]

Now that Simons was responsible for the whole regiment—or what remained of it—his Company B served without a commissioned officer for the remainder of the war. Next in line to command the company was Lt. William Clarkson, but due to a wound, he had been absent from his command all summer, until he was summoned to Richmond in October to appear as a witness in court. Clarkson also never rejoined the regiment.[22] Next in line behind Clarkson was Lieutenant Sinkler, who had been wounded at Cold Harbor, then finally Lieutenant Muckenfuss, who had been captured at Weldon railroad.[23] Another company without an officer was the Charleston Riflemen. Lieutenant Lynch had died before leaving Charleston; his successor, Lieutenant Saltus, was in a Union prison; and Capt. William Dove Walter, like Gaillard, Abney, and Sinkler, was retired to the invalid corps on December 23, 1864, due to protracted illness.[24]

On March 3, 1865, after the tragic loss at Town Creek outside of Wilmington, Captain Simons surmised in a letter to Gen. Samuel Cooper, the Confederate Army's adjutant general, that his Twenty-seventh regiment numbered perhaps 40 men.[25] About this same time, all that remained of Hagood's brigade—a mere twelve companies—was consolidated into what amounted to one small regiment under Lt. Col. James H. Rion of the Seventh South Carolina Battalion. Shortly thereafter, the brigade was augmented by the aforementioned North Carolina troops.[26] Following the Battle of Bentonville, and against his wishes, Hagood was dispatched to South Carolina to round up some 900 men who were absent from the brigade, but time was short. He was unable to complete this mission and failed to rejoin his command before the war ended. At the time of his departure, the North Carolina units in his brigade were transferred, leaving his original brigade's effective strength at only 370 men present for duty.[27] These stalwarts remained in the ranks for three and a half more weeks, until—with Richmond in Federal hands, General Lee's army already surrendered at Appomattox, and the Confederate Government fleeing southward—General Johnston surrendered what was left of his gallant army near Greensboro, North Carolina on April 26, 1865. On this solemn occasion, Hagood's entire brigade, commanded by Lieutenant Colonel Rion, numbered only 350 officers and men still in the ranks. Captain Simons was in command of the "Charlestonians' Regiment" and was paroled with the unit's few survivors.[28]

For more than a week before the surrender, the opposing armies had maintained a cease-fire as their generals hammered

Postwar photograph of Thomas Y. Simons. Courtesy Charles
Rowe and the *Charleston Post & Courier.*

out the details, and as one might expect, quite a number of
Confederates simply packed up and left for home before the
surrender was made final. Faced with the fate that awaited a
surrendered army, and driven by depressing news from home,
the men of the "Charlestonians' Regiment" were not immune
to that survival mechanism in all human beings that urges one
to "get while the gettin' is good." These men were aware of
conditions in their city: the destruction of the fire of December 1861 had been made worse by Union artillery batteries on
Morris Island and Black Island, which had maintained a
relentless long-range fire on the city for 545 days. Civilians
had continued to inhabit the lower wards of the city above
and below the 1861 fire line, until the Union shells drove
them northward. This depopulated Charleston, leaving only a
few thousand destitute inhabitants crowded in its northwest

neighborhoods, with three or four families in each household. Those who could, like the families of Colonel Gaillard, Captain Simons, and Lieutenant Clarkson, had fled to points inland like St. Stephens, Eastover, Columbia, or even farther, to the safety of the mountains near Anderson, South Carolina or Asheville and Flat Rock, North Carolina.[29]

On April 23—three days before the official surrender—an officer in Hagood's brigade noted, "Fifteen men of the Twenty-seventh regiment left for home yesterday and today. The division is being rapidly reduced in this way."[30] That statement, taken with Captain Simons' March 3 report to Gen. Samuel Cooper, suggests that the regiment surrendered no more than twenty-five men in North Carolina. Indeed, the regiment probably numbered fewer than that, as doubtless more men had left for home three days later on April 26, when the surrender officially took place. Regardless, in the end the lion's share of the remaining members of the Twenty-seventh belonged to the Charleston Battalion, whose Company D, the Sumter Guards, surrendered nine men.[31] Those who departed early probably walked home penniless, but each officer and enlisted man still in the army's ranks on April 26 was issued over a dollar in silver—the last of the Confederate treasury, though in that atmosphere, adequate funds to get a soldier from North Carolina back home to Charleston.

The official surrender had taken place, weapons had been stacked to be collected by Union quartermasters, and more Southern men faded off into the countryside, but there still remained one final act in the drama: the final disbanding. Once duplicate rolls had been made containing the names of all Confederates surrendered in General Johnston's army, the terms of surrender stipulated that "the troops will march, under their officers, to their respective States, and there be disbanded, all retaining personal property."[32] The point where Hagood's brigade would officially disband was Lancaster Courthouse, South Carolina, and at that event, held on May 3, 1865, a Sumter Guardsman remembered that in this final pathetic march, "the Twenty-seventh led the column with seven men in its ranks; the Twenty-fifth followed next with five; the Seventh battalion, which had not suffered so much in battle as the other regiments, had near a hundred men in ranks; the Twenty-first not quite so large, and the Eleventh regiment, numbering sixteen . . . was the rear guard."[33]

CHAPTER 11

Citizens Once Again

Charleston was a desolate, smoking ruin when the Union Army marched in on the morning of February 18, 1865, thus beginning the twelve-year occupation of the city by Federal troops. Buildings were wrecked by the shellfire, a huge swath of destruction had been cut by the fire of 1861, and abandoned wharves rotted along the once-thriving waterfront. Miles upon miles of streets were pocked with shell craters, choked with weeds, and overrun by vermin and grazing cattle. The outcome of the war crushed the old order and displaced many of Charleston's once-prominent families. In the years that followed the war, the once-proud lower portion of town became crowded with newly freed men and outsiders come to occupy abandoned and confiscated lands and houses given up due to delinquent taxes and the absence of proper owners. The economy was of course destroyed, and a long road to recovery lay ahead. The future was not bright for the officers and men of the Charleston Battalion as they returned home.

Civilian Peter Charles Gaillard returned to Charleston in March of 1865. President Lincoln was assassinated in April, and the radicals in his party were aghast at the attitude of his successor, Sen. Andrew Johnson of Tennessee, who in their opinion made little effort to block the return of ex-Confederates to power in the South. It was in this atmosphere that in November of that year Gaillard was elected by the white electorate as the city's first postwar mayor. When President Johnson was ousted from office by the Radical Republicans at the end of his term, "Radical Reconstruction" (1868-76) began, and the occupying military governor, Gen. R. S. Canby, quickly removed Gaillard and the entire board of aldermen from office on February 28, 1868. For the next eight years, the position of mayor was filled by a series of military governors.[1] Gaillard resumed commercial endeavors, and in 1876, with the return of the city and state governments to home rule, he was appointed "Treasurer of Charleston County," a post he held until his death on Friday, January 11, 1889, at the age of seventy-six. That Friday, "as the words sped from lip to lip 'Colonel Gaillard is dead' the whole heart of the community was bowed with the sense of public and personal bereavement." For much of Gaillard's life he had been a member of the French Huguenot Church on Church Street, and for twenty years he was a church elder. In the final years of his life he founded the Association of Confederate Survivors of Charleston District, and just one year before his death his fellow veterans appointed him president of the Confederate Veterans' Association of Charleston. Peter Gaillard is buried in Magnolia Cemetery just north of the city on Charleston "Neck" along the Cooper River.

Commander of the "Charlestonians' Regiment" at the end was the thirty-four-year-old Charleston attorney, politician, and former slave owner Thomas Y. Simon, captain of the Charleston Light Infantry. Simons was certainly the last original officer and simply one of the last men standing from the Charleston Battalion and the Twenty-seventh regiment. Simons' wife had fled Charleston for the relative safety of upstate, but soon they were reunited. Upon his return to Charleston, Simons practiced law with his Broad Street firm, Simon & Siegling, and moved from his home in the fire-and-shell district on Meeting Street to the less affected neighborhoods on upper Rutledge Avenue. Still a young man at war's end, Simons served as a voice of the old Charleston establishment as the editor of the Charleston Daily Courier, a position he held during Reconstruction, from 1865 until 1873. Simons

Grave of Peter Gaillard, Magnolia Cemetery, Charleston.
Photograph by author.

also continued to dabble in politics, serving as a delegate to the Democratic National Convention in 1868 and 1872, and throughout Reconstruction he served in the Taxpayers Convention. In his mid-forties, Simons' health began to deteriorate. Throughout 1877 and the spring of 1878, he traveled to Europe endeavoring to recuperate, but upon his return to Charleston he died on April 30, 1878.[2] He is also buried at Magnolia Cemetery. Not long before his death, Simons spoke at a reunion of Union and Confederate veterans in Cambridge, Massachusetts, where hardly a dry eye could be found when he proclaimed, "Dead indeed must be the heart which cannot draw inspirations of patriotism from such scenes as this. We are strangers and aliens no longer, but brothers and fellow-citizens of one common country."[3]

Lt. Col. Julius Blake survived imprisonment after his capture at Weldon railroad. His journey through the Federal prison system took him first to the Old Capital Prison in Washington, then to Fort Delaware, and then to Point Lookout, Maryland. Late in October 1864, Blake was sent back to Fort Delaware, where he was exchanged on the last day of the month and returned to the Confederacy through Union-held Fort Pulaski in the Savannah River. When he returned to Charleston, his health was shattered from his ordeal, and on December 13, 1864, he was granted a leave of absence and admitted to a hospital in the city. On January 6, 1865, somewhat recuperated, Blake departed to rejoin his regiment, then near Wilmington. On his arrival he found that General Hagood had dropped him from the army's rolls and relieved him of command, charging that he had overstayed his leave in Charleston. Blake was later cleared of this charge by a board of inquiry.[4] Stemming from an incident at Drewry's Bluff in May of 1864 where, in Hagood's opinion, Blake had failed to obey direct orders to dislodge enemy pickets from a threatening position, the general was, perhaps, too quick to have Blake removed from command. Only Hagood's version of the incident has survived on record until now, and sadly this version—in which he refers to

Blake as "a negative character"—is so spiteful as to make the false statement that the results of the board of inquiry were never announced. Regardless, Blake was never restored to active command of the regiment. After his return to Charleston, Blake also moved to the less-scarred upper portion of the city, where he reestablished himself as a coal merchant. In 1868 he and his wife, Julia, had a daughter named Julia and in 1870 a son named Edward.[5] Blake died in 1903 and is buried at Magnolia.[6]

Samuel Lord, captain of the German Fusiliers, resigned his commission before the unit went to Virginia due to ill health but likely also so that he could accept the position of Confederate district attorney. At war's end Lord was in Charleston and quickly resumed his legal career. By the 1880s he was partner in the firm Lord & Inglesby, with his offices at 33 Broad Street. Unlike others, Lord chose to reside south of the 1861 fire line, at 11 Lamboll Street, in what was at that time a less desirable part of town.[7] Lord died in August of 1899 and is buried at Magnolia.

Francis Turquand Miles, captain of the Calhoun Guards, also resigned before the regiment went to Virginia and accepted a position as surgeon on the Confederacy's Medical Examining Board. Immediately following the war he returned to Charleston, where he "sought to rehabilitate" the College of Medicine and accepted the position of chair of anatomy. Shortly after the war he married Miss Jennie Wardlaw, daughter of an Abbeville, South Carolina judge. Together they had a son, who also became a physician. Miles' abilities were nationally recognized, and in 1868 he accepted a position as professor of anatomy at Washington College in Baltimore, Maryland. What followed was a long and distinguished career: 1869-80 as professor of nervous diseases at the University of Maryland; 1880-82 as president of the American Neurological Association; and numerous writings on the brain and nervous system. Francis Miles died on July 30, 1903, in Baltimore at the age of seventy-six.

William Sinkler, the only bona-fide planter in the Charleston Battalion's officer corps, sat out the final months of the war due to his leg wound received at Cold Harbor. Sinkler moved to Christ Church Parish across the Cooper River from Charleston, where he continued in his prewar endeavor as a planter with his wife, Mary, and their five children, two of whom were born after the war. Though wage labor and sharecropping were the only means by which to cultivate large tracts of land in a South free of slavery, Sinkler apparently succeeded to some degree, for in 1870 his land holdings were valued at $3,000.[8] Like many planters, Sinkler turned to phosphate mining in the 1880s.[9] Extracting phosphate from the marl found in the low-country riverbeds for use in producing fertilizer returned the fortunes of many a Charleston planter in the decades following the war. William Sinkler died in November of 1902 and is buried at Magnolia.[10]

Capt. James Mulvaney of the Irish Volunteers, successor to Edward MaGrath and William Ryan, was a true fighter. Captured on the enemy's works at Petersburg, he managed to survive imprisonment at Point Lookout, Maryland, Fort Delaware, Delaware, and Union-controlled Fort Pulaski outside Savannah, Georgia before returning to Charleston in the summer of 1865.[11] Following the conflict he returned to Charleston, where the stout Irish policeman—whose services were not needed in a city occupied by Federal troops— became a successful contractor on Queen Street.[12] Captain Mulvaney died on September 13, 1872, and is buried in St. Lawrence Cemetery along the Cooper River north of the city.

The war record of Lt. William Clarkson of the Charleston Light Infantry ends in October of 1864, when he was summoned to Richmond to appear as a witness in court. From that point it is unclear if he returned to Charleston at all. Family records indicate that he moved to Eastover, South Carolina following the conflict, where his wife had sought refuge once the Federals laid siege to Charleston in 1863. Eastover is located just east of Columbia and just west of Stateburg in Sumter County, where Clarkson had been born in 1832. He and his wife and their eight children (two of whom were born during the war) moved to Charlotte, North Carolina in 1873, where three more children were added to the family. William worked as a conductor on the Southern Railway and died in Charlotte on September 22, 1892, where he is buried in Elmwood Cemetery.[13]

Capt. William Dove Walter was retired to the invalid corps in December of 1864 due to a continued illness. He survived the war but little is known of his postwar career, other than the fact that he died on February 20, 1872, and is buried at Magnolia.

When it was all said and done, over 1,100 men had passed through the ranks of the Charleston Battalion between June of 1862 and the autumn of 1863, a few staying only long enough to gain transfer to other units. This number increases when one factors in the men who joined after the companies became the Twenty-seventh South Carolina. Obviously not every man missing from the Charleston Battalion and the Twenty-seventh regiment at the final surrender had been killed in combat, though the battalion alone had lost no less than 230 dead between 1862 and 1865. A far greater number had been wounded in battle, never to return to the ranks. A healthy subtraction to be considered, as stated frequently throughout this work, is that the men from this unit had "connections." Plenty of them had sought—with success—detached duty in and around Charleston and therefore were never counted in the firing line. In addition, by contrast with the Virginia theatre, the war around Charleston had been more or less static, and because of age and frailty, many of the men of the battalion simply fell out from exhaustion after only a few weeks of marching and fighting in the Old Dominion.

Aside from these subtractions of force, large numbers of

men from the battalion were captured at Weldon railroad and
outside of Wilmington, and for many of these men, prison
meant a death worse than that found on the battlefield. One
such example was that of John A. Manude, the cousin of
Charlestonian Miss Pauline Duffort, who recorded years after
the war:

> My cousin, John M. . . . a corporal in the Charleston Rifle-
> men . . . was taken prisoner and confined in Elmira [New York]
> and from the hardships of prison life soon became prostrated.
> With him, as far as this world is concerned, the darkest hour of
> his life was just after dawn, for when about to be exchanged
> with the prisoners at Point Lookout [Maryland] his strength
> was so much exhausted that he was sinking rapidly. A cup of
> tea was handed him by a companion who also was to be
> exchanged; he drank it with great pleasure, the last spark of
> life was waiting upon the water, and in a few minutes after-
> wards the youthful soldier breathed his last, and now sleeps in
> an unknown grave on the Federal side.[14]

Other men from the battalion who died at Point Lookout
were: Charles Westendorf of the Calhoun Guards; thirty-nine-
year-old L. B. Hames and thirty-nine-year-old John Whitlock
of the Charleston Light Infantry; John Hines and A. A.
McDonald of the Union Light Infantry; nineteen-year-old J. J.
Ball and thirty-eight-year-old E. B. Garrett of the Sumter
Guards; thirty-four-year-old Jacob A. Mack of the Charleston
Riflemen; and forty-five-year-old G. H. Bridges and L. C. Kirby
of Company K, old Company G, the offshoot of the
Charleston Light Infantry.

The Union prisoner-of-war camp at Elmira, New York
claimed the lives of: W. J. Sullivan of the Charleston Light
Infantry; John Flynn, Michael Glenn, Patrick Malone, and
Henry Schroder of the Union Light Infantry and German
Fusiliers; Cornelius Dinan and Roddy Whelan of the Irish Vol-
unteers; S. Chancy, Stockton Cheney, and William B.
Lequeaux (LeQuenn) of the Charleston Riflemen; Robert S.

Bryan of the Calhoun Guards; and J. B. Colin (Conlon), Hosea Fowler, T. M. Hendricks, and P. S. Montgomery of Company K.

In addition, William P. Malloy and J. M. Scott of the Charleston Light Infantry died at the Union prison in Fortress Monroe at Hampton Roads, Virginia. D. W. Pierson of the Union Light Infantry and Charleston Rifleman William C. Bishop also died at Fortress Monroe, while Sumter Guardsman Edwin L. Moses died at Camp Chase, Ohio.

Miraculously, a number of men survived imprisonment and returned to their families in Charleston and other parts of South Carolina. Other survivors made their way back to Charleston from Southern hospitals and the private homes of Virginians and North Carolinians who cared for them and nursed them back to health. Throughout the summer and fall of 1865, these men straggled home, and as time passed they were able to return to the business of living a peaceful life.

Under the occupying military rule, armed militia companies by definition were not allowed, but by the 1870s many veterans had reorganized as "Survivor's Associations," "Social Clubs," or "Rifle Clubs." Most of these organizations were not restricted to the veterans of their parent organizations, though many survivors were, of course, found on their rolls. Men from other wartime companies that failed to reorganize during Reconstruction, along with other men who had come of age during Reconstruction and even some who moved to Charleston in the years following the conflict, were also found in these postwar organizations. An example of such a postwar club was the Charleston Riflemen's Association, formed by the Charleston Riflemen. Pvt. A. Koennecke, who enlisted in the Charleston Riflemen, Company A of the Charleston Battalion, on March 17, 1862, was a steward of the postwar organization.[15] Koennecke was captured at Town Creek in February of 1865 and at war's end was released from the Union prisoner-of-war camp at Point Lookout, Maryland on June 28, 1865.

While most of the battalion's companies were not represented by such organizations in the postwar era, the Irish Volunteers were represented by at least three. In 1872, in an
organization with the original name of "Irish Volunteers,"
fifty-seven-year-old John Burke was third vice-president and
John Conroy, James Cosgrove, and John Preston were war-
dens.[16] All four of these men had enlisted in the Charleston
Battalion as privates in March of 1862. Burke had risen to the
rank of second lieutenant in the battalion before being
retired to the invalid corps in August of 1864.[17] Conroy had
been wounded at Drewry's Bluff, and when he returned to
duty, he was one of the few Irish Volunteers to escape capture
at Weldon railroad, only to be captured six months later at
Town Creek on February 20, 1865. He was released at Point
Lookout, Maryland on May 13, 1865.[18] As for Cosgrove, his
service record ended in August of 1864 with him listed as
"Sick at Hospital in Charleston."[19] Preston, like Conroy, survived Weldon railroad only to be captured at Town Creek. Preston was released from Fort Delaware, Delaware on June 17,
1865.[20]

Fellow Irishmen, Pvts. Dennis O'Neill and F. L. O'Neill
were respectively second vice-president and president of the
postwar "Irish Volunteer Rifle Club," and Pvt. James Walsh
became secretary of the "Irish Rifle Club."[21] Dennis O'Neill
was detached from the battalion in April of 1863 and spent
the remainder of the war on an ironclad in Charleston Harbor, while Walsh shared the fate of the majority of his comrades and was captured at Weldon railroad. Walsh was
exchanged on January 17, 1865, but he was in such poor
health that he was admitted to Jackson Hospital in Richmond
and subsequently granted a sixty-day furlough on February 1,
1865. He never rejoined the regiment.[22] By a lucky twist of
fate, F. L. O'Neill had been detached as a signal operator in
Charleston throughout 1863 and 1864 and therefore was not
present during the battles in which many of his Irish comrades were killed, wounded, or captured. He later rejoined

the "Charlestonians' Regiment" after the evacuation of Charleston, which enabled him to be counted amongst the final few surrendered with Captain Simons in North Carolina.[23]

In April of 1871 a group of younger Charlestonians formed the "Sumter Rifle Club," and in November of 1875 many of the surviving members of the Sumter Guards joined too. Not long afterward, the tattered flag of the guards was placed in care of the club and its name was officially changed to "Sumter Guards Rifle Club." This organization continued until Reconstruction ended, when the state militia was reorganized.[24] By the early 1880s the Sumter Guards were again a state militia company, as were the Irish Volunteers, Charleston Riflemen, and German Fusiliers. Forty-two-year-old Morris Quinlivan, a veteran of the Charleston Battalion who enlisted in the Irish Volunteers in April of 1862, served at this time as first lieutenant of that postwar militia company. Serving as first lieutenant of the postwar Fusiliers was J. J. Boesch, who enlisted in June of 1863 in the battalion's German Fusiliers. Still part of Charleston's Fourth Brigade, these companies were at that time included in the First Regiment of Rifles instead of their old militia status in the Seventeenth Regiment of Infantry.[25] The Charleston Riflemen had disappeared by the turn of the twentieth century, but the Sumter Guards remained, serving as National Guard in Charleston's Second Battalion of Infantry. Also serving in the National Guard were the German Fusiliers and Irish Volunteers, who appropriately were placed in Charleston's "First Infantry Battalion"—none other than the old Charleston Battalion.

One by one they passed into the next life. Over the years these men no doubt bumped elbows at church, board meetings, funerals of their aged comrades, or survivors' gatherings where they reminisced about their battlefield exploits. As the years went by and they became frail and fewer in number, perhaps they simply nodded to one another as they passed on the streets of Charleston. Yet still, when eye met eye—without speaking—they relived the hardships they had endured, the terrible carnage they had witnessed, and the gallant acts they had triumphed in. Whether they had been young men or old men in Charleston during the 1860s, the war had been the event of their lifetime, and they had risen to the challenge in the defense of their city, their state, and their country.

"All honor to the glorious name and deathless fame of 'Gaillard's Charleston Battalion'"

APPENDIX A

"Charge of Hagood's Brigade"

Scarce seven hundred men they stand
  In tattered, rude array,
A remnant of that gallant band,
  Who erstwhile held the sea-girt strand
Of Morris' Isle, with iron hand
  'Gainst Yankees' hated sway.

Secessionville their banner claims,
  And Sumter held 'mid smoke and flames
And the dark battle on the streams
    Of Pocotaligo;
  And Walthall's Junction's hard-earned fight,
  And Drewry's bluff's embattled height,
  Whence, at the gray dawn of the light,
    They rushed upon the foe.

Tattered and torn those banners now,
But not less proud each lofty brow,
  Untaught as yet to yield;
With mien unblenched, unfaltering eye,
Forward, where bombshells shrieking fly
Flecking with smoke the azure sky
  On Weldon's fated field.

Sweeps from the woods the bold array,
Not theirs to falter in the fray,

Monument to Hagood's brigade at the battle of Weldon railroad, south of Petersburg, Virginia. Fort Wadsworth, in the background, was built after Hagood's attack, to protect the Union possession of the railroad. Photograph by author.

No men more sternly trained than they
    To meet their deadly doom;
While from a hundred throats agape,
A hundred sulphurous flames escape,
Round shot, and canister, and grape,
    The thundering cannon's boom!

    Swift, on their flank, with fearful crash
    Shrapnel and ball commingling clash,
    And bursting shells, with lurid flash,
        Their dazzled sight confound;
    Trembles the earth beneath their feet,
    Along their front a rattling sheet
    Of leaden hail concentric meet,
        And numbers strew the ground.

On, o'er the dying and the dead,
O'er mangled limb and gory head,
With martial look, with martial tread,
March Hagood's men to bloody bed,
    Honor their sole reward;
Himself doth lead the battle line,
    Himself those banners guard.

    They win the height, those gallant few,
    A fiercer struggle to renew,
    Resolved as gallant men to do
        Or sink in glory's shroud;
    But scarcely gain its stubborn crest,
    Ere, from the ensign's murdered breast,
    An impious foe has dared to wrest
        That banner proud.

Upon him, Hagood, in thy might!
Flash on thy soul th'immortal light
Of those brave deeds that blazon bright

Our Southern Cross.
He dies. Unfurl its folds again,
Let it wave proudly o'er the plain;
The dying shall forget their pain,
    Count not their loss.

Then, rallying to your chieftain's call,
Ploughed through by cannon-shot and ball,
Hemmed in, as by a living wall,
    Cleave back your way,
Those bannered deeds their soul inspire,
Borne amid sheets of forked fire,
By the Two Hundred who retire
    Of that array.

Ah, Carolina! well the tear
May dew thy cheek; thy clasped hands rear
In passion o'er their tombless bier,
    Thy fallen chivalry!
Malony, mirror of the brave,
And Sellers lie in glorious grave;
No prouder fate than theirs, who gave
    Their lives for Liberty.[1]

APPENDIX B

Charleston Battalion Roster
2/1862-9/1863

Name	Co.	Rank	Enlistment
Frost, R. M.	Staff	P/Hosp.	
	Stew.	10/1/1862	
Gaillard, Peter C.	Staff	Lt. Col.	
Hernander,			
Benjamin	Staff	P/Musician	3/1/1863
Kay, Joseph	Staff	P	8/4/1863
Legg, M. B. A.	Staff	Staff	6/20/1863
Poole, W. J.	Staff	P	6/20/1863
Pressley, J. L.	Staff	Asst. Surg.	10/1/1862
Smith, R. Pressley	Staff	Capt. Rgt.	
		QM	5/5/1862
Turner, G. W.	Staff	P/Musician	3/1/1863
Webb, W. G.	Staff	P/Musician	3/24/1862
COMPANY A			
Adams, C. B. C.	A	P	3/17/1862
Adicks	A	P	3/1/1863
Adicks, H.	A	P	3/17/1862
Adkins	A	P	6/6/1863
Alexander, S. B.	A	P	3/17/1862
Anderson	A	P	5/28/1863
Andrews, C. H.	A	P	3/17/1862
Badger, D. E.	A	Cpl.	3/17/1862
Badger, James	A		Not on rolls

Badger, Joseph	A	P	3/17/1862
Bail, W.	A	P	3/19/1862
Barclay, James B.	A	P	3/19/1862
Bee	A	P	3/15/1863
Bee, J. N.	A	P	3/24/1862
Ben	A	Cook, Colored	Not reg. enlisted
Bishop	A	P	6/6/1863
Blake, Julius A.	A	Capt.	3/17/1862
Brandon	A	P	6/25/1863
Brown, A.	A	P	4/16/1863
Buchanan, Thomas	A	P	3/17/1862
Campbell, G. A.	A	P	3/17/1862
Carstons, C. J.	A	P	3/17/1862
Carstons, E. H., Jr.	A	P	3/17/1862
Carstons, E. H., Sr.	A	P	3/17/1862
Chancy, S.	A	P	Not on rolls
Chaplin, B. D.	A	Cpl.	3/17/1862
Chase, James P.	A	P	3/17/1862
Cheney, Stockton	A	P	3/17/1862
Cohen	A	P	6/6/1863
Collier, Joseph H.	A	P	3/17/1862
Collins, Samuel F.	A	P	3/18/1862
Crolly, Thomas	A	P	5/1/1863
Cudwoth, A. G.	A	5th Sgt.	3/17/1862
Cuthbert, G.	A	Musician, Colored	3/17/1862
Danner, John M.	A	P	3/17/1862
Davy	A	P	8/13/1863
Dodd	A	P	6/6/1863
Du Bois, J. J.	A	P	3/17/1862
Eagan	A	P	9/15/1862
Evans, W. H.	A	P	3/17/1862

Farley	A	P	4/29/1863
Fevers	A	Cook, Colored	3/17/1862
Furr, A. J.	A	P	3/17/1862
George	A	Cook, Colored	3/17/1862
Gibson, George B.	A	P	3/17/1862
Gibson, W. A.	A	P	3/24/1862
Gouteveiner, J. G.	A	P	3/17/1862
Gouteveiner, J. O.	A	P	3/17/1862
Goverman, P. L.	A	P	6/20/1863
Gowan, John F.	A	P	3/17/1862
Gradick, G. W.	A	P	3/17/1862
Green, W. H.	A	P	3/17/1862
Guy, J. W.	A	P	3/17/1862
Ham, H. U.	A	P	3/17/1862
Ham, William J.	A	P	3/17/1862
Hampton	A	P	6/6/1863
Hannemann	A	P	6/6/1863
Harris	A	P	1863
Howard (Howell), Joseph L.	A	P	3/17/1862
Hurst, J. M., Jr.	A	P	3/17/1862
Jeanerette, E. N.	A	P	3/17/1862
Johnson	A	Cook, Colored	3/17/1862
Jordan, E. W.	A	P	3/17/1862
Kelly, J. A.	A	P	3/17/1862
Koch, W. P. F.	A	P	3/17/1862
Koennecke, A.	A	P	3/17/1862
Lambers, J. Francis	A	P	3/17/1862
Lawrence	A	P	6/6/1863
Lawrens (Laurens), J. J.	A	P	6/16/1863
Lequeux (LeQuen), W. B.	A	P	1/28/1863
Lynch, Francis R.	A	2d Lt.	3/17/1862

McAbee	A	P	6/10/1863
McIntosh, D. A.	A	P	3/17/1862
March	A	Musician, Colored	3/17/1862
Menude, John	A	P	3/17/1862
Michael, E. A.	A	P	3/17/1862
Michaelsis, C. O.	A	P	3/17/1862
Middleton	A	Drummer, Colored	3/17/1862
Millar, W. L.	A	P	4/14/1862
Miller, W. C.	A	P	Not on rolls
Mood, W. S.	A	P	3/17/1862
Mood, William G.	A	P	3/17/1862
Newton	A	P	1/1/1863
Newton, H. D.	A	Hosp. Stew.	3/17/1862
Nolte, J. O.	A	P	3/17/1862
Oxlade, Thomas	A	Cpl.	3/17/1862
Patterson, E. R.	A	Sgt.	3/17/1862
Patterson, W. D.	A	P	3/19/1862
Pelot, B. S.	A	P	3/17/1862
Petterson, P. W.	A	P	3/17/1862
Pollard	A	P	6/6/1863
Poole, E. W.	A	Cpl.	3/17/1862
Pooser, E. W.	A	3rd Sgt.	3/17/1862
Powell, A. B.	A	P	4/16/1863
Reardon, Robert	A	P	3/17/1862
Rhodes, James	A	P	3/17/1862
Rhodes, 2nd	A	P	12/1/1862
Riggs	A	P	5/7/1863
Roche, E. L.	A	P	3/17/1862
Rose	A	P	7/1/1863
Ross	A	P	7/1/1863
Rowand, Robert	A	P	3/17/1862
Ryan	A	P	8/1/1863
Saltus, James C.	A	Bvt. 2d Lt.	3/17/1862
Sassard, James	A	P	3/17/1862
Sergeant	A	P	8/5/1862

Seybt, George W.	A	Sgt.	3/17/1862
Seyle	A	P	12/26/1862
Sires, S. W.	A	P	3/17/1862
Smith, B. F.	A	P	3/17/1862
Smith, Joseph	A	P	2/22/1862
Smith, N. T.	A	P	3/17/1862
Smythe, A. H.	A	P	3/17/1862
Speissegger, L. R.	A	P	3/26/1862
Stewart, M.	A	Musician	3/17/1862
Stienmeyer, J. W.	A	P	3/17/1862
Stinton, H. L.	A	Sgt.	3/17/1862
Strain, W. H.	A	P	3/18/1862
Suares, B. M.	A	P	3/17/1862
Thompson, J. H.	A	P	3/17/1862
Thompson, 2nd	A	P	1/28/1863
Trimm, W. J.	A	P	3/17/1862
Turner, S. S.	A	P	3/17/1862
Walter, William D.	A	1st Lt.	3/17/1862
Welling, S. M.	A	P	3/17/1862
Wheeler, James G.	A	P	6/3/1863
Whitmore, L. B.	A	P	3/17/1862
Wilder, J. D.	A	P	6/6/1863
Williams	A	P	6/10/1863
Wood, James J.	A	P	3/17/1862
Young, Henry	A	P	3/17/1862
Zimmerman, W. A.	A	P	4/13/1862

COMPANY B

Addison, J.	B	P	1/10/1863
Addison, J. M.	B	P	3/24/1862
Anderson, J.	B		Not on rolls
Anderson, William	B-G	P	10/1/1862
Andrews, John	B	P	4/16/1862
Arnold, Aaron	B	P	5/7/1863
Arnold, J. W.	B	P	2/17/1863
Astle, J. S.	B	P	3/24/1862
Bates, G. W.	B-G	P	3/20/1863

Bates, H. D.	B	P	12/9/1862
Bee, J. N.	B	P	3/24/1862
Belve, H. H.	B	P	6/22/1863
Blackwood, Charles	B	P	2/25/1863
Blocker, W. H.	B	P	3/24/1862
Bluett, A. J.	B	P	12/9/1862
Boring, W. H.	B	P	3/24/1862
Boyd, C. W.	B	P	3/24/1862
Boyd, J. T.	B	P	8/26/1863
Bragg, D. W.	B	P	3/10/1863
Bridges, G. H.	B-G	P	2/17/1863
Brown, A.	B	P	3/24/1862
Brown, C. J. H.	B	P	3/24/1862
Brown, F. T. A.	B	P	3/24/1862
Buckeister, W. C.	B	P	3/24/1862
Burdell, Robert	B	P	3/24/1862
Burns, Edward	B	P	12/15/1862
Cahill, M	B	P	9/1/1862
Canton, R.	B	P	12/31/1862
Carey, T.	B	P	4/16/1862
Carlton, J. T.	B-G	P	4/10/1863
Carlton, M. S.	B-G	P	2/17/1863
Chamberlain, H. A.	B	Cpl.	3/24/1862
Chapman, M. B	B-G	Cpl.	2/25/1863
Chase, W.	B	Musician, Colored	3/25/1862
Christmas, A. J.	B	P	3/6/1863
Clarkson, W. B.	B	P	3/24/1862
Clarkson, William	B-G	1st Lt.; Capt.	3/24/1862
Cobia, H. B.	B	P	3/24/1862
Collins, J. A.	B-G	P	3/23/1863
Conlin, J.	B-G	P	3/24/1862
Conroy, T.	B	P	12/13/1862
Crocker, W.	B	P	2/17/1863
Cronin, John	B	P	1/31/1863

Crosby, J. J.	B-G	P	3/24/1862
Davidson, H. M.	B-G	P	2/26/1863
Davidson, T. L.	B	P	3/24/1862
Deveaux, W. P.	B	P	3/24/1862
Deverin, W.	B	P	4/16/1862
Dixon, Issac	B	P	3/24/1862
Donohoe, J.	B	P	4/16/1862
Dougherty, William	B	P	2/1/1863
Doughtery, C.	B	P	2/17/1863
Doyle, Andrew	B	Musician	11/28/1862
Doyle, G.W.	B	P	3/24/1862
Doyle, J.	B	P	3/24/1862
Duberry, D.J.	B-G	P	3/10/1863
Duplessis, A.	B	P	10/24/1862
Dupre, J.C.	B	P	3/24/1862
Dupree, Joseph	B	P	8/7/1862
Eagan, John	B	P	3/24/1862
Eagan, T.H.	B	P	3/24/1862
Edward	B	Drummer, Colored	4/6/1863
Edwards, N.	B-G	P	3/7/1863
Edwards, W.P.	B-G	P	3/20/1863
Eskew, Y.D	B-G	P	3/5/1863
Farmer, D.A.	B	P	2/17/1863
Fitch, B.F.	B	P	10/7/1862
Flint, D.	B	P	2/17/1863
Foster, B.H.	B	P	2/17/1863
Foster, J.J.	B-G	P	2/17/1863
Fowler, H. R.	B	P	2/17/1863
Fowler, Hosea	B-G	P	2/17/1863
Fraiser (Fraser), W.	B	P	10/1862
Friend, R.	B	P	3/24/1862
Gardner, James B.	B-G	Sgt.	3/24/1862
Gentry, H.	B-G	P	3/10/1863
Gibbes, J.R.	B	P	3/24/1862
Gibbon, M.	B	P	10/1/1862

Gibson, W.A.	B	P	3/24/1862
Gilhooly, P.	B	P	4/16/1862
Goforth, J.P.	B-G	P	6/30/1863
Graser, J.G.	B	P	8/26/1863
Griffin, Thomas B.	B-G	P	3/10/1863
Gruber, C.A.	B	P	3/24/1862
Halsall, W.H.	B	P	3/24/1862
Hambright, J.H.	B	P	2/17/1863
Hamby, A.M.	B-G	P	2/17/1863
Hames, F.	B-G	P	2/17/1863
Hames, L.B.	B-G	P	2/17/1863
Hammett, J.B.N.	B	P	3/24/1862
Hanahan, J., Jr.	B	P	3/24/1862
Hanahan, W.	B	P	3/24/1862
Harrington, T.	B	P	3/24/1862
Harris, J. G.	B-G	P	2/17/1863
Harris, W. L.	B-G	P	12/15/1862
Harvey, A.G.	B	P	2/17/1863
Harvey, J.	B-G	P	3/23/1863
Heller, W.	B-G	P	3/24/1862
Hendricks, T.M.	B-G	P	2/17/1863
Herbert, W.C.	B	P	3/24/1862
Heynes, J.C.	B	P	1/1/1863
Heynes, J.S.	B	P	1/1/1863
Hill, William, Jr.	B	P	2/17/1863
Hines, D.	B	P	3/24/1863
Hiott, William O.	B	P	8/19/1863
Hodges, J. Fletcher	B	2d Lt.	Not on rolls
Hoffmeyer, G	B	P	11/13/1862
Hughes, Thomas	B	P	8/19/1862
Hullender, D. D.	B	P	4/7/1863
Hullender, M.	B-G	P	2/17/1863

Jackson, W.	B	P	10/1862
Jacob	B	Cook, Colored	6/1862
Johnson, C. T.	B	Cpl.	3/24/1862
Johnson, J. W.	B	P	6/1863
Johnson, Paul J.	B	P	3/24/1862
Johnson, Paul T.	B	P	3/24/1862
Jowelt, J. J.	B	P	3/24/1862
Kanapaux, A. E.	B	P	12/27/1862
Karrigan, A.M.	B	P	5/12/1863
Kelly, J.	B	P	3/24/1862
Kerrigan, A. M.	B	P	No dates
Kirby, J. M.	B-G	P	11/1/1862
Kirby, L.	B-G	P	2/25/1863
Kirby, L. C.	B-G	P	3/18/1863
Knight, D.	B	P	2/14/1863
Knight, F.	B	P	2/24/1862
Lacy, M.	B	P	4/16/1862
Lake, Edward	B	P	8/1/1863
Lake, John	B	P	1/13/1863
Lamb, W. J.	B	P	3/24/1862
Landreth, Peter	B	P	2/1/1863
Lawton, A.	B	Musician	9/1/1863
Leahay, Michael	B	P	8/28/1862
Lee, M. C.	B	P	3/20/1863
Lett, T. H.	B	P	3/24/1862
Lindsay, C.	B	P	8/21/1863
Lindsay, W. H.	B-G	P	3/24/1862
Lotzen, H. T.	B-G	P	10/22/1862
Lucas, George	B-G	P	10/29/1862
Mabry, C. H.	B	P	2/17/1863
McAteer, Samuel	B	P	3/5/1863
McCabee, C.	B	P	3/24/1862
McCartney, H.	B	P	4/16/1862
McDowell, W. G.	B-G	P	2/25/1863

McElrath, D. T.	B-G	P	2/25/1863
McElrath, John	B-G	P	2/25/1863
McKinney, J.	B	P	4/16/1862
McKittenick, J. C.	B	P	2/17/1863
McLean, D.	B	P	8/29/1862
McMahan, R. D.	B	P	3/24/1862
McMannus, R. E.	B	P	8/14/1862
McSweeney, M.	B-G	P	4/16/1862
Manly	B-G	Cook, Colored	3/1862
Masterman, Alfred H.	B	2nd Lt.	3/24/1862
Masterman, E. J.	B	P	5/1/1862
Masterman, February	B	Cook, Colored	3/24/1862
Masterman, Jacob	B	Cook, Colored	5/1/1862
Masterman, William	B	P	5/24/1862
Maul, B.	B-G	P	9/1/1862
Molloy, W. P.	B	P	2/17/1863
Montgomery, P. S.	B-G	P	2/17/1863
Morrissey, P.	B	P	10/13/1862
Moses, Willis	B	P	2/17/1862
Muckenfuss, A. W.	B	Sgt.	3/24/1862
Murphy, T.	B	P	10/17/1862
Murray, Thomas	B	P	3/24/1862
Nesbit, S. J.	B	P	2/25/1863
Noonan, C.	B	P	4/16/1862
O'Brian, L.	B	P	3/24/1862
Ostrich, A.	B	P	3/24/1862
Page, J. C.	B-G	P	3/10/1863

Page, L.	B	P	No dates
Page, W. C.	B	P	3/2/1863
Pearson, C. A.	B	P	3/17/1863
Pearson, J. T.	B-G	P	2/17/1863
Perkson, J.	B	P	2/17/1863
Perry, A. J.	B-G	P	4/11/1863
Petsh, E.	B	P	1/1/1863
Phelan, Thomas	B	P	7/18/1862
Phoenix, C.	B	Cook, Colored	7/1/1862
Plaspohl, John	B	P	7/23/1863
Poole, E. U.	B-G	P	3/3/1863
Poole, Luther	B-G	P	2/17/1863
Powers, J. A.	B-G	P	3/7/1863
Pozinanski	B	P	3/24/1862
Quinn, A. R.	B-G	P	2/17/1863
Quinn, L. C.	B-G	P	2/17/1863
Ralph, D.	B	Cook, Colored	7/1/1862
Rantin, J. M.	B	P	3/24/1862
Ray, Wilson	B-G	P	2/17/1863
Renyolds, W. T.	B	P	2/17/1863
Rodgers, James	B-G	P	5/5/1863
Ronan, J.	B	P	4/16/1862
Sauls, B.	B	P	3/24/1862
Seabrook, S. E.	B	Cpl.	3/24/1862
Seifarth, C. C.	B	P	3/24/1862
Sheridan, J. T.	B		Not on rolls
Sheridan, P. M.	B	P	3/24/1862
Sheridan, T. F.	B	P	3/24/1862
Simons, A. D.	B-G	P	3/24/1862
Simons, M.	B	P	3/24/1862
Simons, Thomas Y.	B	Capt.	3/24/1862
Sineath, J. S.	B	P	4/12/1862
Sinkler, N.	B	P	3/24/1862
Sinkler, William	B	2d Lt.	3/24/1862

Smith, Cannon	B-G	P	2/25/1863
Smith, James	B	P	4/16/1862
Smith, James	B	P	2/17/1863
Smith, N.	B	P	2/17/1863
Staley, William	B	P	2/13/1863
Stevens, J. W.	B	P	3/7/1863
Stintion, T. H.	B	P	3/24/4862
Stuart, H.	B	P	4/16/1862
Sullivan, W. J.	B	P	11/1/1862
Summerall, W. H.	B	P	3/24/1862
Sutcliffe, W. H.	B	P	3/24/1862
Sweeny, James	B	P	2/8/1863
Symmes, George W.	B	P	3/24/1862
Symmes, John H.	B	Sgt.	3/24/1862
Taylor, William	B	P	8/7/1862
Thompson, W.	B	P	10/1863
Timmons, A. J.	B-G	P	5/20/1863
Todd, E. W.	B	P	4/9/1862
Torlay, H.	B	P	8/9/1863
Turner, H. H.	B-G	P	3/1/1863
Van Riper, H.	B	P	8/1/1863
Vaughn, Joel	B	P	2/14/1863
Vaughn, Robert	B	P	5/5/1863
Vaughn, W. S.	B-G	P	3/13/1863
Walsh, James	B	P	4/16/1862
Webb, Walter	B	P	3/24/1862
Wheeler, J. G.	B	P	4/9/1862
White, Joseph	B	P	10/1862
William	B-G	Cook, Colored	3/1863
Williams, E.	B-G	P	6/10/1863
Wood, H. J.	B	P	2/17/1863
Wood, R. M.	B	P	2/25/1862
Wright, J. D.	B	Sgt.	3/24/1862
Wright, William	B	P	3/24/1862

Young,
William D.	B-G	P	3/1/1863

COMPANY C

Allemong,			
Alex A.	C	3d Lt.	4/7/1862
Allen	C	P	6/1863
Arney, William	C	P	4/1862
Beckman, W. W.	C	Cpl.	3/1862
Bee, S.	C	P	3/1862
Bee, W. G.	C	P	3/1862
Bernard, Phillip	C	Musician	4/1862
Bingo, Dick	C	Cook, Colored	4/1862
Blanton	C	P	3/1863
Brady, Patrick	C	P	4/1862
Bresman,			
Thomas	C	P	4/1862
Brooks, Robert	C	P	4/1862
Burke, John	C	1st Sgt.	4/1862
Burke, John	C	P	4/1862
Callahan, James	C	P	4/1863
Cambert, George	C	P	4/1862
Carmody, Jeremiah	C	P	4/1862
Carroll, James	C	P	4/1862
Carroll, Patrick	C	P	4/1862
Carson, Robert	C	P	4/1862
Cavanah, Thomas	C	P	4/1862
Chandler, W. N.	C	P	3/1863
Coffee, John	C	P	4/1862
Connelly, Thomas	C	P	8/1862
Connley, Martin	C	P	4/1862
Conroy, John	C	P	4/1862
Corcoran, James	C	P	4/1862
Cosgrove, James	C	P	4/1862
Cosgrove, William	C	P	4/1863

Costlee, Patrick	C	P	1863
Crowley, Richard	C	P	3/1863
Cullenton, Patrick	C	P	4/1862
Cullinane, William	C	P	4/1862
Culliton, Nicholas	C	P	4/1862
Cummings, James	C	P	4/1862
Daly, Patrick	C	P	8/1862
Derry, James	C	P	4/1862
Dinan, Cornelius	C	P	1/1/1863
Divine, John L.	C	P	4/1862
Dodds, George	C	P	3/1863
Doherty, Luke	C	P	4/1862
Doogan, Patrick	C	P	10/1862
Driscoll, Timothy	C	P	5/1863
Dubose, Thomas	C	Cook, Colored	6/1863
Dulin, James	C	P	4/1862
Dunn, John	C	P	4/1862
Edmonds, James	C	P	4/1862
Edmonds, John	C	P	4/1862
Egan, Thomas	C	P	4/1862
Elliot, W. S.	C	P	4/1862
Ellis, Charles	C	P	3/1863
Feehan, John	C	P	4/1862
Fitzgerald, Steven	C	P	4/1862
Flaherty, Thomas	C	P	3/1863
Flannigan, Patrick	C	P	4/1863
Flemming, Peter	C	P	4/1862
Fludd, Luke	C	P	3/1863
Flynn, James	C	P	4/1862
Fowler, James	C	P	3/1863
Gaffney, R. M.	C	P	3/29/1863

Geams, G. P.	C	P	5/1863
Gleason, Thomas	C	P	4/1862
Gralton, Daniel	C	P	4/1862
Gratton, Michael	C	P	4/1862
Gray, R.	C	P	12/1862
Green, F. J.	C	P	3/1862
Grey, James	C	P	4/1862
Haffner, M.	C	P	2/23/1863
Hamilton, J. H.	C	P	4/12/1862
Hancock, John	C	P	4/7/1862
Hanley, Edward	C	P	1/10/1863
Hanley, John	C	P	9/17/1862
Hanley, Patrick	C	P	11/18/1862
Hardee, William	C	P	4/15/1863
Harrington, William	C	P	4/7/1862
Hartigan, Patrick	C	P	4/7/1862
Hartnet (Hartwell), M.	C	P	4/7/1862
Hayden, Thomas	C	P	4/7/1862
Henry	C	Musician, Colored	4/7/1862
Hill, L.	C	P	5/5/1863
Hogan, Patrick	C	P	5/1863
Hogan, Patrick R.	C	Cpl.	4/4/1862
Hogan, Thomas L.	C	P	4/9/1863
Howard, Dan	C	P	4/7/1863
Hughes, Thomas	C	P	2/7/1863
Hurley, Jerry	C	P	4/7/1862
Jackson, Thomas	C	P	9/18/1862
Jager, John Adolphus	C	P	1/15/1863
Kay, Joseph	C	P	3/11/863
Kenny, Peter	C	P	4/7/1862
King, James	C	P	3/15/1863
King, John	C	Drummer	12/31/1862

King, Thomas	C	Musician	4/24/1863
Lannigan, Edward	C	3d Cpl.	4/7/1862
Lee, Edward	C	4th Cpl.	4/7/1862
Lee, Maurice	C	P	4/7/1862
Lee, Patrick	C	P	5/1/1862
Lewis	C	Cook, Colored	4/7/1862
Liddy, John	C	P	4/7/1862
Lipscomb, William M.	C	P	5/1/1863
Loftus, Ruben	C	P	4/7/1862
McCormick, John	C	P	12/20/1862
McDonald, James	C	P	9/20/1862
McLadoon, Patrick	C	P	4/7/1862
McMahn, John	C	P	3/22/1863
McMangle, James	C	P	4/7/1862
McSweeney, Eugene	C	P	4/7/1862
Maddigan, Lawrence	C	P	4/7/1862
MaGrath, Edward	C	Capt.	2/17/1862
Maguire, John	C	P	4/7/1862
Maher, John	C	P	4/7/1862
MaKamison, G.	C	P	5/5/1863
Malone, James	C	P	12/12/1862
Malone, Thomas	C	P	4/13/1863
Maloney, J.	C	P	4/22/1863
Maloney, Thomas	C	P	4/7/1862
Manion, Patrick	C	P	4/7/1862
Manion, Thomas	C	P	5/4/1863
Marammison, G.	C	P	5/5/1863
Martin, Peter	C	P	3/12/1863
Martin, William	C	P	4/7/1862
May, John	C	P	4/7/1862
Middleton, T., Jr.	C	P	3/24/1862

Miller, Charles	C	P	4/7/1862
Minahan, T.	C	P	4/7/1862
Moran, Michael	C	4th Sgt.	4/7/1862
Morgan, Bernard	C	P	3/21/1863
Moses, E. L.	C	P	3/24/1862
Muldoon, J.	C	P	4/7/1862
Mulvaney, James M.	C	1st Lt.; Capt.	4/7/1862
Murphy, James	C	P	4/13/1863
Murphy, Joseph	C	P	6/21/1863
Murphy, John P.	C	P	4/7/1862
Murphy, Michael	C	P	4/7/1862
Norton, R.	C	5th Cpl.	1863
Nunan, John	C	P	4/7/1862
O'Brian, Luke	C	P	4/7/1862
O'Neill, Dennis	C	P	4/7/1862
O'Neill, F. L.	C	P	4/7/1862
O'Neill, James	C	P	1/22/1863
O'Neill, Patrick	C	P	10/1/1862
Peter	C	Cook, Colored	4/7/1862
Phillips	C	P	6/27/1863
Phillips, J. M.	C	P	3/29/1863
Powers, Edward	C	P	4/7/1862
Powers, J. F.	C	P	3/5/1863
Preston, John F.	C	P	4/7/1862
Quinlivan, Morris	C	P	4/7/1862
Ramey, Thomas	C	P	5/31/1863
Reynolds, Samuel	C	P	4/1/1863
Richardson, James	C	P	7/12/1863
Riley, Phillip	C	P	4/7/1862
Rooney, J. C.	C	P	12/31/1862
Warren, Christy	C	P	4/7/1862
Warren, John	C	P	11/11/1862
Wheelan, Edward	C	P	1/21/1863
Wheelan, Roddy	C	P	5/24/1863
Wiley, R	C	P	6/10/1863

Wilson, A. B.	C	P	3/24/1862
Wise, R.	C	P	4/24/1863
Wise, Thomas	C	P	1/6/1863

COMPANY D

Abrahams, T. H.	D	P	3/24/1862
Alley, J. A.	D	P	3/12/1863
Arlington, C. H.	D	P	5/1/1863
Armstrong, A. D.	D	P	3/24/1862
Arnold, Thomas	D	P	3/24/1862
Atkinson, T. W.	D	P	2/27/1863
Austin, Samuel	D	P	2/15/1863
Axson, W. J.	D	P	3/24/1862
Bailey, W. A.	D	P	3/20/1862
Ball, J. J.	D	P	4/10/1863
Ball, Y. J.	D	P	2/15/1863
Ballentine, G. P.	D	P	2/28/1863
Barbot, A. A.	D	P	3/24/1862
Barbot, Anthony	D	P	3/24/1862
Barbot, Peter J.	D	2d Lt.	3/24/1862
Barksdale, J. A.	D	P	4/14/1863
Barksdale, J. C.	D	P	4/14/1863
Beadle, R. T.	D	P	2/15/1863
Beason, S.	D	P	2/15/1863
Beckman, W. W.	D	P	3/24/1863
Bee, S.	D	P	3/24/1862
Bee, W. E.	D	P	3/24/1862
Blanton, L. L.	D	P	2/18/1863
Brown, A. J.	D	P	3/23/1863
Brown, J. S.	D	P	3/23/1863
Bryson, J. H.	D	P	2/15/1863
Bryson, T.J.	D	P	12/15/1863
Bullington, D. G.	D	P	4/4/1863
Bumpus, A.	D	P	2/18/1863
Burns, W. L.	D	P	2/28/1863
Butler, John W.	D	P	2/20/1863
Byars, N.	D	P	2/18/1863

Cannon, W. H.	D	P	12/19/1862
Casey, T.	D	P	3/23/1863
Casey, Thomas	D	P	3/23/1863
Cash, M. S.	D	P	2/18/1863
Cay, John A.	D	P	3/24/1862
Chandler, J. W.	D	P	2/15/1863
Chase, Robert	D	Musician	3/24/1862
Cheek, J.	D	P	7/21/1862
Cleary, J. E.	D	P	2/18/1863
Cleary, William	D	P	2/18/1863
Colson, A. C.	D	P	9/22/1862
Cook, J. C.	D	P	2/16/1862
Courtney, John	D	P	3/24/1862
Davenport, J. C.	D	P	7/21/1863
Davis, W. A.	D	P	2/1/1863
Dewees, T. H.	D	P	3/24/1862
Dingle, G. W.	D	P	3/24/1862
Doyle, A.	D	Musician	11/1862
Edgerton, S. F.	D	P	3/24/1862
Edward	D	Drummer	4/6/1863
Edwards, John J.	D	Bvt. 2d Lt.	3/24/1862
Ellison, A. E.	D	P	2/15/1862
Evans, R. C.	D	P	3/24/1862
Fickling, J. H.	D	P	6/10/1863
Fisher, S. W.	D	P	2/26/1863
Fooshee, J.H.	D	P	2/15/1863
Foster, C.	D	P	3/24/1862
Foster, C. B.	D	P	5/8/1862
Foster, H. P.	D	P	7/27/1862
Fowler, J. F.	D	P	2/15/1863
Fowler, W. W.	D	P	2/28/1863
Frouche, A. F.	D	P	5/8/1862
Gadsden, Daniel	D	Cook, Colored	3/24/1862
Garland, W. H.	D	P	7/23/1863
Garrett, E. B.	D	P	2/15/1863
Gibbes, A. S.	D	P	3/24/1862

Gibbes, J. P.	D	P	3/24/1862
Gilliland, A.	D	P	3/24/1862
Graves, W. B.	D	P	2/27/1863
Graves, W. W.	D	P	2/15/1863
Griffin, W. H.	D	P	8/19/1863
Gyles, W. A.	D	P	3/11/1863
Hamilton, J. A.	D	P	4/12/1862
Hamlet, C.	D	P	3/24/1862
Hargraves, J	D	P	3/24/1862
Harrison, F. M.	D	P	2/15/1863
Harrison, J. F.	D	P	2/13/1863
Hasselton, E. E.	D	P	3/24/1862
Helames, J. H.	D	P	2/15/1863
Helames, W. H.	D	P	8/19/1863
Hitch, S. G.	D	P	9/25/1863
Hopkins, C. M.	D	P	3/24/1862
Hopkins, J. Ward	D	1st Lt.; Capt.	3/24/1862
Howland, W. E.	D	Acting QM	3/24/1862
Hughes, T. S.	D	P	9/15/1862
Hyde, Samuel T.	D	P	7/11/1863
Joel, John	D	P	3/10/1862
Johnson, T. N.	D	P	3/24/1862
Johnson, W. W.	D	P	3/24/1862
Kennedy, M. B.	D	P	8/7/1863
King, Henry C.	D	Capt.	3/24/1862
King, Jacob	D	Cook, Colored	3/24/1862
King, W. L.	D	P	3/24/1862
Knight, J. A.	D	P	7/21/1863
Lamotte, H. A.	D	P	3/24/1862
Lance, A. St. John	D	Sgt.	3/24/1862
Levine, S. M.	D	P	3/24/1862
Lindsey, H. A.	D	P	3/24/1862
Lockwood, James	D	Musician	3/24/1862
Lockwood, T. P.	D	P	3/24/1862
Lucious, J. R.	D	P	8/14/1863
McAbbe, W. C.	D	P	2/18/1863

Macbeth, E. W.	D	P	3/24/1862
Macbeth, W. L.	D	P	3/24/1862
McCrady, J. P.	D	P	3/18/1863
McPherson, J. M.	D	P	9/1/1863
Madden, J. A.	D	P	2/15/1863
Madden, M.	D	P	9/24/1863
Madden, Z. L.	D	P	2/15/1863
Mahoney, M.	D	P	2/3/1862
Martin, F. B.	D	P	9/1/1863
Martin, H. H.	D	P	2/15/1863
Martin, L. D.	D	P	2/15/1863
Martin, L. S.	D	P	9/1/1863
Martin, S. V.	D	P	5/6/1863
Milam, William	D	P	3/11/1863
Miler, Daniel	D	P	3/24/1862
Milford, J. W.	D	P	2/15/1863
Moodie, A. G.	D	P	3/30/1862
Moore, R. L.	D	P	2/15/1863
Moore, W. B.	D	P	2/15/1863
Moses, E. L.	D	P	3/24/1862
Nathans, J. N.	D	P	3/24/1862
Nelson, Josiah	D	P	2/15/1863
Nelson, T.	D	P	9/1/1863
Nelson, W. A.	D	P	2/24/1863
Neufville, H. S.	D	P	3/24/1862
Owens, R.	D	P	2/18/1863
Owings, M. J.	D	P	2/15/1863
Pinson, J. H.	D	P	2/15/1863
Pinson, J. R.	D	P	2/15/1863
Pitts, J. Y.	D	P	2/28/1863
Plane, T.	D	P	3/24/1862
Poole, A. B.	D	P	2/15/1863
Poole, F. T.	D	P	8/18/1863
Pope, M. T.	D	P	2/1863
Porcher, H.	D	Cook	2/18/1863
Porter, J. H.	D	P	7/11/1863
Poznanski, G., Jr.	D	P	3/24/1862

Ray, F. F.	D	P	2/18/1863
Ray, J. T.	D	P	2/18/1863
Redden, H.	D	P	9/30/1863
Reeder, R. S.	D	P	2/15/1863
Reid, C. H.	D	P	3/11/1863
Roberts, John F.	D	P	3/24/1862
Roumillat, A. J.	D	P	3/24/1862
St. Arnaud, M. W.	D	Cook	3/9/1863
Saxon, J. F.	D	P	2/28/1863
Saxon, Jack	D	P	3/14/1863
Saylor, H. E.	D	P	3/24/1862
Saylor, J. J.	D	P	5/8/1862
Schaffer, F. J.	D	P	3/24/1862
Shannon, Benjamin	D	P	4/17/1863
Smith, H. A.	D	Sgt.	3/24/1862
Smith, W. S.	D	Sgt.	3/26/1863
Smith, William K.	D	Sgt.	3/24/1862
Smythe, A. H.	D	P	3/17/1862
Sosbee, J. H.	D	P	2/18/1863
Stanley, James	D	P	3/8/1862
Starnes, R. C.	D	Cpl.	2/15/1863
Stegin, J. H.	D	Cpl.	5/8/1862
Stevens, S. N.	D	P	3/24/1862
Stone, M.	D	P	2/15/1863
Stoney, J. D.	D	P	3/24/1862
Strange, Perry	D	P	5/16/1863
Strobel, R. S.	D	P	11/3/1862
Sullivan, M. O.	D	P	5/5/1863
Surau, H. T.	D	P	4/9/1862
Sutton, A. DeR	D	P	4/15/1863
Sweeny, J. R.	D	P	3/24/1862
Taylor, E. G.	D	P	5/9/1863
Tennant, William, Jr.	D	P	3/24/1862
Tennent, Charles J.	D	P	3/24/1862
Tennent, E. S.	D	P	3/24/1862

Terry, E. L.	D	P	5/8/1862
Theus, S.	D	P	3/24/1862
Timms, J. M.	D	P	3/23/1863
Toomer, E. P.	D	P	3/24/1862
Trouche,			
Augustus F. (J.)	D	Sgt.	3/24/1862
Tupper, J., Jr.	D	P	8/11/1863
Turner, John G.	D	P	2/15/1863
Valentine, Hertz	D	P	3/24/1862
Valentine, Isaac D.	D	P	3/24/1862
Walker, F. F	D	P	5/29/1863
Walker, G. W.	D	P	3/24/1862
Walker, John	D	P	2/15/1863
Ware, W. A. J.	D	P	2/15/1863
Watts, R. S.	D	P	2/15/1863
Wells, B. M.	D	P	9/1/1863
Wells, Clement	D	P	2/15/1863
Wells, Joseph T.	D	P	3/24/1862
Wharton, John A.	D	Bvt. 2nd Lt.,	3/24/1862
Wheeler, G. R.	D	P	4/9/1862
Williams, J. C.	D	P	8/14/1863
Williams, W.	D	Sgt.	3/24/1863
Withers, James	D	P	9/1/1863

COMPANY E

Addison, Capers P.	E	P	4/10/1863
Alexander, G.W.	E	P	3/24/1862
Axson, J. Waring	E	2d Lt.	3/24/1862
Axson, W.J.	E	P	3/24/1862
Baker, Barnard E.	E	P	3/24/1862
Baker, Eugene B.	E	P	6/13/1862
Baker, H.H.	E	P	3/24/1862
Barker, W.J.	E	P	11/25/1862
Bird, W.C.	E	P	3/23/1863
Black, Samuel C.	E	5th Sgt.	3/24/1862
Britton, J.F.	E	P	6/11/1862
Britton, R.A.	E	P	3/24/1862
Brooks, Prince	E	P	3/24/1862

Brown, C.			
Pinckney	E	P	3/24/1862
Brown,			
Edmund T.	E	P	3/24/1862
Brown, Josiah S.	E	P	3/24/1862
Bryan, Robert S.	E		Not on rolls
Buckeister,			
Andrew	E	P	8/1/1863
Buist, Charles B.	E	P	3/24/1862
Caldwell, J.W.	E	P	8/23/1863
Caldwell,			
William A.	E	P	7/15/1863
Calvo, Charles			
Augustus	E	3d Sgt.	3/24/1862
Campbell,			
Hamlet	E	P	3/24/1862
Champlain,			
Edward	E	P	Not on rolls
Champlain,			
Jackson C.	E	P	5/6/1862
Cherry, C.H.	E	P	12/22/1862
Cherry, William	E	P	Not on rolls
Choate, H. Eben	E	P	3/24/1862
Choate, Thomas	E	P	12/29/1862
Clayton, David B.	E	P	1/26/1863
Cole, Thomas J.	E	Drummer, Colored	2/18/1863
Cook, Moses	E	Cook, Colored	10/8/1862
Cook, Primus	E	Cook	3/24/1862
Davis, Calvin T.	E	P	3/24/1862
Davis, G.	E	P	4/14/1862
Drummer, Peter	E	Drummer	2/18/1863
DuBerry, W.D.	E	P	5/21/1863
Dunn, E.	E	P	3/24/1862
Easterby,			
J.M (Easterly)	E	3d Lt.	3/24/1862

Easterby, W.N.			
(Easterly)	E	P	3/24/1862
Fengas (Fuegas),			
H.V.	E	P	3/24/1862
Gadsen,			
Thomas, Jr.	E	P	3/24/1862
Gaillard, F.P.	E	P	3/24/1862
Germain, J.P.	E	P	3/24/1862
Gibbes, J.			
Perroneau	E	P	3/29/1862
Hall, C. G.	E	P	3/24/1862
Hall, F. M.	E	P	3/24/1862
Hamett, A. C.	E	P	4/14/1862
Hamett,			
Ripley K. B.	E	P	3/24/1862
Hamlet, C.	E	P	3/24/1862
Heath, M. W.	E	P	3/1/1863
Heriott,			
William C.	E	P	11/21/1862
Hewett, O. H. R.	E	P	3/24/1862
Holmes, Issac	E	P	3/24/1862
Horry, Edward S.	E	P	3/24/1862
Hughes, E. T.	E	P	8/1/1863
Hughes,			
Henry M.	E	P	8/18/1863
Inness, C. M.	E	P	3/24/1862
Issacs, A.	E	P	3/24/1862
Irvine, Dr. Aurelius	E	P	Not on rolls
Jackson, J. F.	E	P	3/24/1862
Jackson, J. M.	E	P	10/15/1862
Jackson, J. W.	E	P	10/15/1862
Jackson,			
Thomas M.	E	P	10/15/1862
Jervey, Lewis	E	P	3/24/1862
Jervey, Theodore D.	E	P	3/24/1862
Johnstone			
(Johnson), R. P.	E	P	5/21/1863

Johnstone (Johnson), W. A.	E	P	3/24/1862
Kiddell, A.	E	P	3/24/1862
Kiddell, Theodore	E	P	Not on rolls
King, C.	E	P	8/1/1863
Kingman, Oliver H.	E	P	2/19/1862
McCaudhrin, A. J.	E	Cpl.	3/24/1862
Martin, T. Ogier	E	P	4/22/1863
Mellinchamp, W. S.	E	P	3/24/1862
Miles, Francis T.	E	Capt.	3/24/1862
Milliken, A. T.	E	Sgt.	3/24/1862
Miot, John C.	E	P	Not on rolls
Moreland, A. M.	E	P	3/24/1862
Moreland, E. M.	E	P	3/24/1862
North, R. E.	E	P	3/1863
Palmer, Barnwell W.	E	1st Lt.	3/24/1862
Parker, Thomas	E	P	3/24/1862
Pettigrew, Daniel	E	P	3/24/1862
Pratt, G. L.	E	P	3/24/1862
Radcliffe, G. W.	E	P	7/21/1863
Randall, E. F.	E	P	3/24/1862
Rankin, G. F.	E	P	3/24/1862
Riely, W. W.	E	P	3/24/1862
Robertson, A. E.	E	P	4/24/1863
Robertson, H. D.	E	P	3/24/1862
Robertson, J. R.	E	Cpl.	3/24/1862
Schmitt, W. A.	E	P	3/24/1862
Schnierle, H. E. V.	E	P	3/24/1862
Seabrook, M.	E	Cook	10/8/1863
Shannon, Benjamin	E	P	4/17/1863
Singleton, C. K.	E	P	1/23/1862

Smith, A.	E	P	3/24/1862
Smith, J. E., Jr.	E	P	3/24/1862
Smith, P.	E	Cook	3/24/1862
Smyser, J. W.	E	Sgt.	3/24/1862
Spady, S. G.	E	Cpl.	3/24/1862
Swinton, R. H.	E	P	1/7/1863
Tennent, G. V.	E	P	3/24/1862
Tennent, J. S.	E	P	3/24/1862
Torrent, J.	E	P	3/24/1862
Trenholm, P. C.	E	Sgt.	3/24/1862
Vincent, W. J.	E	P	3/24/1862
Waring, J. B.	E	P	7/1/1862
Webb, D. C.	E	Sgt.	3/24/1862
Webb, Pitt H. W.	E	P	3/24/1862
Westendorf, James S.	E	P	3/24/1862
Wethersby, F. J.	E	P	5/2/1863

COMPANY F

Anderson, J. R.	F	P	3/15/1862
Ashe, J. J.	F	P	2/17/1863
Ashecraft, B. M.	F	P	2/171863
Bagwell, Joseph B.	F	P	3/12/1863
Bagwell, W. G.	F	P	3/12/1863
Baker, F.	F	P	5/16/1863
Barry, William L.	F	P	2/17/1863
Beard, W. S.	F	P	2/17/1863
Beardin, S. S.	F	P	3/4/1863
Bernstien, N. A.	F	P	3/15/1862
Berry, W. P.	F	P	3/11/1863
Biggers, A. J.	F	P	2/17/1863
Biter, Alex	F	P	3/6/1863
Blake, Charles	F	P	5/1/1863
Boesch, J. J.	F	P	7/6/1863
Bomar, W. B.	F	P	2/171863
Bramman, T. J.	F	P	2/17/1863

Braun, J.	F	P	3/151862
Brauer, Henry	F	P	5/14/1863
Breen, P. J.	F	P	3/15/1862
Brown, George	F	2d Lt.	3/15/1862
Brown, S. S.	F	P	3/151862
Buchanan, Colen	F	P	3/151862
Burnstien, N. A.	F	P	3/15/1862
Butt, J. F.	F	P	4/21/1862
Cahill, M.	F	Drummer	9/1/1862
Caldwell, A. P.	F	P	2/17/1863
Caldwell, S. A.	F	P	3/12/1863
Campbell, James	F	1st Sgt.	3/15/1862
Care, James	F	P	1/19/1863
Cassidy, D.	F	P	4/7/1862
Cassidy, John	F	Cpl.	11/1/1862
Chesney, G. W.	F	P	2/14/1863
Childers, John	F	P	2/17/1863
Comans, William	F	P	3/15/1862
Comerford, William	F	P	3/15/1862
Coneifort, William	F	P	3/15/1862
Connoly, P.	F	P	3/15/1862
Connors, John	F	P	3/15/1862
Cook, H.	F	P	1/19/1863
Cooper, William	F	P	3/151862
Couch, T. R.	F	P	2/25/1863
Daley, T.	F	P	5/1/1862
Dangerfield, Richard	F	P	3/151862
Davis, James	F	P	3/15/1862
Davis, Peter	F	P	3/15/1862
Dawson, J. S.	F	P	2/17/1863
DeChamp, J.	F	P	3/22/1862
Dillion, Martin	F	P	4/22/1862

Dolphin, P	F	P	12/221862
Dorsey, Francis	F	P	3/15/1862
Dover, C.	F	P	2/17/1863
Drummond, J. L.	F	P	2/14/1863
Dugan, R. E.	F	P	3/15/1862
Duncan,			
Alexander	F	P	3/15/1862
Dwyer, John	F	P	3/15/1862
Edwards, J. P.	F	P	2/1863
Edwards, P.	F	P	3/18/1863
Eggerking, F.			
William	F	P	3/15/1862
Epps, B. W.	F	P	2/14/1863
Evans, Luke K.	F	P	3/15/1862
Falls, E. C.	F	P	4/1863
Farris, J. D.	F	P	2/17/1863
Faulbier, A.	F	P	4/24/1862
Ferguson, Robert	F	P	3/15/1862
Flynn, John	F	P	3/151862
Franklin, J.	F	P	3/15/1862
Gallagher, P. B.	F	P	3/15/1862
Gill, E. H.	F	P	2/17/1863
Gill, S. K.	F	P	2/17/1863
Glenn, Michael	F	P	5/16/1862
Goings, A.	F	Cook,	
		Colored	3/151862
Graves, W. W.	F	P	3/15/1862
Gregory, F. M.	F	P	3/151862
Griffith, J. G.	F	P	3/15/1862
Haffner, M.	F	P	2/23/1863
Hamby, A.	F	P	1863
Hannah, P. C.	F	P	2/14/1863
Harrington,			
William	F	P	3/15/1862
Harris, Charles	F	P	3/18/1862
Harshan, H. J.	F	P	2/17/1863

Heigh, T. P.	F	P	2/17/1863
Hendricks, Henry W.	F	Sgt.	3/15/1862
Hendricks, R. F.	F	P	3/15/1862
Henry, Robert Joseph	F	5th Sgt.	3/15/1862
Herbert, J. C.	F	P	3/15/1862
Hesch, C.	F	P	9/23/1862
Hines, W.	F	P	10/15/1862
Hughes, Edward	F	P	3/15/1862
Jackson, Allen	F	P	3/15/1862
Jeffers, B.	F	P	3/12/1863
Jordan, Henry	F	P	3/15/1862
Kelly, John	F	P	7/6/1862
Kelly, T. R.	F	P	1863
Kerrigan, Ambrose	F	P	3/15/1862
Kirby, H. M.	F	P	3/11/1863
Knighton, W. P.	F	P	2/14/1863
Lawton, G. W.	F	P	5/17/1862
Lay, C.	F	P	3/15/1862
Lee, Issac	F	Cook, Colored	3/15/1862
Lindan, C.	F	P	3/15/1862
Lipscomb, William L.	F	P	1863
Livey, E.	F	P	3/15/1862
Lord, Samuel, Jr.	F	1st Lt.; Capt.	3/15/1862
Lowry, S.	F	P	2/16/1862
Malone, Patrick	F	P	3/15/1862
Marcus, K.	F	Cook, Colored	3/15/1862
McCabee, J. P.	F	P	6/25/1863
McCabee, M. P.	F	P	2/14/1863
McCaffrey, James	F	P	3/15/1862
McCarley, J. M.	F	P	2/17/1863
McDonald, A. A.	F	1st Cpl.	3/15/1862

McDovit, John	F	P	3/15/1862
McNeil, John	F	P	3/15/1862
Meyer, F.	F	P	4/21/1862
Michaelis, J. H.	F	P	3/15/1862
Miskilly, J. W.	F	P	2/17/1863
Mooney, J. J.	F	P	3/15/1862
Mulkings, William	F	P	3/15/1862
Nagle, Luke	F	P	3/15/1862
Ober, James	F	P	3/15/1862
O'Brian, Patrick	F		Not on rolls
O'Brian, Mortimer	F	P	3/15/1862
Patrick, C.	F	P	3/25/1862
Paul, Dunbar J.	F	2d Sgt.	3/15/1862
Pearson, D. W.	F	P	5/16/1863
Phillips, L.	F	P	5/16/1863
Poole, W. J.	F	P	6/20/1863
Pressley, J. L.	F	Surgeon	10/1/1862
Pringle, James	F	P	3/15/1862
Quinn, James	F	P	3/15/1862
Quinn, Patrick	F	P	3/15/1862
Quinn, R.	F	P	3/15/1862
Ramos, D.	F	P	3/15/1862
Ramsay, David	F	Capt.; Maj.	3/15/1862
Rees, B. T.	F	P	2/17/1863
Restig, William	F	P	3/15/1862
Reuter, John	F	P	3/15/1862
Rhode, D.	F	P	3/15/1862
Riley, James, I	F	P	3/19/1862
Riley, James, II	F	P	3/19/1862
Robison, A.	F	P	3/15/1862
Robison, J.	F	P	3/15/1862
Roonan, Martin	F	P	3/15/1862
Ruckh, F. J.	F	P	3/15/1862
Ryan, William	F	P	3/20/1862
Scanlan, John	F	P	2/4/1863
Scharlock, E. C.	F	Musician	3/15/1862

Scharlock, W. F.	F	Musician	3/2/1862
Schroder, H.	F	P	3/15/1862
Schulthiess, E. M.	F	P	3/15/1862
Seay, J. H.	F	P	2/17/1863
Seibert, Fredrick	F	P	6/3/1863
Sellers, R. A.	F	P	2/17/1863
Sexton, Samuel	F	P	2/4/1863
Shillinglaw, W. A.	F	P	2/17/1863
Shirrer, J. M.	F	P	2/17/1863
Shoeflin, J.	F	P	5/9/1862
Smalls, J.	F	Cook, Colored	3/15/1862
Smith, E.	F	P	3/10/1863
Smith, E. P.	F	P	2/14/1863
Sobbe, E.	F	P	5/6/1862
Stack, James	F	P	3/15/1862
Stanton, A.	F	P	3/15/1862
Stephens, H.	F	P	2/14/1863
Stephens, W. M.	F	P	2/4/1863
Stone, E. P.	F	P	3/7/1863
Streaney, Patrick	F	P	9/17/1863
Stucke, H.	F	P	10/7/1862
Swift, John	F	P	3/15/1862
Taylor, H.	F	P	3/7/1863
Tewes, J.	F	P	4/9/1862
Thomas, J. A.	F	P	2/17/1863
Thompson, W.	F		Not on rolls
Tierney, M.	F	P	5/17/1862
Titjen, J. H.	F	P	3/15/1862
Turner, G. W.	F	P	3/1/1863
Tweitman, J. H.	F	5th Cpl.	3/15/1862
Ussery, T. B.	F	P	3/15/1862
Walker, Henry	F	1st Lt.	3/15/1862
Watson, C.	F	P	2/17/1862
Weddigan, E.	F	P	5/10/1862
Weiges, H. W.	F	P	3/15/1862

Wendelken, J. W.	F	P	3/15/1862
West, A. J.	F	P	2/17/1863
Wheelan, Thomas	F	P	3/15/1862
Wheelis, H. W.	F	P	3/15/1862
Wheeliss, J. R.	F	P	3/15/1862
Whitaker, Samuel	F	P	3/15/1862
Whitehead, B.	F	P	2/17/1863
Williamson, J.	F	P	3/7/1863
Witt, P. F.	F	P	5/17/1862
Wood, William C.	F	P	3/15/1862
Wooton, J. H.	F	P	2/17/1863
Young, John	F	P	3/15/1862

COMPANY G

Alley, R.	G	P	7/2/1863
Bishop, H.	G	P	6/16/1863
Bishop, W. P.	G	P	6/13/1863
Cannon, T. H.	G	P	7/2/1863
Cantrell, E.	G	P	7/31/1863
Cantrell, J. D.	G	P	7/25/1863
Carter, S. M.	G	P	7/2/1863
Castleberry, J. H.	G	P	7/25/1863
Chapman, W. D.	G	P	7/1/1863
Cooksey, T. L.	G	P	7/2/1863
Floyd, John	G	P	7/8/1863
Ford, M. D.	G	P	7/4/1863
Hawkins, W. E.	G	P	6/25/1863
Henderson, M.	G	P	6/29/1863
Hollander, John	G	P	Not on rolls
Hollander, Mathew	G	P	Not on rolls
Jeffery	G	Cook, Colored	6/14/1863
Kay, James	G	P	8/4/1863
Kleiner, Karl	G	P	Not on rolls

Lewis, Posar	G	P	7/1/1863
Littlejohn, George	G	P	Not on rolls
Littlejohn, John	G	P	Not on rolls
McDowell, Robert	G	P	Not on rolls
Miller, E. B.	G	P	6/30/1863
Page, Henry	G	P	Not on rolls
Paris, W. B.	G	P	7/2/1863
Perry, John	G	P	Not on rolls
Perry, Robert	G	P	Not on rolls
Perry, W. L.	G	P	7/1/1863
Perry, W. S.	G	P	7/1/1863
Poole, Jas. M.	G	P	Not on rolls
Quinn, Russell	G	P	Not on rolls
Seay, Henry	G	P	Not on rolls
Seay, R. B.	G	P	7/10/1863
Smith, Alfred	G	P	7/25/1863
Spell, J. D.	G	P	7/13/1863
Thomas	G	Cook, Colored	8/14/1863
Turner, B. O.	G	P	7/11/1863
Turner, T. H.	G	Sgt.	6/12/1863
Turner, W.	G	P	Not on rolls
Wilson, William	G	P	8/4/1863[1]

APPENDIX C

Charleston Battalion Deaths

**Charleston Battalion deaths listed
as First South Carolina Infantry Battalion**

Name	Co.	Rank	Died	Where
Anderson, J.	B	Pvt.	6/19/1862	Secessionville
Andrews, John	B	Pvt.	6/14/1862	James Island
Arnold, Aaron	B	Pvt.	8/10/1863	na
Baker, Eugene	E	Cpl.	8/18/1863	Bty. Wagner
Conroy, Timothy	B	Pvt.	8/19/1863	Bty. Wagner
Davis, James	F	Pvt.	6/16/1862	Secessionville
Easterby, Washington	E	Pvt.	9/27/1862	Columbia
Edgerton, Samuel Fields	D	Pvt.	6/17/1862	Secessionville
Edwards, John C.	B	Pvt.	7/18/1863	Bty. Wagner
Edwards, John Jones	B	3d Lt.	6/16/1862	Secessionville
Edwards, Newman	G	Pvt.	8/24/1863	Bty. Wagner
Fourcher, C.	D	Pvt.	8/28/1863	Charleston
Gardner, James B.	G	1st Lt.	9/10/1863	Bty. Wagner
Gilhooly, P.	B	Pvt.	6/16/1862	Secessionville
Gillroach, P.	B	Pvt.	6/24/1862	Secessionville
Hammet, J.B.N.	B	Pvt.	6/16/1862	Secessionville
Henry, J. R. J.	C	Sgt.	6/16/1862	Secessionville
Henry, R.S.	F	Sgt.	6/16/1862	Secessionville
Howard, Daniel	C	Pvt.	6/16/1862	Secessionville
Hughes, Henry M.	E	Pvt.	9/4/1863	Bty. Wagner
Hurst, James M.	A	1st Sgt.	7/26/1863	Beaufort
Hyde, Samuel Tupper	D	Pvt.	7/18/1863	Bty. Wagner

Kelly, J.A.	A	Pvt.	6/3/1862	Legare's Place
Lambers, J. Francis	A	Sgt.	7/18/1863	Bty. Wagner
Leahey, Michael	B	Pvt.	9/15/1862	Charleston
Maddigan, Lawrence	C	4th Sgt.	12/5/1862	Charleston
Maher, John	C	Pvt.	12/2/1862	na
Martin, T. Ogier	E	Pvt.	8/17/1863	Bty. Wagner
Nesbit, S. J.	B	Pvt.	7/18/1863	Bty. Wagner
Parker, Thomas	A	Pvt.	6/16/1862	Secessionville
Perkson, J.	B	Pvt.	na	na
Petsch, Emanuel	B	Pvt.	na	na
Poznanaki, Gustavus	D	Pvt.	6/16/1862	Secessionville
Ryan, William H.	I	Capt.	7/18/1863	Bty. Wagner
Sexton, J.A.	F	Pvt.	3/27/1863	na
Sexton, Samuel	F	Pvt.	8/11/1863	Columbia
Smith, Cannon	G	Pvt.		Morris Island
Stevens, W.H.	F	Pvt.		na
Toole, M.	C	Pvt.	7/18/1863	Bty. Wagner
Valentine, Isaac D.	D	Cpl.	6/16/1862	Secessionville
Walker, Henry P.	F	2d Lt.	8/9/1862	Ft. Pulaski

Charleston Battalion deaths in the Twenty-seventh South Carolina Infantry
Note: Companies correspond with the Twenty-seventh, not the Charleston Battalion. Example: Co. A = old Co. E.

Name	Co.	Rank	Died	Where
Addison, Capers P.	A (E)	Pvt.	5/7/1864	Walthall Junct.
Adicks, Henry	I (A)	Pvt.	8/26/1864	Petersburg, VA
Aldrich, C. F.	D	Pvt.	6/16/1864	Hare's Hill, VA
Alexander, J. W.	D	Pvt.	2/17/1865	Richmond, VA
Allemong, Alexander A.	H (C)	1st Lt.	6/22/1864	Petersburg, VA
Armstrong, Archibald D.	D	Pvt.	8/15/1865	Chester, SC
Atkinson, J. H.	D	Pvt.	5/15/1864	na
Atkinson, Thomas	D	Pvt.	6/1/1864	Cold Harbor, VA
Axson, J. Waring	A (E)	Capt.	6/24/1864	Petersburg, VA
Baker, V.	A (E)	Pvt.	10/26/1864	Richmond, VA
Ball, J. J.	D	Pvt.	12/18/1864	Pt. Lookout, MD
Barksdale, James C.	D	Pvt.	6/24/1864	na
Barnett, J. S.	B	Pvt.	7/5/1864	Petersburg, VA
Bates, Henry D.	B	Pvt.	6/24/1864	Petersburg, VA
Beadle, R. T.	D	Cpl.	6/18/1864	Petersburg, VA
Beckman, William W.	D	1st Sgt.	6/25/1864	Petersburg, VA
Bee, Saniford	D	Pvt.	10/4/1864	At home
Bee, William Edwards	D	Pvt.	5/9/1864	Swift Creek, VA
Biggers, Andrew Jackson	C (F)	Pvt.	7/19/1864	Petersburg, VA
Bishops, William C.	I (A)	Pvt.	7/25/1864	Fts. Monroe, VA
Bodom, H.	A (E)	Pvt.	na	Virginia
Bowers, L. S.	B	Pvt.	5/7/1864	Walthall Junct.
Boyd, Charles J.	B	Cpl.	5/7/1864	Walthall Junct.
Bridges, G. H.	K (G)	Pvt.	7/25/1864	Pt. Lookout, MD
Brown, Charles Pinckney	A (E)	Pvt.	5/14/1864	Drewry's Bluff, VA
Brown, George W.	C (F)	Capt.	6/21/1864	Petersburg, VA
Bryan, William	B	Pvt.	5/9/1864	Swift Creek, VA
Bryson, John H.	D	Pvt.	7/25/1864	Petersburg, VA

Bryson, T. J.	D	Pvt.	6/16/1864	Petersburg, VA
Butt, John F.	C (F)	Pvt.	5/9/1864	Charleston
Caldwell, A. P.	C (F)	Pvt.	7/4/1864	Richmond, VA
Cantrell, E.	K (G)	Pvt.	5/16/1864	Drewry's Bluf, VA
Carroll, James	H (C)	Pvt.	6/24/1864	Petersburg, VA
Champlin, A. J.	A (E)	Pvt.	8/25/1864	Petersburg, VA
Chaney, S.	I (A)	Pvt.	9/27/1864	Elmira, NY
Chapman, Warren D.	K (G)	Cpl.	6/2/1864	Drewry's Bluff, VA
Cheney, D. Stockton	I (A)	Pvt.	9/28/1864	Elmira, NY
Chesney, George W.	C (F)	Pvt.	6/6/1864	Petersburg, VA
Childers, J.	C (F)	Pvt.	6/29/1864	Richmond, VA
Choate, Henry E.	A (E)	Pvt.	6/15/1865	At home
Christmas, Andrew J.	B	Pvt.	4/7/1864	Petersburg, VA
Cocksey, J. L.	K (G)	Pvt.	5/16/1864	Drewry's Bluff, VA
Collier, Joseph	A (E)	Pvt.	6/15/1865	At home
Conlin, J. B.	K (G)	Pvt.	9/22/1864	Elmira, NY
Cook, A. W.	D	Pvt.	6/26/1864	na
Cook, James C.	D	Pvt.	6/24/1864	Petersburg, VA
Cooksey, T. L.	K (G)	Pvt.	5/16/1864	Drewry's Bluff, VA
Cooper, William	C (F)	Pvt.	10/3/1864	Petersburg, VA
Coster, William	C (F)	Pvt.	8/26/1864	Petersburg, VA
Crosby, J. J.	K (G)	Pvt.	5/17/1864	Drewry's Bluff, VA
Davis, P.	C (F)	Pvt.	6/29/1864	Petersburg, VA
Davis, William A.	D	Pvt.	8/21/1864	Ream's Stn., VA
Dinan, Cornelius	H (C)	Pvt.	8/14/1864	Elmira, NY
Drummond, John F.	C (F)	Pvt.	9/22/1864	na
Fitch, B. F.	B	Pvt.	6/24/1864	Petersburg, VA
Flynn, John	C (F)	Pvt.	8/15/1864	Elmira, NY
Foster, Berryman H.	B	Pvt.	5/26/1864	Petersburg, VA
Foster, Charles Bernard	D	Pvt.	9/17/1864	Alexandria, VA
Fowler, Hosea	K (G)	Pvt.	2/3/1865	Elmira, NY
Fowler, James F.	D	Pvt.	7/1/1864	Petersburg, VA
Frederick, Charles	D	Pvt.	6/16/1864	Hare's Hill, VA
Garrett, E. B.	D	Pvt.	2/12/1865	Pt. Lookout, MD

Garrett, T. B.	D	Pvt.	8/5/1864	na
Gelling, George Brown	C (F)	2nd Lt.	6/16/1864	Hare's Hill, VA
Glenn, Michael	C (F)	Pvt.	1/31/1865	Elmira, NY
Goforth, J. Preston	K (G)	Pvt.	7/16/1864	Petersburg, VA
Grant, A. A.	D	Pvt.	2/20/1865	Town Creek, NC
Griffin, T. B.	K (G)	Pvt.	8/17/1864	Petersburg, VA
Haines, W. L.	B	Pvt.	5/16/1864	Drewry's Bluff, VA
Hames, L. B.	B	Pvt.	4/4/1865	Pt. Lookout, MD
Harris, William L.	B	Pvt.	5/16/1864	Drewry's Bluff, VA
Harvey, A. G.	B	Pvt.	na	na
Hendricks, T. M.	K (G)	Pvt.	11/14/1864	Elmira, NY
Hines, John	C (F)	Pvt.	4/8/1865	Pt. Lookout, MD
Hogan, Patrick J.	H (C)	Pvt.	6/19/1864	Petersburg, VA
Hopkins, J. Ward	D	Capt.	6/16/1864	Hare's Hill, VA
James, John F.	A (E)	Pvt.	7/4/1864	Petersburg, VA
Jeffers, B.	C (F)	Pvt.	3/20/1865	Richmond, VA
Johnson, William W.	D	Pvt.	9/28/1864	Weldon RR, VA
Kenney, Peter	H (C)	Pvt.	9/1/1864	Greensboro, NC
Kiddell, Theodore	A (E)	Pvt.	5/7/1864	Walthall Junct.
Kirby, H. M.	C (F)	Capt.	5/16/1864	Richmond, VA
Kirby, L. C.	K (G)	Pvt.	4/11/1865	Pt. Lookout, MD
Klance, John	na	Pvt.	8/3/1864	Weldon RR, VA
Lance, Archibald St. John	D	2d Lt.	5/14/1864	Drewry's Bluff, VA
Lawton, George W.	C (F)	Pvt.	8/1/1864	Charlotte, NC
Lequeaux, William B.	I (A)	Pvt.	9/6/1864	Elmira, NY
Love, P. P.	H (C)	Lt.	na	Petersburg, VA
McDonald, A. A.	C (F)	Pvt.	4/22/1865	Pt. Lookout, MD
McElrath, David T.	B	Pvt.	8/23/1864	Petersburg, VA
Mack, Jacob A.	I (A)	Pvt.	9/10/1864	Pt. Lookout, MD
McSweeney, Miles	K (G)	1st Sgt.	6/13/1864	Petersburg, VA
Madden, Moses	D	Pvt.	6/23/1864	na
Malloy, William P.	B	Pvt.	11/2/1864	Fts. Monroe, VA
Malone, Patrick	C (F)	Pvt.	11/20/1864	Elmira, NY
Manude, John A.	H (C)	Cpl.	10/26/1864	Pt. Lookout, MD

Martin, S. V.	D	Pvt.	6/25/1864	Drewry's Bluff, VA
Masterman, Alfred H.	B	2d Lt.	5/7/1864	Walthall Junct
Mellichamp, William S.	A (E)	Pvt.	3/2/1864	Charleston
Menude, John A.	I (A)	Cpl.	10/21/1864	Pt. Lookout, MD
Milford, J. W.	D	Pvt.	7/8/1864	Petersburg, VA
Miskelly, J. W.	C (F)	Pvt.	5/20/1864	Petersburg, VA
Molloy, W. P.	A (E)	Pvt.	na	At sea
Montgomery, Prater S. G.	K (G)	2d Sgt.	2/9/1865	Elmira, NY
Moses, Edwin L.	D	Pvt.	6/11/1865	Camp Chase, OH
Neill, Daniel	B	Pvt.	5/7/1864	Walthall Junct
Nelson, Josiah	D	Pvt.	11/30/1864	Richmond, VA
Nelson, W. A.	D	Pvt.	2/10/1864	James Island, SC
Palmer, Barnwell W.	A (E)	Capt.	6/16/1864	Hare's Hill, Va.
Pearson, Thomas	B	Pvt.	9/23/1864	Petersburg, VA
Pierson, D. W.	C (F)	Pvt.	na	Fts. Monroe, VA
Pierson, Thomas J.	B	Pvt.	9/28/1864	Petersburg, VA
Pringle, James	C (F)	Cpl.	6/24/1864	Petersburg, VA
Quinn, L. C.	K (G)	Pvt.	6/24/1864	Petersburg, VA
Rees, B. F.	C (F)	Pvt.	7/17/1864	Richmond, VA
Rhode, D.	C (F)	Pvt.	5/16/1864	Drewry's Bluff, VA
Rook, Samuel L.	A (E)	Pvt.	1/16/1865	Elmira, NY
Ryan, Thomas	H	Pvt.	na	Richmond, VA
Saylor, Henry E.	D	Sgt.	8/23/1865	Columbia
Scheflin, J.	C (F)	Pvt.	5/16/1864	Drewry's Bluff, VA
Schnierle, Vincent	A (E)	Pvt.	6/16/1864	Hare's Hill, VA
Schroder, Henry	C (F)	Pvt.	3/4/1865	Elmira, NY
Scott, J. M.	B	Pvt.	8/1/1864	Fts. Monroe, VA
Seabrook, E. Smyley	B	Cpl.	8/5/1864	Richmond, VA
Seay, R. B.	K (G)	2d Lt.	5/14/1864	Drewry's Bluff, VA
Sellers, R. A.	C (F)	Pvt.	7/27/1864	Richmond, VA
Seybet, George W. B.	I (A)	1st Sgt.	6/18/1864	Petersburg, VA
Sheehan, Patrick	H (C)	Pvt.	6/24/1864	Petersburg, VA
Smith, Henry Abbott	D	1st Sgt.	8/24/1864	Weldon RR, VA
Spady, Southey G.	A (E)	Sgt.	12/18/1864	Pt. Lookout, MD

Starnes, Robert C.	D	Cpl.	8/24/1864	Weldon RR, VA
Strain, William H.	I (A)	Pvt.	6/15/1864	na
Sullivan, W. J.	B	Pvt.	3/4/1865	Elmira, NY
Tennet, Gilbert V.	A (E)	Pvt.	na	Charleston
Todd, James	H (C)	Pvt.	6/17/1864	Petersburg, VA
Vaughn, G. P.	A (E)	Pvt.	8/10/1864	Richmond, VA
Vaughn, Joel	B	Pvt.	6/3/1864	Bermuda Hundred
Vaughn, R. B.	B	Pvt.	7/21/1864	Richmond, VA
Warren, Christopher	H (C)	Pvt.	8/2/1864	Petersburg, VA
Warren, John	H (C)	Pvt.	6/26/1864	Petersburg, VA
Watson, Cornelius	C (F)	Pvt.	3/23/1865	Kittrell Spgs, NC
Watson, John Drayton	D	Pvt.	7/11/1864	Richmond, VA
Webb, Daniel C.	A	1st Sgt.	6/12/1864	Petersburg, VA
Westendorf, Charles	A (E)	Pvt.	4/4/1865	Pt. Lookout, MD
Whelan, Edward	H (C)	Pvt.	5/15/1864	Drewry's Bluff, VA
Whelan, Roddy	H (C)	Pvt.	10/4/1864	Elmira, NY
White, R. M.	A (E)	Pvt.	6/18/1864	Petersburg, VA
Whitehead, B. T.	C (F)	Pvt.	8/31/1864	Richmond, VA
Whitlock, John	B	Pvt.	3/12/1865	Pt. Lookout, MD
Wilder, John	I (A)	Pvt.	7/15/1864	Petersburg, VA
Wright, James D.	B	2d Sgt.	na	Fayetteville, NC
Yon, R. A.	I (A)	Sgt.	2/12/1865	Richmond, VA
Young, W. D.	B	Pvt.	na	Fayetteville, NC

Died between 1862 and 4/1864 but all credited to Twenty-seventh rather than First South Carolina Infantry Battalion

Name	Co.	Rank	Died	Where
Adams, H.A	Pvt.		11/1/1862	Richmond, VA
Bailey, William A.	D	Pvt.	8/6/1863	Bty. Wagner
Ball, T. J.	D	Pvt.	9/1/1863	na
Ballentine, George P.	D	Pvt.	8/10/1863	Bty. Wagner
Bearde, W. S.	C	Pvt.	8/15/1863	na
Bragg, D. W.	K	Pvt.	10/1/1863	na
Brice, J. A.	C	Pvt.	2/3/1864	Charleston
Brown, Fred T. A.	B	Pvt.	11/14/1862	Charleston
Burns, P.	B	Pvt.	8/19/1863	Bty. Wagner
Collins, Samuel	I	Pvt.	12/24/1862	King Street, Charleston
Dodd, N. G.	I	Pvt.	9/14/1863	Columbia
Foster, J. J.	K	Pvt.	10/15/1863	na
Fourcher, J. Henry	D	Pvt.	8/23/1863	Charleston
Fowler, W. W.	D	Pvt.	7/20/1863	Bty. Wagner
Gill, S. H.	C	Pvt.	4/15/1863	Bermuda Hundred
Graves, W. B.	D	Pvt.	8/9/1863	na
Graves, W. W.	D	Pvt.	7/16/1863	na
Haseltine, Edward, E.	D	Pvt.	10/31/1862	Charleston
Kelly, John	C	Pvt.	8/15/1863	na
King, Henry C.	D	Cpt.	6/16/1862	Secessionville
Lake, Edward	B	Pvt.	11/18/1863	Ft. Sumter, SC
Lake, John	B	Pvt.	9/28/1863	At home
Lamotte, Henry J.	D	Pvt.	2/27/1863	na
Lawton, Amos B.	B	Pvt.	11/10/1862	na
Lewis, Posey	K	Pvt.	2/14/1864	Pt. Lookout, MD
Lindsay, Henry A.	D	Pvt.	3/6/1863	na
Lynch, Francis R.	I	1st Lt.	10/20/1863	Spartanburg, SC
Martin, Henry H.	D	Pvt.	8/7/1863	na
Morrisey, Patrick	B	Pvt.	10/5/1863	Columbia

Pope, M. T.	D	Pvt.	8/19/1863	na
Reeves	A	Pvt.	6/15/1862	Charleston
Smith, Horace Waring	A	Pvt.	2/15/1864	Charleston
Smith, William Kirkwood	D	1st Sgt.	7/18/1863	Bty. Wagner
Stone, M.	D	Pvt.	7/20/1863	Bty. Wagner
Suares, Basil Manly	A	Pvt.	2/3/1863	Charleston
Tennet, Edward S.	D	Pvt.	8/15/1862	Secessionville
Timms, J. M.	D	Pvt.	8/15/1863	Bty. Wagner
Trouche, Augustus J.	D	Sgt.	2/15/1864	Charleston
Ware, W. A. J.	D	Pvt.	7/20/1863	Bty. Wagner
Warton, John	D	Pvt.	10/3/1863	na
Watts, R. S.	D	Pvt.	9/15/1863	na

APPENDIX D

Officer Graves and Markers

Grave of Julius Blake, Magnolia Cemetery, Charleston. Photograph by author.

Marker of George Brown, First Scots Presbyterian
Graveyard, Charleston. Photograph by author.

Marker of Ward Hopkins, First Scots Presbyterian
Graveyard, Charleston. Photograph by author.

Grave of Samuel Lord, Magnolia Cemetery, Charleston. Photograph by author.

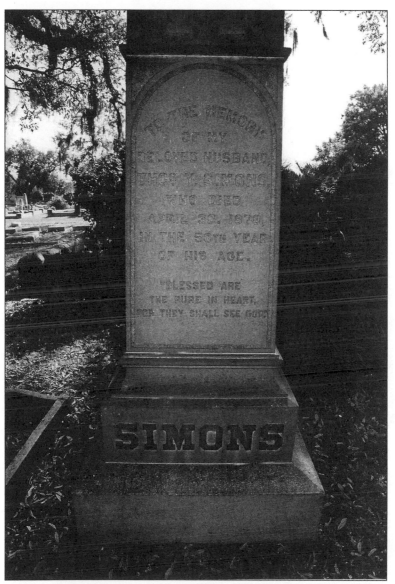

Grave of Thomas Simons, Magnolia Cemetery, Charleston. Photograph by author.

Notes

Chapter 1

1. Flynn, 23.
2. Ibid.
3. *The South Carolina Historical Society Magazine,* vol. 88, 108-10.
4. Meyer, 6-7.
5. McPhereson, 168.
6. Cauthen, 110-11.
7. Ibid.

Chapter 2

1. Burton, 15.
2. Swanberg, 22.
3. *Charleston Daily Courier,* December 20, 1860.
4. Ibid., December 21, 1860.
5. *Military Collector & Historian,* vol. 3, 57.
6. Ibid., vol. 42.
7. Ibid., vol. 3, 60.
8. Ibid., vol. 42.
9. Ibid., vol. 3, 60.
10. *Shole's Directory of the City of Charleston—1881-89,* 45-46.
11. *Military Collector & Historian,* vol. 3, 60.
12. *Shole's Directory of the City of Charleston—1881-89,* 45.
13. *Charleston Mercury,* December 18, 1860.
14. *Military Collector & Historian,* vol. 3, 58.
15. Ibid., vol. 42, 108-9.

16. Johnson, 23.

17. *Sketch of the Irish Volunteers,* 432.

18. December 28, 1860.

19. Ravenel, 489.

20. *Charleston Daily Courier,* December 28, 1860.

21. Burton, 16.

22. Ibid., 13.

23. *Cyclopedia of Eminent and Representative Men of the Carolinas of the Mid-Nineteenth Century,* 658. (Hereafter abbreviated to *Cyclopedia.*)

24. *Official Records of the Union and Confederate Armies in the War of the Rebellion,* vol. 1, 5-9. (Hereafter abbreviated to O.R.; series 1 unless otherwise noted.)

25. "A Brief Chronological Account," 6.

26. Johnston, 7.

27. *Confederate Military History,* vol. 5, 8-11.

28. *Sketch of the Irish Volunteers,* 432.

29. Swanberg, 146-47.

30. *Charleston Mercury,* January 9, 1861.

31. *The South Carolina Historical Society Magazine,* vol. 61, 64.

32. Ibid., 64-65.

33. Burton, 38.

34. *The South Carolina Historical Society Magazine,* vol. 61, 64-65.

35. Ibid.

36. *Charleston Mercury,* February 4, 1861.

37. Ibid., February 15, 1861.

38. Marszalek, 10-11.

39. *Charleston Mercury,* March 1, 1861.

40. Hagood, 29.

41. Marszalek, 11; and Muhnlenfeld and Woodward, 45.

42. Marszalek, 11.

43. Cauthen, 115.

44. Roman, vol. 1, 29.

45. Ibid.

46. Marszalek, 24.

47. O.R., vol. 1, 45.

48. Ibid., 59.
49. *Sumter Guard: Past, Present and Future,* 3.
50. Ibid., 4.
51. Alexander, "Reminiscence of Duty in a Rifle Regiment on Sullivan's Island in 1861 on the Eve of the Civil War."
52. *Confederate Military History,* vol. 6, 5.
53. *Southern Historical Society Papers,* vol. 14, 185.
54. *Sketch of the Irish Volunteers;* McCrady, 14-15.
55. Freeman, vol. 1, 7.
56. O.R., vol. 2, 944.
57. *Charleston Mercury,* July 4, 1861.
58. Cauthen, 136.
59. "Volunteers for Confederate Service and State Service," 15.
60. *Charleston Mercury,* July 27, 1861.
61. *The South Carolina Historical Society Magazine,* vol. 61, 69.
62. Order Book #34.
63. *The South Carolina Historical Society Magazine,* vol. 61, 67-68.
64. Ibid., 66-67.
65. Order Books # 46, #49, #56.
66. Johnson, 24.
67. O.R., vol. 6, 309.
68. Burton, 77.
69. O.R., vol. 6, 326.
70. Order Book #171.
71. Order Book # 141.
72. *Recollections and Reminiscences,* vol. 3, 67.
73. O.R., vol. 6, 351.
74. Marszalek, 105.
75. *Charleston Daily Courier,* February 25, 1862.

Chapter 3

1. Cauthen, 138.
2. Ibid., 144.
3. *Charleston Daily Courier,* February 8, 1862.
4. Order Book #231.
5. Ibid.

6. *Charleston Daily Courier*, February 17, 1862.
7. Ibid., February 13, 1862.
8. Ibid., February 23 and 24, 1862.
9. Ibid., February 21 and 24, 1862.
10. Compiled Service Records for the Charleston Battalion.
11. *Charleston Daily Courier.*
12. *Charleston Mercury,* February 26, 1862.
13. *Record and Roll of the German Fusiliers,* no page numbers.
14. *Charleston Mercury,* March 7, 1862.
15. *Charleston Daily Courier,* March 10, 1862.
16. Ibid.
17. *Charleston Mercury,* March 11, 1862.
18. Ibid., March 17, 1862.
19. Ibid., March 10, 1862.
20. O.R., supplement, S.C. vol., 394.
21. Compiled Service Records for the Charleston Battalion.
22. Moore, 14-15.
23. Schreadley, 152-53.
24. Compiled Service Records for the Twenty-fourth South Carolina Infantry.
25. Hagood, 206-8.

Chapter 4
1. Hagy, 1859 and 1860, no page numbers.
2. 1860 South Carolina Census, 209.
3. Hagy, 1859 and 1860.
4. Ibid.
5. *Charleston Yearbook,* vol. 85, 542.
6. Hagy, 1860.
7. Compiled Service Records for the Charleston Battalion.
8. Ibid.
9. *The South Carolina Historical Society Magazine,* vol. 65, 198.
10. Ibid., vol. 55, 197.
11. Hagy, 1860; and Clarkson Family.
12. 1860 South Carolina Census, 159.
13. *Charleston Mercury,* February 15, 1862.

14. Ibid., March 5, 1862.
15. Hagy, 1860.
16. Ibid.; and Compiled Service Records for the Charleston Battalion.
17. Hagy, 1860.
18. Ibid., 1859.
19. Salley.
20. Compiled Service Records for the Charleston Battalion.
21. *Sketch of the Irish Volunteers,* 432.
22. Hagy, 1860.
23. *Charleston Mercury,* June 19, 1862.
24. Hagy, 1860.
25. Ibid., 1859 and 1860; and Bolchoz.
26. Hagy, 1859 and 1860.
27. *Charleston Mercury,* June 19, 1862.
28. *Sumter Guard: Past, Present and Future,* 3.
29. Salley, 5.
30. *Charleston Daily Courier,* February 15, 1862.
31. *Charleston Mercury,* February 17, 1862.
32. Compiled Service Records for the Charleston Battalion.
33. Hagy, 1860.
34. *Cyclopedia,* 658.
35. Hagy, 1859.
36. Ibid., 1860.
37. Meyer, 214.
38. Hagy, 1859.
39. Compiled Service Records for the Charleston Battalion.
40. Hagy, 1859.
41. Hagood, 207.
42. 1860 South Carolina Census, 232.
43. Hagy, 1859.
44. Ibid., 1860.
45. Ibid.
46. 1860 South Carolina Census, 264.
47. Memminger and Ostendoeff, 5-6.
48. *Record and Roll of the German Fusiliers.*

49. *Charleston Mercury,* February 17, 1862.
50. Compiled Service Records for the Charleston Battalion.
51. "In Memory of Colonel Gaillard."
52. *Recollections and Reminiscences,* vol. 3, 67.
53. Hagy, 1859.
54. Hagood, 207.
55. *Confederate Commissions Book,* 1862.
56. Compiled Service Records for the Charleston Battalion.
57. *Confederate Commissions Book,* 1862.
58. Compiled Service Records for the Charleston Battalion.
59. Powers, 267.
60. Ibid., 279.
61. 1860 Slave Schedules, no page numbers.
62. Ibid.
63. Ibid.
64. Ibid.
65. Ibid.
66. McPhereson, 34.
67. 1860 Slave Schedules.
68. Ibid.
69. Ibid.
70. Ibid.
71. Ibid.
72. O.R., ser. 4, vol. 1, 1,080.
73. Johnston, 2-3.
74. McPhereson, 86.
75. Lonn, 31.
76. Ibid., 4.
77. Ibid.
78. Powers, 42.
79. Ibid., 46.
80. Hagy, 1859 and 1860.
81. Ibid.
82. Ibid.; and 1860 South Carolina Census.
83. Ibid.
84. Ibid.

85. Hagood, 208.
86. Compiled Service Records for the Charleston Battalion.
87. Hagood, 235.
88. May and Faunt, 118.
89. *The South Carolina Historical Society Magazine,* vol. 7, 43.
90. Hagy, 1859.
91. *The South Carolina Historical Society Magazine,* vol. 7, 43.
92. Hagood, 208.
93. *Sketch of the Irish Volunteers,* 19.
94. Ostendorff, 6-7.
95. *Charleston Mercury,* February 4, 1861.
96. Wiley, 330-31.
97. Fox's Regimental Losses, O.R., 505.
98. Kirkland, all entries are in alphabetical order.
99. *The Civil War in South Carolina.*
100. Fox's Regimental Losses, O.R., 518.
101. O.R., vol. 14, 530.
102. Brennan, 20.

Chapter 5

1. O.R., vol. 14, 512.
2. Hagood, 87.
3..O.R., vol. 14, 535.
4. Ibid., 538.
5. Ibid., 575.
6. Brennan, 71-72.
7. Ibid., 69.
8. Ibid., 77-78.
9. Walter B. Capers, 52.
10. Ibid., 53.
11. Brennan, 79.
12. *Charleston Mercury,* June 4, 1862.
13. Walter B. Capers, 53.
14. O.R., vol. 14, 29-30.
15. Ibid.
16. Ibid., 30.

17. *Sketch of the Irish Volunteers,* 433.

18. Compiled Service Records for the Charleston Battalion.

19. *Charleston Mercury,* June 4, 1862.

20. Compiled Service Records for the Charleston Battalion.

21. Gaillard's report found in *Memory Rolls,* reel 3.

22. Ibid.

23. *Charleston Daily Courier,* June 4, 1862.

24. O.R., vol. 14, 51-52.

25. *Southern Historical Society Papers,* vol. 16, 145.

26. O.R., vol. 14, 58-60.

27. Ibid., 95.

28. Brennan, 172-73.

29. Ibid., 181.

30. O.R., vol. 14, 93.

31. *Charleston Mercury,* June 19, 1862.

32. *Charleston Daily Courier,* June 18, 1862; and *Cyclopedia,* 658.

33. *Charleston Mercury,* June 19, 1862.

34. O.R., vol. 14, 97.

35. *Charleston Mercury,* June 19, 1862.

36. *Sketch of the Irish Volunteers,* 27.

37. Brennan, 203-5.

38. *Charleston Mercury,* June 19, 1862; and *Sketch of the Irish Volunteers,* 27.

39. *Charleston Mercury,* June 18, 1862.

40. O.R., vol. 14, 94.

41. *Charleston Mercury,* June 18, 1862.

42. Ibid., June 19, 1862.

43. Brennan, 258.

44. O.R., vol. 14, 90.

45. *New York Herald,* June 24, 1862.

46. Figures drawn from Compiled Service Records, O.R., *Memory Rolls,* Confederate States Army Casualty List and Narrative, Roll of Honor, period newspapers, and various secondary sources on the battle.

47. *The South Carolina Historical Society Magazine,* vol. 63, 144.

48. *Charleston Mercury,* June 19, 1862.
49. Ibid.
50. Ibid.
51. Compiled Service Records for the Charleston Battalion.
52. Woodward, 390.
53. O.R., vol. 14, 97.
54. *Charleston Daily Courier,* June 26, 1862.
55. O.R., vol. 14, 95.
56. Ibid., 92.
57. *Charleston Daily Courier,* June 22, 1862.
58. *Muster and Pay Rolls.*

Chapter 6
1. O.R., vol. 14, 582.
2. *Charleston Mercury,* July 9, 1862.
3. *Charleston Daily Courier,* July 7, 1862.
4. *Charleston Mercury.*
5. Compiled Service Records for the Charleston Battalion; and Ellison Capers, 579.
6. Sparkman, 2.
7. Compiled Service Records for the Charleston Battalion.
8. *Charleston Daily Courier,* December 8, 1862.
9. Compiled Service Records for the Charleston Battalion.
10. Ibid.
11. Ibid.
12. Fraser, 256.
13. Compiled Service Records for the Charleston Battalion.
14. *Charleston Daily Courier,* January 1, 1863.
15 O.R., vol. 14, 624, 823; and vol. 28, pt. 2, 161-62.
16. Compiled Service Records for the Charleston Battalion.
17. Ibid.
18. *Charleston Mercury,* April 10, 1863.
19. Compiled Service Records for the Charleston Battalion; and 1860 South Carolina Census.
20. Compiled Service Records for the Charleston Battalion.
21. Ibid.

22. Ibid.; and Hagy, 1860.
23. Compiled Service Records for the Charleston Battalion.
24. Ibid.
25. Wiley, 290.
26. Compiled Service Records for the Charleston Battalion.
27. Ibid.
28. *Charleston Daily Courier,* February 18, 1863.
29. *Charleston Mercury,* March 31, 1863.
30. Ibid., April 6, 1863.
31. O.R., vol. 14, 264-65.
32. Ibid.
33. Wise, 34.
34. Ibid., 35.

Chapter 7
1. *Charleston Daily Courier,* July 10, 1863.
2. O.R., vol. 28, pt. 1, 65.
3. Wise, 61, 226.
4. *Charleston Daily Courier,* July 10, 1863.
5. Wise, 58.
6. O.R., vol. 28, pt. 2, 188.
7. Ibid.
8. Wise, 227.
9. Ibid., 66.
10. O.R., vol. 28, pt. 2, 191.
11. Ibid., 415.
12. Ibid., 202.
13. Johnson, 101.
14. Honor, 101.
15. O.R., vol 28, pt. 1, 418.
16. Ibid., 543.
17. *Southern Historical Society Papers,* vol. 20, 175.
18. *Charleston Daily Courier,* July 21, 1863.
19. O.R., vol. 28, pt. 1, 418, 544.
20. Ibid., 544-45.
21. Ibid., 346-47.

22. Ibid., 362.

23. Trudeau, 80.

24. O.R., vol. 28, pt. 1, 362.

25. Ibid., 347.

26. Trudeau, 82.

27. O.R., vol. 28, pt. 1, 418.

28. Ibid., 419.

29. Ibid., 544-45.

30. Ibid., 418.

31. Ibid., 543.

32. *Charleston Mercury*, July 21, 1863.

33 *Charleston Daily Courier*, July 21, 1863.

34. O.R., vol. 28, pt. 1, 362.

35. Ibid., 418.

36. Ibid., 347.

37. Wise, 108.

38. O.R., vol. 28, pt. 1, 348.

39. Wise, 109.

40. Johnston, 11.

41. O.R., vol. 28, pt. 1, 544.

42. *Charleston Daily Courier*, July 21, 1863.

43. *Charleston Mercury*, July 21, 1863.

44. *Charleston Daily Courier*, July 21, 1863.

45. O.R., vol. 28, pt. 1, 419.

46. *Charleston Daily Courier*, July 21, 1863.

47. O.R., vol. 28, pt. 1, 419.

48. Wise, 111.

49. O.R., vol. 28, pt. 1, 419; and *Charleston Yearbook*, vol. 84, 369.

50. *Southern Historical Society Papers*, vol. 12, 138.

51. O.R., vol. 28, pt.1, 202.

52. *Southern Historical Society Papers*, vol. 20, 176.

53. Bradshaw, 121.

54. Compiled Service Records for the Charleston Battalion.

55. Figures drawn from Compiled Service Records, O.R., *Memory Rolls*, Confederate States Army Casualty List and Narrative,

Roll of Honor, period newspapers, and various secondary sources on the battle.
56. Honor, 109.
57. July 20 and 21, 1863.

Chapter 8
1. *Charleston Mercury,* August 5, 1863.
2. *Charleston Yearbook,* vol. 84, 369.
3. July 23, 1863.
4. O.R., vol. 28, pt. 2, 211.
5. Compiled Service Records for the Charleston Battalion.
6. Special Order No. 264, O.R., vol. 28, pt. 2, 249.
7. O.R., vol. 28, pt. 1, 454.
8. Compiled Service Records for the Charleston Battalion.
9. Johnson, 143.
10. O.R., vol. 28, pt. 1, 339.
11. "In Memory of Colonel Gaillard," 4.
12. O.R., vol. 28, pt. 1, 441.
13. Ibid., 63.
14. Compiled Service Records for the Charleston Battalion.
15. O.R., vol. 28, pt.1, 499.
16. Johnson, 138.
17. Ibid., 147.
18. Ibid., appendix cvii.
19. O.R., vol. 28, pt. 1, 7.
20. *Charleston Mercury,* September 8, 1863.
21. Wise, 205-7.
22. O.R., vol. 28, pt. 1, 726.
23. Ibid.
24. O.R., vol. 28, pt. 1, 125.
25. *Charleston Mercury,* September 10, 1863.
26. Ibid.
27. *Record and Roll of the German Fusiliers.*
28. Johnson, 161-62.
29. O.R., vol. 28, pt. 1, 125.
30. Ibid., 726-27.

31. Honor, 159.
32. O.R., vol. 28, pt. 1, 725.
33. Ibid., 727.
34. Ibid., 724.
35. September 10, 1863.
36. Confederate War Department Casualties Lists and Reports, Morris Island.

Chapter 9
1. Hagood, 208.
2. O.R., ser. 4, vol. 2, 815.
3. Warner, 121.
4. Hagood, 210.
5. Ibid., 195.
6. Ibid.
7. Compiled Service Records for the First Battalion South Carolina Sharpshooters.
8. 1860 South Carolina Census.
9. City of Charleston Directory, 1860.
10. 1860 South Carolina Census.
11. Compiled Service Records for the Charleston Battalion.
12. Compiled Service Records for the First Battalion South Carolina Sharpshooters.
13. Meyer, 193.
14. Chapman, 246-49.
15. O.R., vol. 14, 181.
16.. Hagood, 213.
17. *Southern Historical Society Papers,* vol. 14, 38.
18. Phelps, 92.
19. Hagood, 203.
20. O.R., vol. 25, pt. 1, 152.
21. Hagood, 217-19.
22. O.R., vol. 36, pt. 2, 253.
23. Ibid., 252.
24. Kirkland.
25. Sifakis, 105.

26. O.R., vol. 36, pt. 2, 254.
27. See appendix C of this book.
28. Chapman, 474.
29. Catton, 162-63.
30. Hagood, 260.
31. O.R., vol. 40, pt. 1, 804.
32. Ibid., vol. 42, pt. 1, 936.
33. Ibid., 431.
34. Dedmondt, 113.
35. O.R., vol. 42, pt. 1, 936.
36. Izlar, 96.
37. Ibid., 937.
38. Hagood, 315; and Compiled Service Records for the Charleston Battalion.
39. Hagood, 315-17.
40. Ibid., 328.
41. Fonvielle, 554.
42. O.R., vol. 46, pt. 2, 1,138.
43. Ibid., vol. 47, pt. 3, 732.
44. Ibid., 697.
45. Ibid., pt. 1, 1,080.

Chapter 10
1. Compiled Service Records for the Twenty-seventh South Carolina Infantry.
2. Ibid.
3. O.R., ser. 4, vol. 2, 816, 827; and ser. 1, vol. 28, pt. 1, 396-97.
4. Compiled Service Records for the Twenty-seventh South Carolina Infantry.
5. Ibid.
6. Transcripts of the South Carolina Medical Association, 203.
7. Compiled Service Records for the Twenty-seventh South Carolina Infantry.
8. Ibid.
9. Hagood, 267.
10. Kirkland.

11. O.R., vol. 40, pt. 1, 801.
12. Compiled Service Records for the Twenty-seventh South Carolina Infantry.
13. Ibid.
14. Hagood, 278-79.
15. *Recollections and Reminiscence,* vol. 6, 434-37.
16. Hagood, 299; and *Sketch of the Irish Volunteers,* 29.
17. Hagood, 285, 299.
18. "In Memory of Colonel Gaillard."
19. Fonvielle, 389; and O.R., vol. 41, pt. 2, 1,187.
20. Hagood, 312.
21. Compiled Service Records for the Twenty-seventh South Carolina Infantry.
22. Ibid.
23. Ibid.
24. Ibid.
25. Ibid.
26. Hagood, 351.
27. O.R., vol. 47, pt. 3, 745.
28. Ibid., p. 1, 1,062; pt. 3, 732; and Compiled Service Records for the Twenty-seventh South Carolina Infantry.
29. Compiled Service Records for the Twenty-seventh South Carolina Infantry.
30. Hagood, 370.
31. Bolchoz.
32. Roman, vol. 2, 407.
33. Hagood, 372.

Chapter 11
1. Powers, 86, 96; and Ripley, 307.
2. May and Faunt, 209.
3. *The South Carolina Historical Society Magazine,* vol. 65, 198.
4. Compiled Service Records for the Twenty-seventh South Carolina Infantry.
5. 1870 South Carolina Census.
6. *Record of Burials at Magnolia Cemetery.*

7. *Shole's Directory of the City of Charleston—1882.*

8. 1870 South Carolina Census.

9. *Shole's Directory of the City of Charleston—1882.*

10. *Record of Burials at Magnolia Cemetery.*

11. Ripley, 309.

12. City of Charleston Directory, 1866.

13. Clarkson Family.

14. *Our Women in the War,* 53.

15. City of Charleston Directory, 1872.

16. Ibid.

17. Compiled Service Records for the Twenty-seventh South Carolina Infantry.

18. Ibid.

19. Ibid.

20. Ibid.

21. City of Charleston Directory, 1872.

22. Compiled Service Records for the Twenty-seventh South Carolina Infantry.

23. Ibid.

24 *Sumter Guard: Past, Present and Future,* 4.

25. *Shole's Directory of the City of Charleston—1882.*

Appendix A
1. Wharton, 181-83.

Appendix B
1. Compiled Service Records for the Charleston Battalion.

Bibliography

UNPUBLISHED SOURCES

Abstracts of Troop Strength, 1861. South Carolina Department of Archives and History, Columbia. S192023 233L01.

Alexander, George W. "Reminiscence of Duty in a Rifle Regiment on Sullivan's Island in 1861 on the Eve of the Civil War." South Carolina Historical Society, ca. 1895.

Bacot-Huger Family. Papers. South Carolina Historical Society, Charleston.

Bolchoz, Abney. (Historian and holder of records of the Sumter Guards.) Papers.

City of Charleston Directory. Charleston County Library. Microfilm.

The Civil War in South Carolina. Eastern Digital Resources, Clearwater, S.C. CD ROM.

Clarkson Family. Papers. Manakin-Sabot, Va.

Compiled Service Records for the Charleston Battalion. Charleston County Library. Microfilm reels 149-51.

Compiled Service Records for the First Battalion South Carolina Sharpshooters. Charleston County Library. Microfilm reel 152.

Compiled Service Records for the Twenty-fifth South Carolina Infantry. Charleston County Library. Microfilm reels 343-49.

Compiled Service Records for the Twenty-fourth South Carolina Infantry. Charleston County Library. Microfilm reels 337-42.

Compiled Service Records for the Twenty-seventh South Carolina Infantry. Charleston County Library. Microfilm reels 355-60.

Confederate Commissions Book. South Carolina Department of Archives and History, Columbia. S192107 233K07.

Confederate States Army Casualty List and Narrative. South Carolina Department of Archives and History, Columbia. Microfilm reel 3, microcopy m836.

Confederate War Department Casualties Lists and Reports, Morris Island. South Carolina Department of Archives and History, Columbia. Microfilm reel CW 1211.

1880 South Carolina Census. Charleston County Library.

1870 South Carolina Census. Charleston County Library.

1860 Slave Schedules. Charleston County Library.

1860 South Carolina Census. Charleston County Library.

Honor, Theodore A. Letters. Archives of Appalachia, East Tennessee State University, Johnson City, Tenn.

McCrady, Col. Edward. Paper presented at the Irish Volunteers Memorial Meeting, Charleston, 1877.

Memory Rolls. South Carolina Department of Archives and History, Columbia. Microfilm.

Muster and Pay Rolls, Company E, Charleston Battalion. South Carolina Historical Society, Charleston.

Order Book, 1861-62, S.C. Militia, Fourth Brigade, Second Division. Wilmot G. DeSaussure Collection. South Carolina Historical Society.

Record and Roll of the German Fusiliers. Handwritten. S108118 370B01. South Carolina Department of Archives and History, Columbia.

Record of Burials at Magnolia Cemetery. Charleston County Library. Microfilm reel 1C.

Salley, F. M. *History of the Irish Volunteers Company.* Copied from handwritten original by Agnes P. Lyons as part of the WPA Project No. 624: 65-33-775, 1933-36. South Carolina Room, Charleston County Library.

Sparkman, Mary. "General Beauregard's Headquarters in Charleston 1862-1864." MS. South Carolina Historical Society, Charleston.

NEWSPAPERS

Charleston Daily Courier, 1860-65. Charleston County Library. Microfilm.

Charleston Mercury, 1860-65. Charleston County Library. Microfilm.

New York Herald, 1860-65. Charleston County Library. CD ROM.

Richmond Examiner 1860-65. Charleston County Library. CD ROM.

PERIODICALS AND MAGAZINES

Military Collector & Historian 3 (September 1951): 53-60; 42 (Winter 1990): 108-55.

The South Carolina Historical Society Magazine. Vol. 7, 55, 61, 63, 65, 88. Charleston: South Carolina Historical Society.

PUBLISHED BOOKS, DIARIES, MEMOIRS, PAMPHLETS

Bradshaw, Timothy. *Battery Wagner.* Columbia, S.C.: Palmetto Historical Works, 1993.

Brennan, Patrick. *Secessionville: Assault on Charleston.* Campbell, Calif.: Savas Publishing Co., 1996.

"A Brief Chronological Account of the Raising of Troops for State and Confederate Service." *South Carolina Pamphlets and Miscellaneous* (n.d.).

Burton, E. Milby. *The Siege of Charleston, 1861-1865.* Columbia: University of South Carolina Press, 1970.

Capers, Ellison. *Confederate Military History—South Carolina.* Vol. 5. Wilmington, N.C.: Broadfoot, 1987.

Capers, Walter B. *The Soldier Bishop, Ellison Capers.* New York: Neale Publishing Co., 1912.

Catton, Bruce. *The Army of the Potomac.* Vol. 3. Garden City, N.Y.: Doubleday & Co., 1953.

Cauthen, Charles E. *South Carolina Goes to War, 1860-1865.* Chapel Hill: University of North Carolina Press, 1950.

Chapman, John A. *History of Edgefield County from the Earliest Settlements to 1897.* Reprint, Spartanburg, S.C.: The Reprint Co., 1980.

Charleston City Directory 1859. Charleston: Walker, Evans and Cogswell, 1859.

Charleston Yearbook. Charleston: Nelson Southern Printing, 1880-1950.

Confederate Military History. 12 vols. Atlanta: Confederate, 1899.

Confederate States Roster—South Carolina Roster. Vol. 2. Wilmington, N.C.: Broadfoot, 1998.

Crute, Joseph H. *Units of the Confederate States Army.* Frederick, Md.: Old Soldier Books, 1987.

Cyclopedia of Eminent and Representative Men of the Carolinas of the Mid-Nineteenth Century. Madison, Ga.: Brant and Fuller, 1892.

Dedmondt, Glenn. *The Flags of Civil War South Carolina.* Gretna, La.: Pelican Publishing Co., 2000.

Doubleday, Abner. *Reminiscences of Forts Sumter and Moultrie in 1860-61.* Charleston: The Nautical & Aviation Publishing Co. of America, 1998.

Flynn, Jean Martin. *The Militia in Antebellum South Carolina Society.* Spartanburg, S.C.: The Reprint Co., 1991.

Fonvielle, Chris E., Jr. *The Wilmington Campaign: Last Rays of Departing Hope.* Mechanicsburg, Pa.: Stackpole Books, 2001.

Fraser, Walter J., Jr. *Charleston Charleston.* Columbia: University of South Carolina Press, 1989.

Freeman, Douglas S. *Lee's Lieutenants.* 3 vols. New York: Charles Scribner's Sons, 1946.

Hagood, Johnson. *Memoirs of the War in Secession.* Reprint, Camden, S.C.: Fox Books, 1997.

Hagy, James W. *On the Eve of the Civil War: The City of Charleston*

Directory for 1859 & 1860. Baltimore: Genealogical Publishing Co., 2000.

"In Memory of Colonel Gaillard." *South Carolina Pamphlets and Miscellaneous* 83, no. 10 (n.d.).

Izlar, William Valmore. *Edisto Rifles.* Oxford, Miss.: Guild Bindery Press, n.d.

Johnson, John. *The Defense of Charleston Harbor, Including Fort Sumter and Adjacent Islands.* Reprint, Germantown, Tenn.: Guild Bindery Press, 1994.

Johnston, Terry A. *Him on the One Side and Me on the Other.* Columbia: University of South Carolina Press, 1999.

Kelly, H. A., and W. L. Burrage, ed. *Dictionary of American Medical Biographies.* Westport, Conn.: Greenwood Press, 1984.

Kirkland, Randolph W., Jr. *Broken Fortunes.* Charleston: South Carolina Historical Society, 1995.

Landrum, J. B. O. *History of Spartanburg County.* Atlanta: Franklin Printing and Publishing Co., 1900.

Lonn, Ella. *Foreigners in the Confederacy.* Chapel Hill: University of North Carolina Press, 1940.

McPhereson, James M. *Ordeal by Fire.* New York: McGraw-Hill, 1992.

Marszalek, John F., ed. *The Diary of Miss Emma Holmes.* Baton Rouge: Louisiana State University Press, 1979.

May, John Amsa, and Joan Reynolds Faunt. *South Carolina Secedes.* Columbia: University of South Carolina Press, 1960.

Memminger, R. Withers, and J. Hernie Ostendoeff. *History of the German Fusiliers of Charleston, South Carolina.* Charleston: Charleston Library Society, 1892.

Meyer, Jack Allen. *South Carolina in the Mexican War.* Columbia: South Carolina Department of Archives and History, 1996.

Moore, Albert Burton. *Conscription and Conflict in the Confederacy.* New York: McGraw-Hill, 1924. Reprint, Columbia: University of South Carolina Press, 1996.

Muhnlenfeld, Elisabeth, and C. Vann Woodward. *The Private Mary Chesnut.* New York: Oxford University Press, 1984.

Official Records of the Union and Confederate Armies in the War of the Rebellion. Washington, D.C.: Government Printing Office, 1880-1901.

Ostendorff, Louis F. *An Historical Sketch of the Washington Light Infantry*. Charleston, 1943.

Our Women in the War: The Lives They Lived; the Deaths They Died. Charleston: The News & Courier Book Presses, 1885.

Phelps, W. Chris. *The Bombardment of Charleston: 1863-1865*. Gretna, La.: Pelican Publishing Co., 2002.

Powers, Bernard. *Black Charlestonians*. Fayetteville: University of Arkansas Press, 1994.

Ravenel, St. Julien. *Charleston: The Place and the People*. New York: Macmillan, 1931.

Recollections and Reminiscences, 1861-1865 through World War I, South Carolina Division, United Daughters of the Confederacy. Vol. 3, 6. N.p., 1992.

Ripley, Warren, ed. *Siege Train: The Journal of a Confederate Artilleryman in the Defense of Charleston*. Columbia: University of South Carolina Press, 1986.

Rivers, William James. *Rivers' Account of the Raising of Troops in South Carolina for State and Confederate Service, 1861-1865*. Columbia, S.C.: The Bryan Printing Co., 1899.

Roman, Alfred. *The Military Operations of General Beauregard*. 2 vols. New York: Da Capo Press, 1994.

Schiller, Herbert M. *The Bermuda Hundred Campaign*. Dayton, Ohio: Morningside House, 1988.

Schreadley, R. L. *The Washington Light Infantry in Peace and War*. Spartanburg, S.C.: The Reprint Co., 1997.

Shole's Directory of the City of Charleston—1881-89. Charleston, S.C.: Shole's & Co., 1881-89.

Sifakis, Stewart. *Compendium of Confederate Armies*. New York: Facts on File, 1995.

Sketch of the Irish Volunteers. Charleston: News and Courier Book and Job Presses, 1878.

Southern Historical Society Papers. 52 vols. Wilmington, N.C.: Broadfoot, 1992.

Stauffer, Michael E. *South Carolina's Antebellum Militia*.

Columbia: South Carolina Department of Archives and History, 1991.

Stone, Lawrence. "Prosopography." In *Historical Studies Today,* edited by Felix Gilbert and Stephen R. Graubard. New York: W. W. Norton and Co., 1972.

Sumter Guard: Past, Present and Future. Charleston, S.C.: Walker, Evans & Cogswell, 1921.

Swanberg, W. A. *First Blood: The Story of Fort Sumter.* New York: Scribner's, 1957.

Transcripts of the South Carolina Medical Association. 1904.

Trudeau, Noah A. *Like Men of War: Black Troops in the Civil War 1862-1865.* Edison, N.J.: Castle Books, 2002.

"Volunteers for Confederate Service and State Service, to the Close of the Year 1861." *South Carolina Pamphlets and Miscellaneous* (n.d.).

Warner, Ezra J. *Generals in Gray.* Baton Rouge: Louisiana State University Press, 1959.

Wharton, H. M. *War Songs and Poems of the Southern Confederacy 1861-1865.* Edison, N.J.: Castle Books, 2000.

Wiley, Bell I. *The Life of Johnny Reb: The Common Soldier of the Confederacy.* Reprint, Baton Rouge: Louisiana State University Press, 1978.

Williams, Harry T. *Napoleon in Gray.* Baton Rouge: Louisiana State University Press, 1955.

Wise, Stephen R. *Gate of Hell.* Columbia: University of South Carolina Press, 1994.

Woodward, C. Vann. *Mary Chestnut's Civil War.* New Haven: Yale University Press, 1981.

Acknowledgments

I grew up in Chester, Virginia—once the sleepy little railroad link between Richmond, Virginia ten miles to the north and Petersburg ten miles to the south. On an Easter visit with my family back in Chester one year, after I had moved to Charleston, where I was attending college, I picked up a copy of Hagood's memoirs at the Petersburg National Battlefield bookstore, and in it I discovered the general's curious sketches of the Charleston Battalion and the Twenty-seventh South Carolina Infantry. As I read through the book I learned more of their exploits in Virginia and I thought it an incredible irony that this unit, "claimed by Charlestonians as their Regiment," had tramped over the same ground that I had come to know so well growing up. After long, hot days of skateboarding, as teenagers my friends and I often swam in the Appomattox River at Port Walthall, where these Charlestonians were initiated into the 1864 Virginia campaign. My father and I used to fish in Swift Creek, and as a boy of twelve I rode my bicycle each day across Swift Creek to visit a girl who lived in present-day Colonial Heights, Virginia. The south side of the bridge that spans the creek was the position held by the Twenty-seventh South Carolina during the battle of Swift Creek on May 9, 1864. When I was fifteen, my first real job was at the Bellwood Drive-In Theatre on Route 301, "Jeff Davis Highway," the old Richmond-Petersburg Turnpike, whose parking lot and movie screens sat on the same piece of ground fought over by the Twenty-seventh at Drewry's Bluff,

279

May 16, 1864. I felt a connection with these men—abstract though it was—and I began to gather information on this regiment, with specific interest in the Charleston Battalion, clearly the Charlestonian element of the Charlestonians Regiment. I quickly discovered that beyond the sketches provided by General Hagood in his memoir, no definitive volume yet existed on this distinctively Charlestonian organization, and thus, I felt compelled to one day tell their story.

First and foremost, this work would not have been possible without the encouragement and assistance of my mentor, Dr. Clark Reynolds, professor of history at the College of Charleston, who permitted me to write my senior thesis on the Charleston Battalion, which ultimately served as the foundation for this work. Though by the time I studied under "Doc" Reynolds he had shifted his historical focus to the ancient Minoan civilization on the Mediterranean island of Crete, he had been reared on Civil War history, and I suppose for the nostalgia of it he honored me with his guidance and direction. Thank you, sir! And yes, he forced me to use the term "prosopographic." Look it up!

Of course, years of time for travel, research, and writing were robbed from my wife, Aimee, and our three children, Tucker, Addie-Belle, and Lucy, as well as from my business partners, Trae Rhodes and Dennis Stiles, all of whom were good sports, however, and very supportive along the way. Aside from working full time at the Medical University of South Carolina and raising three children besides, Aimee also put in a lot of hours helping me finish this project. My good friend and Charleston historian Mike Brown helped transcribe the microfilm service records of the Charleston Battalion, while friends and co-workers Andrea Fisher and Harry Dinwiddie assisted in sorting them all out and transferring the data to floppy disks. Other friends and co-workers Carolyn Nations and Kelly Johnson helped me wrestle with my endnotes, among other tasks.

Although my task was to research the whole Charleston Battalion, there is one man out there who knows everything there is to know about the Sumter Guard, Company D of the battalion, and his name is Abney Curry Bolchoz, Sr. He has helped me tremendously with my research. Mr. Bolchoz is a member of the current Sumter Guard organization, the last vestige of the Charleston Battalion, and he has spent years compiling genealogical and biographical information on the Sumter Guard, which one day he will publish. He is also a member of the Secessionville Camp of the Sons of Confederate Veterans, many of whose members have given me support and encouragement, as have those in the Fort Sumter Camp of the S.C.V., of which I am a member.

John L. Dangerfield, president of the Twenty-seventh South Carolina reenactors unit, supplied the ragged Rebel detail used for the jacket image. These unreconstructed rascals are Shea Mclean, Lee Ginn, Mike Sarvis of the Twenty-seventh, and Steve Burt of the Twenty-fifth South Carolina, who sadly died of pancreatic cancer in the fall of 2003. My good friend Terry Manier of "Point Blank Design" transformed the modern image of these men into what appears to be nothing short of a faded old tintype found in someone's attic 139 years after the event.

In addition, much local assistance was given by the staffs of the library at the Citadel Military Academy, the Waring Historical Library on the campus of the Medical University of South Carolina, and the Charleston County Library. In particular, Liz Newcombe and Lish Thompson in the South Carolina Room at the county library provided me with much assistance. Sherry Summers of the St. Lawrence Cemetery and Janet Clegg of Magnolia Cemetery provided a great service in helping me locate the gravesites of many members of the Charleston Battalion. Many thanks must also be extended to the staffs of the South Carolina Department of Archives and History and the Confederate Relic Room in Columbia, South Carolina.

Dr. Herbert Schiller graciously permitted me to use several maps from his study of the Bermuda Hundred campaign to illustrate the positions of the Charleston Battalion and the

Twenty-seventh South Carolina at Port Walthall, Swift Creek, and Drewry's Bluff in Virginia. Heather Milne from the Museum of the Confederacy in Richmond, Virginia and Jill Pascoe from Pamplin Historical Park at Petersburg, Virginia allowed the photographic reproduction of two flags from the Charleston Battalion and the Twenty-seventh South Carolina, respectively the flag of the Charleston Light Infantry and the Charleston Depot battle flag captured at Weldon railroad. W. Eric Emerson, Ph.D., director of the South Carolina Historical Society, who has recently completed a manuscript on the Charleston Light Dragoons, was kind enough to read the work, and Mike Coker from the society helped me track down several maps and images used in the work. Finally, I owe a great deal of thanks to my friends and Charleston Civil War historians Eric Wright and Charles Hunt for patiently reading and scrutinizing my manuscript, pointing out errors, and, at the very least, feigning interest while I talked about my research.

Thank you all.

Index